"THE DARDENS HAVE REALLY PREPARED A FEAST!"
—*Amsterdam News*

Heartwarming and mouth-watering recipes for—

Sweet Potato Biscuits • Southern Fried Corn • Chicken Purlo • Hungarian Beef Goulash • • Baked Grits • Artelia's Hush Puppies • Drop Dumplings • Aunt Norma's Banana Fruit Punch • Ora Witte's White Fruitcake • Cousin Johnnie K's Macaroni and Shrimp Salad • Aunt Marjorie Palmer's Every-Kind-Of-Cookie Dough

And Hundreds of Others, Including:

Aunt Lillian's Violet Vanishing Cream and Special Flower Sachet • Aunt Alice's Plant Beverage •

And Complete Recipes For—

• Uncle Bud's Fourth-Of-July-Bash •

"A downhome treasury . . . which generously shares family memories and recipes. . . . This is big-happy-family fare, warmly anecdotal and highly likable."
—*Kirkus Reviews*

"AN INTRIGUING GLIMPSE OF A SPECIAL ERA AND A SPECIAL FAMILY."
—*New York Post*

SPOONBREAD
and
STRAWBERRY WINE

Recipes and Reminiscences of a Family

Norma Jean and Carole Darden

with line drawings by Doug Jamieson

FAWCETT CREST • NEW YORK

**Dedicated to
"Bud" and Mamie Jean**

SPOONBREAD AND STRAWBERRY WINE

THIS BOOK CONTAINS THE COMPLETE TEXT OF THE
ORIGINAL HARDCOVER EDITION.

Published by Fawcett Crest Books, a unit of CBS Publications, the
Consumer Publishing Division of CBS Inc., by arrangement with
Doubleday and Company, Inc.

ISBN: 0-449-24264-1

Printed in the United States of America

First Fawcett Crest Printing: February 1980

10 9 8 7 6 5 4 3 2 1

※

Contents

※

On the Road
RECIPES FROM FRIENDS & NEIGHBORS 252

♥

Acknowledgements

♠

Maxine McKendry and **Bernadine Morris**
who were there at the conception

Wally Amos and **the Rosicas**
who shone the light

Jean Naggar, Marie Brown and **Terri Soreco**
who had confidence

Hattie, Jed, Scott, Diana and **E.J.**
who pushed

Ed Lloyd, Carole's husband
for his support

H.A., S.H., and **M.W.**
for their encouragement

Peggy, Cordell, Jeanie, Louella, Barbara and
Lola
who typed

The host of cousins
who gave generously of their time,
recipes, and reminiscences

and

The many friends
who so cheerfully tested and partook.

Introduction

❀❖❀❖❀❖❀❖❀❖❀

We are two sisters who love to cook, especially together. During a small party we were giving the conversation drifted into talk of ethnic heritages. We mentioned that we were definitely home-grown, since our grandfather, Papa Darden, had been a slave and a great-grandmother whom we knew nothing about had been a Cherokee Amerind. A guest offhandedly remarked that we must have a lot of old-time recipes. It seemed a strange statement at the time, for we had never viewed our genealogy in precisely that way. However, someplace deep down in our imaginations a chord had been struck.

Yes! We were indeed the heirs to many old and wonderful recipes, but had never thought to collect them. Growing up around the large families of our mother and father who were scattered throughout the South, Midwest, and West had exposed us to some spectacular dishes that for the most part we had taken for granted and could not reproduce.

At the same time we realized that we had many relatives whom we knew very little about. Our father had been the youngest child in a family so spread in age that many had died before we were born, and our mother had been separated from her well-dispersed family by distance. A chat with our Aunt Maude, now in her nineties, hastened our desires to jot down some of the family stories and recipes before time had erased them. So we decided to make a pilgrimage back to the old spots of our childhood.

As children, we had always been intrigued by the women in our family as they moved about in their kitchens, often preparing meals for large numbers of people. Each one worked in a distinct rhythm, and from the essence of who they were came unique culinary expressions. They rarely measured or even tasted their food but were guided, we guessed, by the aroma, appearance, and perhaps some magical instincts unknown to us.

We felt it was time to capture that elusive magic, strengthen family ties, and learn more about our ancestors' history and tradition. So we initiated correspondence with a myriad of long-lost relatives and friends, and decided to hit the road for Petersburg, Virginia; Wilson, North Carolina; Opelika, Alabama; Delaware, Ohio; and points in between.

It had been a while since we had been united with our relatives for any occasions other than weddings or funerals. Memories of longer stays flooded our minds: like catching June bugs and making mud pies under Aunt Lizzie's peach tree; watching Cousin Artelia making dandelion wine; and listening to our Uncle William's ham radio set. And how evenings with Aunt Norma would find us in freshly ironed dresses and polished white Mary Jane shoes, walking down the mainly dirt roads of Wilson, calling on the neighbors or sitting in the *balcony* of the local movie house (yes, those were the separate and unequal days), followed by a trip to old man Shade's drugstore (with its slow-turning ceiling fan) for pineapple ice. Other evenings in Wilson would find us sitting on Uncle C.L.'s front porch swing, smelling his cigar as he, the local mortician, would relate (forgive us) how many "bodies" he had versus his competitor up the road.

In our recent travels we encouraged people to talk about the times of their youth—their hopes, dreams, highs, lows, and of course thoughts on food. To our delight, many had collections of old photographs that gave a greater sense of reality to their reminiscences. We scouted out old-timers who had known departed family members and combed through their memory boxes. Our composite picture of the ambitious, high-spirited Darden family from North Carolina was in total contrast to the more sober, religious Ohio-based Sampsons, our mother's family. But both revealed seriousness of purpose and flashes of humor. Unfortunately, we could not trace our family roots past our grandparents, and this was frustrating; but such was the effect of slavery and its resulting destruction of family ties.

Nonetheless, our journey was immensely successful for us, and after returning to New York City we amazed ourselves with the short time it took us to acquire such skills as wine making, canning and preserving, breadmaking, and even preparing homemade cosmetics—all parts of our family's repertoire. Some of our recipes were a bit sketchy, so we cooked a lot (and ate a lot), creating miracles and catastrophies in order to pinpoint measurements for you.

We have divided this book into two main sections, the Dardens and the Sampsons, and each chapter includes a photograph, a personal anecdotal sketch, and the recipes which that relative was most fond of or noted for, such as Uncle Asa's favorite meal—chicken-in-the-pot and devil's food cake, Uncle John's ice-cream making, and Aunt Maude's candies and confections. We have many family members, so we have provided two family trees for clarification. There are also four miscellaneous chapters: "Holiday Time with the Winner Sisters" and "New Year's Day Dinner at our House," which include complete menus and recipes for those celebrations; "Funerals," which suggests an assortment of cakes and pies to take to a bereaved family; and "On the Road," which contains recipes received from friends during our travels.

So, you see, this book is the reflection of our pilgrimage "home," which revealed to us not only good food but the origins, early struggles, and life-styles of our family. Our mother used to tell us that good food inspires good thoughts, good talk, and an atmosphere of happiness. It was in such an atmosphere that this book grew, and it is therefore a testimonial to those who lovingly fed us and at the same time gave us a better sense of ourselves by sharing themselves.

Norma Jean and Carole Darden
August 1976

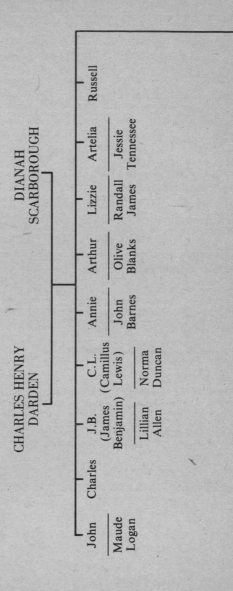

THE DARDENS

CHARLES HENRY
DARDEN

DIANAH
SCARBOROUGH

John	Charles	J.B. (James Benjamin)	C.L. (Camillus Lewis)	Annie	Arthur	Lizzie	Artelia	Russell
Maude Logan		Lillian Allen	Norma Duncan	John Barnes	Olive Blanks	Randall James	Jessie Tennessee	

THE SAMPSONS

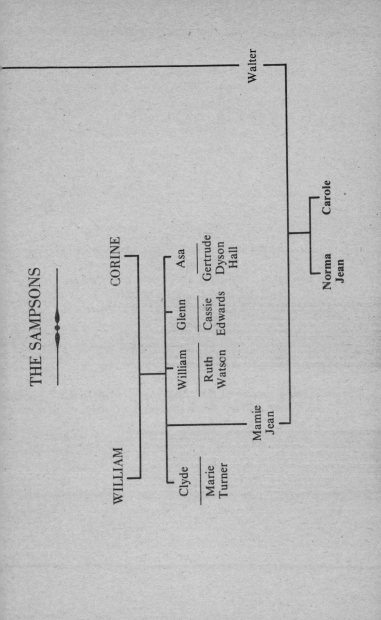

WILLIAM

CORINE

Clyde
Marie
Turner

William
Ruth
Watson

Glenn
Cassie
Edwards

Asa
Gertrude
Dyson
Hall

Mamie
Jean

Walter

Norma
Jean

Carole

Papa Darden's Grace

Heavenly Father,
From the abundance of Your streams, fields
and earth
You have seen fit to bless our table,
And we are grateful.
We pray for Your constant guidance in all
things

and

Let us never forget
To give thanks for the way You have
Blessed the hands of the cook.
Amen.

Papa Darden

Gentle, wise, ingenious—these are the adjectives most used to describe him by those who knew him. Family legend has it that in 1868, at the age of fourteen, Charles Henry Darden walked into Wilson, North Carolina. He had no money, no relatives, no friends there, and no one knew where he had come from—he wouldn't say. Somehow, somewhere in his mysterious fourteen years he had gained considerable skill as a blacksmith and could make and repair wheels. These abilities allowed him to eke out a small living and to put together the long wooden toolbox that was to become his trademark as he traveled door to door repairing broken locks and sharpening knives. In a short time he established a good reputation and at seventeen was able to open a small repair shop at the end of the main street in Wilson.

Charles Darden's future in his new town was shaped by a chance encounter. While attending a church social, he met and fell desperately in love with the perky and haughty young lady who was serving the lemonade. She was Dianah Scarborough, a fourteen-year-old seamstress and daughter of a freeborn couple who owned a small confectionery store in Wilson. Charles was shy, but not too shy to propose after a few breathless meetings. However, the Scarboroughs were firm in their answer of "No." After all, Charles was new to town, a stranger of untested character, and Dianah had many suitors. With the added pressure of love denied, Charles literally hammered his way out of this dilemma. Working with wood, glass, and iron, he produced washing boards, ax handles, troughs for animals; shoed horses, and made and repaired wagons and carriages. His business quickly prospered. Within a year's time after their first meeting, the Scarboroughs were sufficiently impressed by Charles's diligence and his quiet persistence in wooing their daughter to reverse their previous stand and welcome the marriage.

The first of thirteen children (ten lived), a son, John, was born when Dianah was sixteen, and the rest followed in rapid succession. As the family grew, so did the business. Because of his skill as a carpenter, Charles was asked to make coffins. As requests multiplied, he realized the need for a funeral establishment and became the first black undertaker in the State of North Carolina. But wagons, wheels, and coffins did not content such an enterprising soul.

Ever mindful of the needs of his expanding family, as well as those of the community, he began growing vegetables and fruits in volume and opened a little store to sell his produce. His hot roasted peanuts, melons, and the soda water were popular items, but the thing that brought the customers in was Charles Darden's own homemade wines. Wine making was his hobby. He used whatever fruits were in season and was especially known for his grape, dried peach, and watermelon wines. People seemed to enjoy his presence and gathered at the store for wine and discussion.

By the middle 1870s politics was the subject most discussed by folks who came into the store. There were three black senators and nineteen black members of the House in the North Carolina legislature in those post-Civil War days and all black folks took an optimistic interest in voting. Charles Henry was a forceful, sometimes humorous speaker, who never used profanity, never smoked or drank—even his own wines. His opinions were valued and sought after and it was known that he harbored political aspirations. Wilson was a small, slow-paced, rather quiet tobacco town with about 4,000 citizens, 40 per cent of whom were black, so things looked encouraging for black political progress. But by 1875, Reconstruction had given way to terrorism. In Wilson as well as throughout the rest of the South, the Ku Klux Klan had spread its sheets. Voting was over. First by intimidation and finally by law, blacks were banned from the ballot box. Political power as a tool for black advancement had failed, so Charles Henry Darden focused his energies on his business, the education of his family, and the leadership of his community. He was convinced that economic self-reliance now held the key to the survival of the black community.

Papa Darden would have been about nine when the Emancipation Proclamation was signed, but he did not talk about being a slave. Never did he tell his family about a single day in his life before the day he came to town as his own man. He merely set an example. Always self-contained, even in tense times he radiated optimism and confidence. He became head of the trustee board of his church,

Papa Darden visits son Walter T.'s first office in Newark, New Jersey.

17

which he attended twice on Sundays and once during the week, and led his family in an orderly life. As his children grew, they were put to work, before and after school, in the repair shop, the funeral parlor, store, or garden.

The evening hours were sometimes spent playing ball, sewing, having a candy pull or brushing up a musical talent. But most often, the children were asked to recite their homework. The one thing above all others that Charles Darden desired for his children was the thing he himself had been denied—a formal education. He was naturally swift with mathematics and somehow had learned to read, and to write in a clear hand, but all in all, he only had the equivalent of a fourth-grade education.

Wilson did not have a high school for black youngsters, so all ten Darden children had to be sent some distance away to larger towns at the age of thirteen. Papa Darden was seldom known to travel, yet he attended the graduations, from elementary to graduate school, of every one of his children. Without a doubt, he must have been the proudest "papa" in the group, for in his lifetime, against many odds, he saw three sons become physicians, two become lawyers, and two become morticians, while two of his daughters became teachers and one a nurse. In addition, he assisted many other neighborhood children to attain higher education.

It was a fitting tribute that when Wilson built a high school for black students, it was named Charles H. Darden High for the inspiration his life had given the community.

Papa Darden died before we were born and we truly regret that we never knew him.

GRANDDADDY AND WINE

Our father, "Bud," remembers that Papa Darden experimented a great deal before perfecting his concoctions and placing them on the "local market" in his store at ten cents a water glass. As our father tells it, one glass would make the buyer stay and talk. Talking usually led to a second glass. But he never knew anyone to go past three without needing assistance home. Granddaddy made his wines in quantity and served them from a spigoted barrel. Bud also claims that the pan placed on the ground to catch the spigot drippings used to fill with so many flies too drunk to wobble away that it depleted the fly population for a five-mile radius.

The recipes that follow are a near approximation of Granddaddy's original recipes, based upon our father's memories and our own experiments. But we have limited our quantities to approximately two gallons, since most people do not have room in their homes for spigoted barrels.

Equipment for Wine Making

1. *Stone crocks or plastic pails able to hold 3-5 gallons.* Aesthetically, we prefer crocks. However, plastic pails are more convenient for making large quantities, since stone crocks are extremely heavy to handle and sometimes crack.
2. A clean cloth to cover the crock in order to prevent bug visits. Tea towels will do.
3. A *long wooden spoon for stirring.* Metal is taboo because it seriously affects the wine flavor.
4. A *large cooking vessel*—able to hold 5-10 quarts (for dried fruit wine).
5. A *straining bag made of cheesecloth*—for squeezing the juice from the fruit base. These are obtainable in wine-making equipment stores, but you can easily make one yourself. It should be about 15 inches long and 8 inches wide. Muslin can also be used.
6. A very large bowl in which to strain the wine.
7. *Gallon jugs with screw-on fermentation locks.* We prefer glass rather than pottery jugs. First, you can watch the wine at work, which is really good fun. Second, you can determine when fermentation has ceased by the lack of activity (small air bubbles rising to the top), and, third, you can see if the wine is clear enough for final bottling. The fermentation locks allow the air bubbles caused by fermentation to escape without letting any air in. If these are not obtainable, corks can be used.
8. *Clear plastic or rubber tubing, about 4 feet long for siphoning.* This can be bought at a drugstore.
9. A *large plastic funnel.*
10. *Wine bottles and corks or screw-on tops.*
11. *An assortment of small bottles and jars*—for storage of excess wine.
12. *Wine rack*—to store your prized vintages.

STEPS AND TIPS ON HOW TO MAKE WINE

Wine making requires patience and a willingness to experiment. Try our method and use it to create your own.

There are four main steps in wine making. The first step is to mix the fruit and liquid in a crock or pail and put it in a warm place (60-75°) to ferment. At this stage the mixture will bubble, hiss, and give off an extremely strong odor until it turns to wine.

After the wine has quieted, the second step is to extract the liquid from the fruit pulp by straining it through a funnel lined with cheesecloth into gallon jugs. The jugs are then topped with fermentation locks filled with water or with corks loosely placed, so that air given off during the fermentation process can escape. Extra wine is stored in smaller jars, but try not to leave more than a two-inch air space at the top of any vessel for better brewing action. During this stage a quieter, slower fermentation occurs. Now the wine should be allowed to rest undisturbed for at least a month or until it clears.

As the wine clears, a layer of sediment settles at the bottom of the jug, so the third step in wine making is siphoning the wine off the sediment with a plastic tube and into a second jug. This process is called "racking." It is very important to siphon rather than pour because too much contact with air can turn good wine into bad vinegar. The extra wine stored in small bottles can be used to replenish the loss in volume due to discarding the layer of sediment. The wine now rests again. Some wines require two rackings, but if after two to four months no sediment has formed, fermentation (bubbling) has ceased, and the wine is perfectly clear, a second racking will not be needed and the wine is ready for bottling.

The fourth step is the final bottling and corking. The clear wine should be siphoned from the jug into wine bottles, leaving about an inch of air space at the top and corked tightly. Lay the bottles on their sides (preferably in a wine rack) to keep the corks moist and to prevent them from shrinking and popping out. The wine should then be stored in a cool dark place where it can be aged for a period of six months to two years or longer.

Be sure to keep a thorough written record of the entire process. This should include the kind of wine and the dates of the four steps. In this way you can keep an accurate account of fermentation, clearing, and aging times of different wines as you strive to find which is the most pleasing to your taste.

It should be noted that some wines are drinkable after the second step, but, like most good things, they mellow with age.

STRAWBERRY WINE

(Our Favorite)

7 pounds strawberries   Juice of 1 lemon
2 gallons boiling water   5 pounds sugar

Mash strawberries in a crock. Add boiling water and lemon juice, and stir vigorously. Cover with a cloth and let stand for 1 week, stirring once every day. Strain through a cheesecloth bag into a large bowl and discard fruit. Return to a clean crock. Stir in sugar, cover with a cloth, and let stand for 1 more week, stirring once every day. Transfer through a funnel to gallon jugs. Top with fermentation lock or cork loosely. Rack after about 3 months. Bottle when fermentation has ceased and wine is clear. Age for 1 year.

Yield: Approximately 2½ gallons.

~~~~~~

DANDELION WINE

9 cups dandelion petals   1 gallon boiling water
  (discard stems and pods)   3 pounds sugar
1 lemon, unpeeled, sliced   1 pound light raisins
  thin   1 package wine yeast* or
1 orange, unpeeled, sliced   active dry yeast (¼-
  thin   ounce)

*Obtainable in stores specializing in wine making.

Pick the dandelions on a hot, dry day, when petals are fully open and fairly bug free. Wash them well to remove any hidden insects. Pluck petals, measure and place them in a crock, adding the lemon and orange slices. Pour a gallon of boiling water over them and stir well. Cover with a tea towel and let stand for 10 days. Strain off liquid through a cheesecloth bag into a large bowl and discard petals and fruit slices. Return to a clean crock. Stir in sugar and raisins, then the yeast. Cover and leave undisturbed for 3 days. Strain into gallon jugs topped with fermentation locks or loose corks. Rack (see Index) after 3 months. Bottle when fermentation has ceased and the wine is clear. Age for 6 months to 1 year.

Yield: Approximately 1½ gallons.

DRIED PEACH (OR APRICOT) WINE

(Very Sweet)

3 pounds dried peaches (or apricots)
1½ gallons cold water
4½ pounds sugar

1 package wine yeast* or
1 (¼-ounce) package active dry yeast

*Obtainable in stores specializing in wine making.

Soak peaches in 1½ gallons of cold water overnight. Place peaches and water in a large cooking vessel. Bring to a boil and let simmer for about 5 minutes. Let mixture cool to the point where it can be handled easily. Then strain it through a cheesecloth bag into a crock, using your hands or any other method you can think of to press out as much liquid as possible. Stir in sugar. When the mixture cools to room temperature, sprinkle yeast on top and cover. After 12 hours, stir yeast into the mixture. Let stand for 1 week, stirring daily. Transfer to gallon jugs, place fermentation locks or corks on them, and allow the wine to continue fermentation undisturbed. Rack after 3 months. Bottle when wine has cleared and fermentation has ceased. Age for 9 months to a year.

Yield: Approximately 2 gallons.

This is a delicious, rather sweet wine that can be used in many ways other than sipping it straight. We have tried the following:

1. Mixed with a fresh fruit compote
2. Mixed with champagne as a punch
3. Served on the rocks, straight or with soda water, and garnished with a sprig of mint
4. As a substitute for rum when making cakes, such as baba cake
5. As a substitute for brandy in brandying fresh peaches

Another feature is the dried peach pulp that remains after the liquid has been strained off the original mixture. It has innumerable uses. Sweeten to taste, and try it in the following ways: 1. As a pie, tart, or crepe filling 2. In pancake or flapjack batter   3. In a ham, sparerib, or pork roast glaze   4. In breads and muffins.

BLACKBERRY WINE

A few years ago we made the discovery that our back yard had been blessed by the winds or the birds with rambling wild blackberry bushes.

That first summer the yield was only 2 pounds of small but delicious berries. We contacted the mother of a dear friend who was kind enough to pick 4 more pounds of a larger variety that grows near her home in Virginia. She sent them to us and we made blackberry wine.

6 pounds blackberries, washed   5 pounds sugar
2 gallons boiling water

Place berries in a large crock. Pour the boiling water over them. Stir, cover, and let stand for 10 days. Strain through a cheesecloth bag into a large bowl. Return to a clean crock. Add the sugar, stirring vigorously. Cover and leave for another week, stirring daily for the first 3 days. Transfer to jugs and top with fermentation locks or cork loosely. Rack (see Index) after about 3 months. Bottle after fermentation has ceased and the wine has cleared. Age for 6 months.

Yield: Approximately 2½ gallons.

⋅⊹❊ ❧⊹⋅

RICE AND RAISIN WINE

1 pound dark raisins   1 orange, unpeeled, sliced
2 pounds raw rice   1 gallon warm water
2½ pounds sugar   1 (¼-ounce) package
                                     active dry yeast

Place all ingredients in a crock. Stir well, cover, and set in a warm place. Stir daily for the first week and every other day for the second week. Let stand undisturbed for 2 weeks. After 1 month, strain into a gallon jug. Top with fermentation locks or cork loosely. Rack (see Index) after 3 months. Sediment produced from rice frequently takes quite a while to settle, so the wine may have to be racked again. Have patience and bottle only when crystal clear. Age for at least 1 year, preferably 2.

Yield: Approximately 1 gallon.

WATERMELON WINE

1 large watermelon
Sugar, 4 pounds to each
measured gallon of
watermelon juice

1½ (¼-ounce) packages dry
active yeast

Cut watermelon into several pieces. Remove all red meat from rind. Place red fruit in a cheesecloth bag and squeeze out juice. To each gallon of juice add 4 pounds sugar. Place all ingredients, and yeast, in a crock. Stir vigorously. Cover and let ferment 2 weeks, stirring daily the first week, not at all the second. After 2 weeks, strain through a cheesecloth bag into gallon jugs topped with fermentation locks or cork loosely. Rack (see Index) after about 3 months. (Watermelon wine seems to spoil more easily than other wines, so make certain your equipment is as sterile as possible.) When wine is completely clear, bottle. Age for 1 year.

Yield: Approximately 1½ gallons.

GRAPE WINE

Every year Papa Darden donated this wine to his church for sacramental ceremonies, and we are sure that afterward the pastor looked out on many smiling parishioners in his congregation.

1½ gallons grapes (we use wine or jelly grapes)
1½ gallons water
6 pounds sugar

Wash, stem, and place undamaged grapes in a crock. Mash them a bit with a wooden spoon, taking care not to crush open the seeds. Boil the 1½ gallons of water and when lukewarm pour over grapes. Let the mixture stand for 10 days, stirring daily for the first 3 days. At the end of 10 days, discard the grapes, which will be floating on the top, and strain the remaining liquid through a cheesecloth bag into a large bowl or pan. Measure and pour the liquid back into a clean crock, adding a pound of sugar for each quart of juice. (1½ gallons of grapes yield approximately 6 quarts of juice.) Let stand a week, and then siphon into jugs. Top with fermentation locks or cork loosely. Bottle after the wine has cleared and fermentation has ceased. Age for 6 months.

Yield: Approximately 1½ gallons.

OLD-FASHIONED PERSIMMON BEER

Brother Sheridan, a long-time Wilson resident, told us how the old folks used to brew this one. No one that we know makes this anymore, but it was once considered an old-time treat. You may not wish to make it either, but it's a recipe worth recording nonetheless.

Pine straw—2–3 bunches of needles from a pine tree
Wild persimmons—enough to fill a 2-gallon crock with a spigot
   (about 4 dozen).
1 cup sugar

Place pine straws at the bottom of the crock. Fill crock with whole persimmons, leaving a 3-inch air space at the top. Sprinkle with sugar. Add warm water to cover. Seal. Let stand for 1 week. Strain free-flowing liquid off through spigot and drink.

Papa Darden's last picture before retiring

PLUM LIGHTNING WINE

For those who want instant gratification, here's a quickie. This wine can be aged but has an exceptionally good flavor when new.

8 pounds red or purple plums	2 (¼-ounce) packages dry active yeast
7 pounds sugar	1½ gallons lukewarm water

Place whole, unpitted plums in a crock. Sprinkle with 5 pounds sugar. Add water and yeast. Stir vigorously, cover, and let stand for 4 weeks. Carefully remove plums and any mold that may have formed. Then strain the liquid into a large bowl. Return liquid to a clean crock and add remaining 2 pounds sugar. Stir daily for 3 days. On the fourth day the wine is ready for a sip. In 2 weeks it's ready for serving or bottling.

Yield: Approximately 2 gallons.

Dianah Scarborough Darden

The personal legacy that our Grandmother Dianah Scarborough left behind is one of passionate pride and determination. Her erect carriage, penetrating gaze, and strong sense of self made an indelible impression on all who met her. In contrast to the easy warmth of Papa Darden and the diplomatic way he approached the public, she could appear stern and aloof and was decidedly outspoken. Yet she was a fiercely loving person and no sacrifice was too great for her to make for family or a friend. Her greatest joy came from church and family, and for both she labored tirelessly and fervently.

Our father tells of an evening when he, a preschooler, had missed the children's matinee of a traveling show in Wilson because he had a cold. Only adults were allowed in the nighttime performance. Unfazed by that news and knowing how much he wanted to see the show, Mama Darden bundled him up and took him to the theater, where she demanded two tickets. When the man in the box office protested, she narrowed her eyes and, with sparks flying, swept past the startled ticket taker and into two seats where her electrically defiant attitude kept them undisturbed for the duration of the show.

A woman with little time for nonsense, Dianah set serious standards for her family and herself. She was adamant, as was Papa Darden, that her children would have a trade that would give them some control over their destinies and that they would be able to offer a service to the community. She was not one to merely accept second-class citizenship, and instilled in each child what was then called "race pride," insisting that they hold their heads high and assert their equality before God and among men.

She was a seamstress by trade, and professional pride kept her particularly interested in the immaculate appearance of her many offspring. After all, they were walking advertisements for her business. The ladies of Wilson—black and white—were well acquainted with her testy temperament, yet they continued to come to her because she could always be relied upon to deck them out in the latest dress and millinery styles, often embellished with her own lace and special touches. She taught her three daughters dressmaking, needlepoint, and other homemaking skills—notably baking, canning, pickling, and preserving—in which she excelled and expected excellence.

Once when a traveling photographer came to Wilson, Mama Darden, anxious to record her family and work for posterity, hired him to make a family portrait. For three days straight, she and the older daughters, Annie and Lizzie, sewed until everyone had a new Sunday outfit. The photographer arrived at the appointed time, set up his equipment, and began shouting instructions from under the black cloth, moving the family back and forth from pose to pose. For two hours on that hot summer day he tested the patience of the family, dressed up in stiff collars, satin, and taffeta. In the end, he collected a partial payment and promised to return in three days. Three weeks went by and the man never returned. Papa Darden

Mama Darden with older sons J.B., Charlie, and John

tried in vain to get Dianah to forget the phony photographer, but she continued to steam for months. And everyone knew that the black cloth, the picture machine, and the man himself would be torn to shreds if Mama Darden ever set sight on him again.

Although she was a churchgoer all her life, one incident sparked a lasting religious experience for Mama Darden and resulted in calming her extremely tempestuous nature. Once when her oldest daughter Annie failed to carry out her sewing instructions, Dianah's notorious temper flared, and she threw an iron at the wall. But Annie made an unexpected turn and was struck and knocked unconscious. When Annie could not be revived, Dianah, beside herself with grief, dispatched her son John to find a doctor. Dianah prayed and prayed—vowing to change her ways if Annie recovered. John returned from an hour's run without having found a doctor to see about poor Annie. No doctor was needed, for after what seemed like an eternity Annie opened her eyes. Dianah, true to her commitment, emanated a sense of calm—unless unduly provoked—for the rest of her life.

29

There are still those in Wilson who tell us that Dianah worked herself into the grave. But, perfectionist that she was, she could not be stopped. Toward the end of her life, when she was feeling poorly and had taken to her bed, she told a visiting neighbor that her life had been fulfilled and blessed by her many children. Dianah died in the arms of her youngest son, Bud, our father, who was then nine years old. Her last words to him were: "When God sent me you, He must have wrapped up a little piece of Himself." And that was how she felt about them all.

MAMA DARDEN'S CANNING AND PRESERVING

They say that Dianah Darden would attack all that had to be done with the energy of a whirlwind. And there were so many things to be done for a family the size of hers—curing the meat in the smokehouse, making the soap, boiling the clothes for laundry, and baking. But canning and preserving were the things that gave her the most satisfaction. She felt that the whole process just seemed to pull her into the rhythm of the universe. She'd plant her seeds in the spring, pick and prepare the vegetables and fruits from the earth in summer and fall, and serve them in the winter.

We can thank Mrs. Elizabeth Sheridan of Wilson, North Carolina, and our Cousin Thelma Byers, whose mother, Annie, watched Mama Darden and was able to pass along many delicious recipes. All of the following pickles, relishes, and preserves may be refrigerated and eaten at once, but we have included processing times for those who want to put a little something up for the wintertime.

Equipment for Canning and Preserving

1. *Jars:* Self-sealing Mason jars may be purchased at most hardware and grocery stores. They are recognizable by their flat lids and separate screw-on bands.

2. *Water-Bath Canner:* A large pot with a tight-fitting lid and a rack or wire basket inside that prevents jars from touching the bottom or sides. It can be bought in hardware stores or you can improvise by using a big pot with a cake rack placed inside. Be sure, though, that the pot has a tight lid and is large enough so that the jars do not touch the side or bottom of the pot or each other to prevent cracking, and that it is deep enough for water to come 2 inches above the jars, allowing 2 inches more for boiling space.

3. Large kettles capable of holding 6–8 quarts (do not use copper, iron, or brass).

4. Slotted spoons for removing food from kettles.

5. Food mill or blender for puréeing and grinding.

6. Ladle, funnel, or dipper for filling jars.

7. Tongs for lifting jars in and out of water-bath canner.

8. Jelly jars.

9. Paraffin for sealing jellies.

SEALING

To create a vacuum seal and to keep food in Mason jars air-tight and bacteria free, jars must be processed (boiled) in the water of a water-bath canner, then cooled. Heat melts the sealing compound on the flat lids, and as the hot contents of the jars cool, the lids contract and seal so that no air can enter the jars. A musical ping can be heard as this occurs.

CANNING

Always select choice, firm, ripe produce for canning and be sure to wash it well, cutting out and discarding any damaged spots. Wash jars and tops in hot soapy water and rinse well in hot water before using. Jars that are to be processed do not need to be sterilized, but it is best to sterilize jelly and jam glasses by boiling them for 15 minutes. There are two standard methods for preparing food for processing: cold and hot pack.

Cold Pack: Raw fruits or vegetables are placed in clean jars and hot water or syrup is poured over the contents, leaving a ½-inch air space at the top. The flat lids and bands are then screwed on and the jars placed in the water-bath canner or a large pot that has been filled with enough hot water to cover the height of the jars by 2 inches. The pot is then covered and the jars processed (boiled) for the time indicated in the recipe.

31

Hot Pack: Fruits or vegetables that have been cooked in water or syrup are packed while still boiling hot in heated clean jars (they may be heated either by rinsing in very hot water or by leaving in the oven at 250° for at least 15 minutes). When filled, the tops are screwed in place and the jars processed for the time indicated in recipe.

EXAMPLES: EASY CANNED FRUIT—COLD PACK

3 pounds fresh peaches,
2 tablespoons mild honey*
    per quart jar

Boiling water
Dash of cinnamon (optional)

Wash, peel, and slice fruit. Pack in 2 heated pint jars or 1 quart jar. Put full tablespoons of honey on top of fruit and add boiling water, leaving a ½-inch space at the top. Add a dash of cinnamon if a slightly spicy flavor is desired. Screw on lids and place in warm water in a water-bath canner. Make sure that jars are completely covered with water, cover, and bring to a boil. Process time is counted from the time of boil. Allow 25 minutes for pints; 30 minutes for quarts. Then remove jars. Cool away from drafts, on racks or towels. As jars cool, the lids will seal.

* You can cover the fruit with a syrup composed of ½ cup of sugar and 2 cups of water if you wish. We prefer honey, though.

EASY CANNED FRUIT—HOT PACK

3 pounds fresh peaches,
    pears, etc.
½ cup mild honey or sugar

2 cups water
Cinnamon stick (optional)

Wash, peel, and slice fruit. Then cook in syrup of honey or sugar and the 2 cups of water. More or less sugar or honey may be added according to your taste. Simmer until boiling hot and tender, then place in heated jars (1 quart or 2 pints), leaving ½-inch space at the top. Be sure that no spilled fruit lingers on rims, as that will interfere with the sealing process. Screw on lids, place in hot water in the water-bath canner, adding water to cover if necessary. Cover pot, bring to a boil, and process pints for 20 minutes and quarts for 25 minutes. Remove from canner and allow to seal. Some people feel that the hot pack gives better flavor, and others prefer cold pack for truer color. Try both methods to find out which suits you better.

Extra Canning Tips and Steps

1. If air pockets form in jars after filling them, run a knife along the side of jar to dispel them.
2. If water should boil below the height of jar during processing, have boiling water handy to replenish it.
3. Screwing bands may be used over and over, but the flat self-sealing lids only once.
4. Always remove bands and check lids 12 hours after canning to make sure lids are sealed tight and cannot be removed without prying. (Refrigerate and eat food if not properly sealed or else completely reprocess.)
5. Label each jar with contents and date of canning.
6. Store jars in a cool, fairly dry place. Properly stored food will keep its color and flavor for at least 2 years.
7. If you wish 10 quarts of canned fruit, start out with half a bushel of fresh fruit.

VERY SPICY PICKLED PEACHES

5 pounds fresh peaches
2½ cups cider or white vinegar
4 cups dark brown sugar
2 cups white sugar
½ cup water
2 tablespoons pickling spice
Bay leaves

Blanch peaches for easy removal of skin by dipping them in boiling water for 1 minute, then dipping them in cold water. Halve and remove pits. In a large saucepan combine vinegar, sugars, and ½ cup water. Boil until a thin syrup forms—a few minutes. Add peaches. Continue boiling until peaches are tender. Immediately spoon peaches into 2 quart jars, pouring over them the syrup in which they have been cooked, leaving a ½-inch space at the top. Sprinkle 1 tablespoon (use 1½ teaspoons for more subtle flavor) of pickling spice on top of each jar. Slide 1 bay leaf toward the side of each jar. To seal, process pints for 10 minutes, quarts for 15 minutes. (Excess syrup can be used for pickling plums or as basting sauce for pork or beef roasts.)

Yield: 2 quarts.

BREAD AND BUTTER PICKLES

5 large cucumbers, unpeeled, sliced
3 large onions, sliced
¼ cup salt
1 cup cider or white vinegar
1 cup water
¾ cup sugar

¼ teaspoon turmeric
½ teaspoon celery seed
½ teaspoon mustard seed
½ teaspoon powdered ginger
½ teaspoon dill weed or seed

Combine cucumbers with onions. Add salt, let stand for 2 hours, then rinse in cold water and drain. Heat vinegar, 1 cup water, sugar, turmeric, celery seed, mustard seed, ginger, and dill weed to boiling point. Add cucumbers and onions. Simmer for about 5 minutes or until cucumbers are greenish and somewhat translucent. Pack while hot into heated jars. To seal, process pints for 5 minutes, quarts for 10 minutes.

Yield: 2 quarts.

SOUR PICKLES

8 small pickling cucumbers, 3–5 inches long
¼ cup salt
1 quart water

1 cup cider or white vinegar
3 cups water
1 teaspoon mustard seed

Place cucumbers in brine composed of salt and 1 quart water. After 2 days, drain and place in a saucepan with vinegar and 3 cups water. Bring to a low boil and simmer for 5 minutes, then pack pickles in a hot quart jar, sprinkle with mustard seed, and cover with the hot vinegar. To seal, process quart for 10 minutes.

Yield: 1 quart.

WATERMELON RIND PICKLES

pound watermelon rind
quart water
¼ teaspoon slaked lime
  (calcium hydroxide, can
  be purchased at
  drugstores)
½ tablespoon mace
stick cinnamon

½ tablespoon whole cloves
½ tablespoon allspice
¾ teaspoon powdered ginger
2 cups sugar
1½ cups cider or white
  vinegar
2 cups water

With a sharp knife, cut the thick rind of a melon into squares 1–2 inches thick. Remove outside green skin and any remaining fruit. Soak rind for 3 hours in water with slaked lime, which will make the pickles crisp. (Soak rind in ½ cup salt for 6 hours if slaked lime is unobtainable.) Then drain and rinse well in cold water. Cover with ice water and let stand for about an hour. Then cook in water to cover until tender (10 minutes). Combine spices, sugar, and vinegar in a kettle and bring to a rapid boil, then simmer for 10 minutes. Add rind and enough water to cover if needed. Boil very gently— almost a simmer—until the melon cubes are transparent and tender. This should take about 10 minutes more. Turn into 2 hot pint jars. To seal, process pints for 5 minutes and quarts for 10 minutes.

Yield: 2 pints.

PICKLED PEPPERS

About 1 dozen hot red and
  green chili peppers

1 cup cider or white vinegar
2 teaspoons sugar

Fill a pint jar with whole hot red and green peppers. Add vinegar and sugar. Screw on top and let set for 2 weeks. Use as a hot sauce seasoning. Excellent on fried fish, pigs' feet, or anything else that needs spicing up.

Yield: 1 pint.

BEET RELISH—A QUICK CONDIMENT

3 cups peeled, chopped
   cooked beets
⅔ cup sugar
½ cup cider or white vinegar

¼ cup prepared horseradish
¼ teaspoon salt
¼ teaspoon celery seed

Mix ingredients. Chill for several hours to blend flavors before serving.

Yield: about 1 quart.

HOME CANNED TOMATOES

3 pounds tomatoes
1 teaspoon salt per quart jar
Pinch of sugar

Wash and core fresh, firm tomatoes. Blanch and peel them if you like. Stuff whole or quartered tomatoes into as many hot jars as you wish, leaving a ½-inch space at the top. Don't add water—simply allow their own juices to cover them. To each jar add 1 teaspoon salt and a pinch of sugar. Boil in a water-bath canner for 35 minutes for pints and 45 minutes for quarts. Then cool to seal. These beat store canned tomatoes any day. They are good in soups, stews, and sauces as well as plain. (1 bushel of tomatoes yields about 18 quarts.)

Yield: 1 quart.

GREEN OR RED TOMATO CHOWCHOW

3 cups cider vinegar
3 pints white corn syrup
1 dozen green or red
   tomatoes, unpeeled
6 medium-size onions
3 green peppers

1 head green cabbage
6 stalks celery (discard tops)
3 cucumbers (peeling
   optional)
1½ teaspoon salt

Place vinegar and corn syrup in a large saucepan. When mixture comes to a boil, add vegetables, which have previously been chopped, diced, or sliced according to one's own artistic sense. Add salt. Bring to a second boil. Lower heat and simmer slowly for 1 hour, stirring occasionally. Fill 3 quart jars or 6 pint jars, leaving ¼-inch space. To seal, process pints for 10 minutes and quarts for 15 minutes. (When making red tomato chowchow add 1 teaspoon ground cayenne pepper to the above recipe.)

Yield: 3 quarts.

BRANDIED PEACHES

2 pounds small clingstone
   peaches

1 pound sugar
Brandy

Place whole, unpeeled peaches in a large saucepan. Add water to cover and simmer (do not boil) until peaches are tender but still fairly firm. Take out peaches and remove skins. In each of 2 quart jars arrange 1 or 2 peaches and cover with sugar (about ⅛–¼ cup). Add more peaches and more sugar. Continue alternating until the jar is filled. Then pour in enough brandy to cover completely and screw lid on tightly. Store in a dark place for 2 months before serving. For a less pungent peach, add ¼ cup brandy to Easy Canned Fruit—Hot Pack (see Index) before processing in boiling water bath.

Yield: 2 quarts.

PEACH PRESERVES

2 pounds fresh peaches
3½ cups sugar

2 cups water
Juice of ½ lemon

Peel and quarter peaches, discarding pits. Boil sugar and 2 cups water until sugar is dissolved. Add peaches and cook over moderate heat for 8-10 minutes or until syrup is clear and slightly thickened, and the peaches are tender. Cover and let stand overnight. Remove the fruit from the syrup and place in hot self-sealing pint jars. Boil the remaining syrup with the lemon juice, stirring frequently, until syrup reaches the consistency of molasses or honey. Pour this over the peaches and top with self-sealing lids. To seal, process pints and half pints in simmering, not boiling, water for 20 minutes.

Yield: 2 pints.

☆

CHERRY, ORANGE, AND PEACH PRESERVES

4 pounds peaches, peeled and sliced
2 pounds sugar
1 orange, peeled, minced, and rind cut in thin slivers

¼ pound blanched almonds, cut in slivers
Small bottle of maraschino cherries, cut in thin rings, including juice

Mix peaches, sugar, orange and rind, almonds, cherry rings, and cherry juice. Slowly cook everything together stirring frequently for about 45 minutes or until thick (the consistency of honey). Pour into small jelly jars. To seal, process pint and half-pint jars for 10 minutes in simmering water. This makes a very nice Christmas present and you can substitute nectarines if peaches are out of season.

Yield: 4 pints.

FIG PRESERVES

4 pounds unpeeled figs, ripe but firm
3½ pounds sugar
1 teaspoon cinnamon

2 dozen whole cloves
1 teaspoon nutmeg
2 lemons, chopped fine

Wash figs. Leave the skin and a short section of stem on, so as to preserve juices. Let stand in the sugar for 24 hours or until figs make their own juice. Then put in saucepan to simmer (no water added). Add cinnamon, cloves, nutmeg, and lemon bits. Simmer slowly, uncovered for 2–2½ hours, stirring occasionally. Pour into jars while hot. To seal, process half pints or pints in simmering water for 20 minutes.

Yield: 4 pints.

PLUM BUTTER

3 pounds damson plums
2½–3 cups honey, depending upon desired sweetness
Juice and grated rind of ½ lemon

Wash plums and remove stems. Cut in half, remove pits, and place plums in a large saucepan. Add a small amount of water, just enough to prevent burning. Cover and cook over medium heat until soft (about 10–15 minutes). Allow softened fruit to cool slightly. Then purée in a blender or press through a sieve or food mill. Return to saucepan, add honey, lemon juice, and grated lemon rind. Cook, uncovered, over low heat for 2½–3 hours until dark and thick. Pour immediately into heated jars. To seal, process pints for 10 minutes, quarts for 15 minutes.

Yield: Approximately 2½ pints.

PEACH RAISIN CONSERVE

12 peaches
2 cups seedless raisins

4½ oranges, unpeeled
Sugar
1 cup chopped walnut meats

Dip the peaches in boiling water for 1 minute, then dip in cold water to better remove the skins. Halve, remove pits, and slice peaches. Put raisins through a food grinder or chop fine. Wash and thinly slice the oranges, then quarter the slices removing seeds. Combine these ingredients and measure by the cupful. For each cup add an equal amount of sugar. Cook together very slowly until thick (about 30 minutes), stirring frequently. Add nuts and cook for 5 minutes more. Then pour into hot pint jars. To seal, process pints and half pints for 10 minutes.

Yield: 4 pints.

THREE-FRUIT MARMALADE

1 grapefruit	Cold water
1 orange	Sugar
1 lemon	

Grate about a quarter of the rind of each fruit. Then slice each fruit in half (including rinds). Remove seeds and white fibrous centers and discard. Taking half of each fruit, slice as thinly as possible through the rind and pulp. Peel the rind off the remaining halves and cut in thin, narrow strips; chop the fruit pulp. Place all fruit and rind in a bowl; cover with cold water and let stand overnight. The next day, boil rapidly for a half hour in the same water. Cover and again let stand overnight. Measure fruit and for each cupful add 1 cup sugar. Return to stove and boil rapidly for about 45 minutes, stirring often. Toward the end of cooking time, test frequently, until it jells, by dropping a small amount on a cold dish. Runniness indicates that marmalade needs to cook a little longer. Place in 5 half-pint jars. To seal, process pints in simmering water for 10 minutes.

Yield: About 2 pints.

STRAWBERRY JAM

1 pound strawberries	Paraffin for sealing
1 pound powdered sugar	

Slice a quarter of the berries; coarsely mash the rest. Place berries in a heavy saucepan. Add sugar. Cook slowly at first, stirring frequently to prevent sticking. When sugar has melted, bring to a slow, rolling boil and cook for twenty minutes, stirring often. Then pour into sterilized jelly glasses. There are many options for putting up jams and jellies. Ours rarely make it through the month, so we rarely process, but if you would like to seal them, process pints and half pints for 10 minutes in simmering water. We do sometimes use paraffin for short-term sealing. To do so, melt the paraffin in the top of a double boiler and pour a ⅛-inch layer of the liquid wax on top of the hot preserves, tipping the jar in a circular motion to make sure edges are tightly sealed. Prick any bubbles with a pin and let the wax solidify. Leftover paraffin can be stored and reused at a later date. The nice thing about using paraffin to seal jams and jellies is that you can use any attractive glass as a container. Also, a bit of bright cloth and ribbon on the top makes it an attractive gift.

Yield: 1½ pints.

MRS. SHERIDAN'S SCUPPERNONG JELLY

This is a delicious grape indigenous to North Carolina and thereabouts. So if you don't live there and don't know anyone there who could send you some, you may be out of luck. However, Concord grapes may be substituted.

5 pounds red scuppernongs
Sugar

Wash grapes well. Place them in a large saucepan and cook them over medium heat for about 10–15 minutes or until the skins burst (do not add water). Strain through a cheesecloth bag and squeeze all of the juice out. To every 2 cups juice add 1 cup sugar. (For Concord grapes, use ¾ cup of sugar for each cup of juice.) Boil the mixture for about 25 minutes, stirring frequently. Mixture is ready when it drips heavily from a spoon. Pour immediately into hot sterile jelly jars and seal with paraffin (see recipe above).

Yield: Approximately 8 6-ounce jelly jars, depending upon juiciness of grapes.

Uncle John

Uncle John Darden was the oldest son. The dreams and hopes of the family centered on him, and he proved worthy of their confidence. From the beginning, John was a carbon copy of his father, Papa Darden. Even in his youth, he was disarmingly self-assured and knew how to survive and to protect others. But from the age of ten, when he was unable to find medical assistance for his unconscious sister Annie, John had one driving goal, and that was to become a doctor.

At the age of thirteen, he was sent by Papa Darden to high school in Salisbury, North Carolina. Lean years followed as he worked his way through Livingston College, medical school and an internship in Long Island, New York. His was a long, hard struggle, but when he made it the pattern was established that the younger ones would follow. Summer jobs mainly on the railroad and ships took John all over the country. But he always found his way back to Wilson to share what he had seen and learned of the world and to encourage his brothers and sisters in their pursuits. By the time he was ready to put out his shingle in 1903, Wilson already had black medical service, so John went deeper south, settling in Opelika, Alabama, where as the only black doctor in a thirty-mile radius, he was greeted with an eighteen-hour workday.

His overloaded practice in that remote little town almost caused him to lose his fiancée, Maude Jean Logan, who questioned his long absences from her. But Uncle John's persuasive letter saved the wedding day:

Sat. Noon

My own darling Jean:
    Here on the very verge of our approaching happiness comes the saddest news pen could write.... Sweetheart Jean, the condition of half dozen patients demands that I keep constant watch over them for at least three days. Had thought to see you at the cost of their lives; but you would care so much less for me then.... Won't you sympathize with me just a little, the responsibilities on this end and realize that no man under the canopy of heaven could love you more....

Soon after, John, making calls with his new wife in his horse and buggy, became a familiar sight on the narrow dirt roads around the Opelika countryside.

Emulating his father's diversified business tactics, John opened a drugstore on Avenue A, the main street of town. His brother J.B. had just earned his degree in pharmacy from Howard University, so he was recruited as a partner. The two brothers dispensed prescriptions, cosmetics, ice cream, and a lot of good cheer, and the store became a meeting place for the community. Local residents tell us that their Sunday was not complete without a stroll to the drugstore for a chat and a scoop of John's homemade ice cream. After the death of their mother, baby brother Bud, our father, joined the group and, at the age of nine, became the ace soda fountain man, specializing in a tutti-frutti sundae. Eventually Opelika proved to be too quiet for J.B., so, with John's blessings, he returned to medical school in livelier Nashville, Tennessee, leaving the oldest and the youngest brothers together. John was like a second father to Bud, who nicknamed him Toad because of his protruding abdomen.

According to Bud, John was a natural leader of men and was considered the guardian of minority rights. People brought him their sorrows, their joys, and news of gross community injustices. Long outraged at the lack of public medical facilities for black people, he established a private hospital. It was a simple one-story wooden building, but many complicated operations were performed there and many lives saved. Like most country doctors, he had his thumb glued to the pulse of the community and became the town chronicler. He knew who had been born, who had died, and who had moved in or out. Because of his two side jobs as a

Leonard Medical College, now Shaw University, Class of 1901 (John W. Darden—top row, fourth from right)

conscription doctor and the Lee County Jail doctor, he even knew who was inducted into the Army or who was incarcerated. Thus, he had firsthand knowledge of the jailing of people for minor infractions of the law, the assaults on defenseless females, and the countless other indignities perpetuated on blacks. During his time, the air was indeed permeated with clouds of sudden and irrational violence.

Once Dr. John's quick presence of mind was able to avert the lynching of a black stranger. Bud remembers that he and John were in the drugstore when they heard a commotion coming from the street and upstairs, where John's brother-in-law, a dentist, had an office. Dr. John Clark came down to tell them that a stranger seeking refuge from a lynching mob had run into his office quite out of the blue. With no questions asked, John left and returned in a flash with a few fearless and daring black citizens and the white Republican postmaster (a federal appointee in those days when Republicans were considered liberals). The mob had gathered momentum and was threatening to storm the building. But the postmaster, whom John knew to be sympathetic to the plight of blacks, had arrived heavily armed and kept the mob distracted while John and his friends spirited the man out of town. The man's crime? A visitor from Chicago unfamiliar with local customs, he had almost lost his life for taking a seat in an empty white restaurant while waiting for directions to another town.

Some local residents conducted a campaign of harassment against John and Maude, who remained cautious, cool, and armed until the fervor died down. We asked Aunt Maude if John had ever considered leaving town. She answered that in the darkest days in the backwoods of Alabama, he had never wavered in his determination to remain in the community he loved and to aid others.

She also tells us that the balance and harmony so sorely missing in John's hostile environment were supplied by his love of music, of religion, of gardening, and, surprisingly, of fashion. A meticulous dresser, he had developed an appreciation for good fabric and fit from his mother, the seamstress. He was a steward in his church, raised livestock and pigeons, and kept a beautiful flower and vegetable garden, as had his father. However, the talent that set him apart was his melodious baritone voice, and it is said that he could be heard singing a mile away.

In a life that had so many parallels to Papa Darden's, it is interesting to note that after John's death the local black high school was named for him in appreciation for the many things that he had done for the citizens of Opelika.

UNCLE JOHN'S ICE CREAM

Aunt Maude says that Uncle John got a big kick out of making ice cream. She can see him in her mind's eye in the pre-drugstore days—sleeves rolled up, spreading old newspapers, and chipping up a block of ice; packing the ice into the tub of his machine along with coarse salt, churning and whistling, churning and whistling until it was time to lick the dasher. Our father still remembers making the homemade ice cream for the Sunday crowd in his drugstore days. Vanilla and chocolate were the two regular flavors, but every week a special flavor was added from a recipe invented or given by friends.

Once you have tasted John's homemade ice cream, you will become an addict. If you want the true feeling of the old days, buy a wooden hand-crank ice-cream maker. It is wonderful to do things from scratch! However, if taste alone is what you're after, the electric models give you almost the same flavor with half the work.

SPICE ICE CREAM

1 quart milk
2 2-inch sticks of cinnamon
1½ cups sugar
1 teaspoon salt
1 quart heavy cream

2 tablespoons vanilla
½ teaspoon ground
cinnamon
½ teaspoon ground nutmeg
¼ teaspoon ground cloves

Place milk and cinnamon sticks in a large saucepan. Heat almost to boiling, then dissolve sugar and salt in the milk. Let cool. Add cream, vanilla, cinnamon, nutmeg, and cloves. Chill for approximately 2 hours. Remove the cinnamon sticks. Freeze in an ice-cream freezer according to manufacturer's directions.

Yield: About 3 quarts.

FIG ICE CREAM

2 cups milk
6 eggs, separated
1 cup sugar
1 pint heavy cream

½ teaspoon vanilla
1 quart peeled and mashed
figs

Heat milk in a medium-size saucepan. Beat egg yolks and sugar in a bowl. Stirring constantly, slowly pour half of the hot milk over sugar and yolks. When well blended, return entire mixture to saucepan. Cook over medium heat, stirring constantly, until mixture is thick enough to coat spoon. Cool, then chill for 2 hours. Stir in cream. Beat egg whites until stiff and fold into mixture. Add vanilla and figs. Stir well. Freeze in an ice-cream freezer according to manufacturer's directions.

Yield: About 2 quarts.

STRAWBERRY ICE CREAM

3 cups light cream
3 cups heavy cream
2 cups sugar
½ teaspoon salt

2 teaspoons vanilla
3 cups fresh strawberries
(or raspberries)

SPOONBREAD AND STRAWBERRY WINE

Combine light and heavy creams. Stir in sugar and salt until dissolved. Add vanilla. Crush strawberries and put through a sieve, or purée in a blender. Add to cream mixture. Pour into ice-cream freezer and freeze according to manufacturer's directions.

Yield: 2 quarts.

BANANA ICE CREAM

7 cups milk
12 egg yolks
2 teaspoons salt
3 cups sugar

2 tablespoons vanilla
6 ripe large bananas
1 quart heavy cream

Heat milk in a large saucepan, bringing it almost to a boil. In a large bowl, beat egg yolks until light. Add salt. Stirring constantly, slowly pour about half of the milk over the eggs. When well blended, return entire mixture to the saucepan. Add sugar and cook over medium heat, stirring continuously, until mixture is thick enough to coat the spoon. Pour into a large bowl, add vanilla, and chill in refrigerator for 2 hours. Mash the bananas thoroughly with a fork. When the mixture is well chilled, stir in heavy cream and mashed bananas. Freeze in ice-cream freezer according to manufacturer's directions.

Yield: 2½ quarts.

PINEAPPLE ICE CREAM

8 egg yolks
1 cup sugar
¼ teaspoon salt
1 quart milk
½ cup pineapple syrup
(from drained crushed
pineapple)

1 tablespoon vanilla extract
1 pint heavy cream, stiffly
whipped
3 cups drained crushed
pineapple

Beat egg yolks until light and foamy. Add ½ cup sugar and salt. Gradually stir in milk. Pour into a large saucepan. Cook slowly over low heat, stirring constantly. When thick and as smooth as possible, remove from heat and cool. Add the rest of sugar, the pineapple syrup, and the vanilla. Freeze according to your freezer manufacturer's directions. When mixture begins to form a mush, add whipped cream and pineapple. Continue freezing until solid.

Yield: About 2 quarts.

RUM RAISIN ICE CREAM

1½ cups seedless raisins	1 teaspoon salt
¾ cup dark rum	1 quart milk
8 egg yolks	1 quart heavy cream
1½ cups sugar	2 teaspoons vanilla

Chop raisins and soak them in the rum overnight. Beat egg yolks until light and fluffy. Blend in sugar and salt. Scald milk in a large saucepan, bringing it almost to a boil. Pour half of the milk into the yolk mixture, stirring constantly. Return this mixture to the saucepan and cook slowly, stirring until the custard is thick enough to coat the spoon. Remove from heat and let cool. Stir in heavy cream and vanilla, and chill for 2 hours. Freeze according to freezer manufacturer's directions. When mixture becomes mushy, add rum and raisins. Finish freezing.

Yield: About 2 quarts.

TUTTI-FRUTTI ICE CREAM

The most popular ice cream at Uncle John's drugstore.

3 cups light cream	½ cup pineapple sundae topping
3 cups heavy cream	
¾ cups sugar	½ cup chopped maraschino cherries
½ teaspoon salt	
2 teaspoons vanilla	1 cup pecan or walnut sundae topping, drained
½ cup strawberry sundae topping	

Combine light and heavy creams and stir in sugar and salt until dissolved. Add vanilla. Freeze according to freezer manufacturer's directions. When ice cream begins to form a mush, add fruit toppings, cherries, and nuts. Finish freezing.

Yield: 2 quarts.

OLD-FASHIONED FRESH PEACH ICE CREAM

Uncle John got this recipe from his brother-in-law, John Barnes, who made it every Sunday.

1 quart half-and-half milk	2 cups sugar
4 or 5 eggs, depending on size	10–12 freestone peaches, peeled and mashed
2 tablespoons cornstarch	1 pint heavy cream
¼ teaspoon salt	2 tablespoons vanilla

In a large saucepan, blend half-and-half and eggs, well beaten. Combine cornstarch, salt, and sugar. Gradually add this to half-and-half mixture. Cook over low heat, stirring constantly to prevent scorching. Custard is done when it drips heavily from a spoon. Do not overcook! However, if it does curdle, this in no way impairs the quality or taste when frozen. Cool and chill for approximately 2 hours. Stir in mashed peaches, heavy cream and vanilla. Pour into ice-cream freezer. When hardened, remove dasher and lick same with tongue. Pack ice cream with ice and salt or place in ice box until ready to serve.

Yield: 2½ quarts.

BLUEBERRY ICE CREAM

6 cups fresh ripe blueberries	3 cups heavy cream
2 cups sugar	3 cups light cream
½ teaspoon salt	2 teaspoons vanilla

Uncle John in his drugstore

Mash blueberries with a fork. Add 1 cup sugar. Cook over medium heat, stirring constantly, until berries are soft (about 5 minutes). Let cool. Dissolve the remaining sugar and salt in the creams. Add vanilla and berries. Freeze according to ice-cream freezer directions.

Yield: 2 quarts.

CARAMEL ICE CREAM

8 egg yolks	¼ teaspoon salt
1 quart milk	1 tablespoon vanilla
1 cup dark brown sugar, packed	1 pint heavy cream

Beat egg yolks well and place in a large saucepan. Add milk gradually. Cook slowly over low heat, stirring constantly. When thick and smooth, remove from heat. In a smaller saucepan, heat the brown sugar, stirring until melted. Stir this into the custard mixture, along with salt and vanilla. Cool, then chill for 2 hours. Freeze, according to your ice-cream freezer directions, until mushy. Whip heavy cream. Open freezer and add whipped cream. Finish freezing.

Yield: About 1½–2 quarts.

PEANUT BUTTER ICE CREAM

This is a recipe that Uncle John acquired from his neighbor, George Washington Carver, who invented over a hundred uses for the peanut.

2 cups milk	½ cup blanched and ground
3 egg yolks	peanuts (or peanut butter)
½ teaspoon salt	1 teaspoon vanilla
1¼ cups brown sugar	1 quart heavy cream
2 cups cooked prune pulp	

Heat milk in a medium-size saucepan. Beat egg yolks until light. Add salt. Stirring constantly, slowly pour half of the milk over the beaten egg yolks. When well blended, return entire mixture to the saucepan. Add sugar, prune pulp, and ground peanuts. Continue stirring. Cook over medium heat until mixture thickens. Cool, then chill for 2 hours. Add vanilla and cream. Freeze in an ice-cream freezer according to manufacturer's directions. Enjoy a new taste sensation. The peanuts are high in protein and prunes are a good source of iron.

Yield: About 2 quarts.

FRUITCAKE ICE CREAM

A festive holiday treat.

3 cups light cream	1 cup chopped candied
3 cups heavy cream	cherries
1½ cups sugar	1 cup diced candied
½ teaspoon salt	pineapple
2 teaspoons vanilla	½ cup chopped nut meats
1 cup diced candied citron	⅓ cup dark rum

Combine light and heavy creams. Stir in sugar and salt until dissolved. Add vanilla. Freeze according to freezer manufacturer's directions. When ice cream begins to form a mush, add fruit, nut meats, and rum. Finish freezing.

Yield: 2 quarts.

LEMON ICE

Juice of 4 or 5 lemons   4 cups water
2 cups sugar   8 egg whites

Blend lemon juice, sugar, and 4 cups water. Freeze according to manufacturer's directions. Beat egg whites until stiff. Stir this into the lemon mixture as a mush begins to form. Finish freezing.

Yield: About 2 quarts.

Aunt Maude

Aunt Maude was married in 1905 and it was the greatest event in her life. She has been madly in love for seventy years. Even twenty-five years of widowhood have not dimmed her ardor for Uncle John. She remembers the details of their courtship and marriage as though they happened yesterday, and we never tire of hearing their story. She was the belle of the ball in her home town, Montgomery,

Alabama—a stylish dresser and a jazzy dancer with many beaux and no intentions of settling down. On Sundays she played the piano for the Methodist Church, and it was in church that she met John. His church choir had been invited to give a concert at hers. John was the soloist and she was called to accompany him. Well! At the first note of their musical interlude, her ears perked up, and by the end of the song she was completely entranced. And so it was with his melodious voice that the country doctor, most famous for his rendering of "Oh Promise Me," was able to entice Maude to abandon "city" life for the small community of Opelika, Alabama.

It was a decision she never regretted, because life in Opelika was far from dull for her. She made house calls with Uncle John in their horse and buggy, helped with bookkeeping at the drugstore, taught Sunday school, and gave piano lessons. Tuskegee Institute was not too far away, and she and Uncle John were able to cultivate friendships with Booker T. Washington, the founder of the school, and also knew George Washington Carver, the agricultural scientist most acclaimed for his discoveries of more than a hundred uses for the peanut. Some of the great cultural events of the times took place in Tuskegee. Celebrated concert singers Black Patti, Roland Hayes, and Todd Duncan; the famous trial lawyer Clarence Darrow; the actor Will Rogers are just a few of the many famous people John and Maude saw lecture or perform at Tuskegee. Then once a year John would take leave of his busy practice to take her to visit their relatives and to see some of the spots he had been introduced to in his railroad days. They visited Los Angeles, where John's brother Charlie lived, and San Francisco, where her older sister Ida still lives, but Atlantic City, Boston, and Atlanta were their favorite haunts wherever they visited, Maude always kept a peeled eye for potential brides and grooms.

Maude Jean Logan Darden loves romance. She is a great believer in the power and joy of love and can relate the details of every tragic or wildly successful love story in her town for the last five generations. Not surprisingly, she has played matchmaker to countless couples. Two of her matches in the family were her sister Fannie to Dr. John Clark, the local dentist; and John's brother C.L. to Norma Duncan, a young woman from Maude's home town. The latter two were married under the grape arbor in her flower garden.

"It has been a good life, a rich life," she mused recently. "No woman ever had a more perfect husband. John was every inch a man and a gentleman. He was handsome, well dressed, so thoughtful—he knew exactly how to put things. For example, when I first came to Opelika, I had no intention of joining the church because you had to give up dancing and card playing, which I loved

Logan family (from left to right, Maude Jean, her father, the local barber, Fannie, Mother, Ida Mae)

to do. But one day John said that the organist had left and would I mind sharing my talent with the congregation. It was just how he put it. Before I knew it, I was not only providing the music, but teaching Bible class as well. Can't say that I didn't miss my cards and dancing, but I enjoyed pleasing my John and the pupils even more. Ideal companion that he was, he knew that it was truly what I needed, for I had just lost the only child we were to conceive.

"While waiting in our horse and buggy for John to administer to a sick patient, our horse bolted and threw me to the ground. I was pregnant at the time and was not to conceive again. So you see, teaching Sunday school for over sixty years has given me hundreds of children who are now dispersed all over the world."

Aunt Maude says, "Getting old doesn't mean giving up." Every day ninety-four-year-old Aunt Maude puts on her make-up and her pearl choker and earrings. She comes downstairs to greet the day, confident that it will be a good one. "Every day I relive the beautiful moments John and I shared, and I am never lonely."

We wish she could live forever. Aunt Maude, with her sweet sense of romance, is an avid candymaker and here are some of her tried and true recipes for making confections.

SWEETS FROM THE SWEET

Every Valentine's Day we would receive an enormous treat from Aunt Maude: two big shoe boxes, one filled with pecans from the tree in her back yard, and the other with candy—her divinity fudge and pecan brittle. Later we would see the avid candymaker at work in her own kitchen. In the center of the room was a large table covered with a yellow oilcloth tablecloth, and there she assembled her ingredients and applied great concentration to the job at hand. She used pecans in many of her confections because they were plentiful, and she tested the stages of her candymaking by that time-honored method of a drop of syrup into a teacup filled with cold water. However, for the novice candymaker we recommend a candy thermometer.

||||||||||||||||||||||||||||||||||||||||||||||||||||||||||||

EASY PEANUT BRITTLE

(a quickie)

2 cups regular or Spanish peanuts
3 cups sugar

Stir sugar slowly in a large frying pan over low heat. When melted to the color of clear caramel, add nuts. Pour onto a buttered cookie sheet. When cold, break up into small, eatable pieces.

Yield: 2 dozen small pieces.

||||||||||||||||||||||||||||||||||||||||||||||||||

DIVINITY FUDGE

2½ cups sugar
½ cup light corn syrup
½ cup water

2 egg whites, stiffly beaten
1½ cups finely chopped
   pecans
½ teaspoon vanilla

Mix sugar, syrup, and ½ cup water. Boil until a few drops placed in a cup of cold water forms a *soft* ball when rolled between the thumb and second finger (235° on a candy thermometer). Then pour half the boiling mixture over the stiffly beaten egg whites and stir. Return the remaining half of the mixture to the heat and boil until a few drops placed in a cup of cold water form a *hard* ball (260° on a candy thermometer). Then combine with egg white mixture. Add nuts and vanilla, working fast, drop by rounded teaspoons on a buttered cookie sheet.

Yield: About 1 pound candy.

PECAN BRITTLE

1½ cups pecans, halved or in pieces
¼ teaspoon salt
1 cup sugar

½ cup light corn syrup
½ cup water
1½ tablespoons butter

Sprinkle the nuts with salt and warm them in low oven. Mix the sugar, corn syrup, and ½ cup water and heat slowly, stirring until dissolved. Continue cooking over moderate heat. The mixture is ready when a small amount dropped in a cup of cold water becomes brittle (260° on a candy thermometer). Remove from heat and stir in butter and warm nuts. Pour immediately onto a buttered cookie sheet. As soon as cool enough to handle, cut in strips, and wrap in wax paper. Or wait until completely cooled and break into irregular pieces.

Yield: About 1 pound candy.

Aund Maude tells us that candy pullings provided high drama for many a family on a cold evening. Two people would butter their fingers and pull the ends of the candy as far as it would go without breaking, then double it over and pull again. This was repeated until the candy lightened in color and started to harden. At that point they would twist it, roll it, or braid it into long strips. Just before it was completely hard and the participants exhausted, they would cut it with scissors or break it into mouth-sized pieces and enjoy the fruits of their labor.

MOLASSES TAFFY

2 cups brown sugar
1 tablespoon white vinegar
1 cup molasses

¾ cup water
1 tablespoon butter
½ teaspoon baking soda

Boil first 4 ingredients together until a drop placed in a cup of cold water forms a hard ball (260° on a candy thermometer). Stir in butter and baking soda. When mixture stops foaming pour into a buttered cake pan to set until cool enough to handle. Don't let it get too cool or it will be hard to pull.

Yield: Over a pound.

CARAMEL KISSES

Not recommended for denture wearers!

1 cup sugar
¾ cup dark corn syrup
¼ cup butter

1 cup light cream
1 teaspoon vanilla

Slowly cook sugar, corn syrup, butter, and light cream together until 250° is reached on candy thermometer, or until a firm ball can be formed when a drop is placed in a cup of cold water. Remove from heat and add vanilla. Pour into a buttered 9-inch-square pan. Cut into small squares when cool. Wrap individually in wax paper.

Yield: About 36 kisses.

CHOCOLATE-COVERED CANDY

CREAMED FILLING

2 cups sugar
1 cup heavy cream
1 tablespoon light corn syrup
⅛ teaspoon salt

Shredded coconut
2 or 3 drops of peppermint extract, lemon, or orange extract
Candied fruit
Almonds or pecans chopped

59

Place sugar, cream, corn syrup, and salt in a saucepan and cook over low heat until dissolved. Then boil until candy thermometer reaches 238° or mixture forms a soft ball when a few drops are placed in a cup of cold water. Now pour mixture onto a greased large platter and allow it to cool. When barely warm, begin to knead with fingers or a spatula for 5–10 minutes. Texture will then become creamy, smooth, and dough-like. Candy can be chocolate-coated immediately, but taste is improved by ripening. Roll into a ball and store in a covered glass jar in the refrigerator for 2–4 days prior to dipping. When ready to coat (see below), divide candy into 6 sections. Give each section a different flavoring by adding coconut to one, 2 to 3 drops of peppermint, lemon, or orange extract to others. One section may be left plain. Food color may be added for variety as well. Now form each section into balls, squares, ovals, or patties and place on wax paper. Candied fruit and nuts may be pressed into the centers. Now prepare chocolate to coat them.

CHOCOLATE COATING:
2 8-ounce packages semisweet chocolate

To cover the cream fillings, weather is all-important. Pick a cool, sunny day versus a rainy, humid one, so that the candy can dry. Begin by slowly melting the chocolate in the top of a double boiler over boiling water. When 75°–80° is registered on the candy thermometer, it's time to dip. Using a long fork or your fingers, dip each cream filling patty into the chocolate. Make sure candy is coated completely. Then return to wax paper to dry. Coconut, candied fruit, or nuts can be used for decoration on top if you wish. If any chocolate is left after all the patties have been dipped, pour it into a small pan, sprinkle any leftover ingredients on top, and cut in squares when cool. These candies make an attractive gift or charming afterdinner surprise.

Yield: About 1 pound candy.

❖❖❖❖❖❖❖❖❖❖❖❖❖❖❖❖❖❖❖❖❖❖❖❖❖❖❖❖❖❖❖❖❖❖❖❖❖

SHOE LEATHER BALLS

¾ pound dried apricots   Fine granulated sugar
¼ pound dried peaches

Fannie Logan's wedding to Dr. Clark, one of the many arranged by Aunt Maude, the matchmaker

Aunt Maude's recipe for shoe leather candy called for putting the dried fruits through a food grinder, coating a board with fine sugar, placing the fruit on top, rolling the fruit ⅛ inch thick with a rolling pin, and cutting it into 1-inch strips. To accomplish this, you must have very very dry dried fruit. We discovered this the hard way, and if you should end up as we did with fruit too moist and too sugary to be rolled, don't despair. Simply form the fruit into small balls with your fingers and top with a nut, cherry, or a sprinkle of coconut. Either way it produces tasty candy. Store your shoe leather or shoe leather balls in the refrigerator.

Yield: 1 pound.

CANDIED VIOLET OR ROSE PETALS

Candied violets and roses are such sweet and romantic confections—
Aunt Maude uses them as candies and as decorations for cakes and desserts.

30 violet and baby rose petals   1 cup superfine sugar
1 egg white, beaten

Separate petals, wash and dry them. Beat an egg white until foamy.
Dip petals into egg white, then into very fine or sifted granulated
sugar, coating evenly. Let dry in the refrigerator, then store in a
covered container, until ready for use.

GINGERBREAD

Dr. John Clark, Aunt Maude's brother-in-law, invented his own
gingerbread, which she loves to bake.

2 eggs
¾ cup sugar
¾ cup molasses
¾ cup melted butter
2½ cups all-purpose flour
2 teaspoons baking powder
2 teaspoons powdered ginger

1½ teaspoons powdered
  cinnamon
½ teaspoon powdered cloves
½ teaspoon powdered
  nutmeg
½ teaspoon baking soda
½ teaspoon salt
1 cup boiling water

Preheat oven to 350°. Beat eggs well and blend in sugar, molasses,
and melted butter. Sift and measure flour. Add all other dry
ingredients and sift together. Alternate adding the flour and the
boiling water to the batter and beat well until smooth and
bumpless. Pour into a well-greased 9-inch-square pan and bake for
30–40 minutes. Cut into squares and serve warm with whipped
cream.

PEACH GINGERBREAD UPSIDE-DOWN CAKE

Melt 3 tablespoons butter with 4 tablespoons brown sugar in the 9-inch-square pan. Then add 2 chopped fresh peaches or canned peaches to cover bottom of the pan. Pour gingerbread batter over peaches and bake as indicated above. Invert pan to serve upside down with peaches on top. Cut in squares and serve with a generous dot of whipped cream on each portion.

Yield: 9 servings.

PECAN PIE

3 eggs
½ cup dark brown sugar
1 cup dark corn syrup
½ teaspoon salt
1 teaspoon vanilla

¼ cup softened butter
1 cup pecans, broken into pieces
½ cup pecan halves for garnish

9-inch unbaked pie shell (see Index), kept refrigerated until ready for use.

Beat eggs in a medium-size bowl. Add brown sugar, corn syrup, salt, and vanilla. Blend well. Stir in butter and broken pecans. Pour into pie shell. If you like, make a design when placing the pecan halves on top. Bake for 45–50 minutes in a preheated 375° oven.

Yield: About 8 servings.

MERINGUE CUPS

These were the perfect settings for Uncle John's ice creams. He liked them filled with peach ice cream, fresh strawberries, and whipped cream on top.

2 egg whites
⅛ teaspoon cream of tartar

⅔ cup sugar
⅔ cup finely chopped pecans

SPOONBREAD AND STRAWBERRY WINE

Beat egg whites with cream of tartar until foaming. Add sugar little by little until mixture is stiff and glossy. Stir in pecans. Spread by spoonfuls on the bottoms and sides of extremely well-buttered muffin cups or custard cups, or form into little mounds on a buttered cookie sheet. Bake for 25–30 minutes in a preheated 325° over until light golden brown. Cool for 5 minutes. To remove, carefully loosen around the edges with a sharp knife. Let cool completely before filling. They can be stored in the refrigerator for several weeks if not used immediately.

Yield: 1 dozen.

Every family has its "sport." In ours, it was Uncle J.B.—James Benjamin, a hard worker and a hard player. He started his professional life as a druggist, but, encouraged by his older brother John, he went back to Meharry Medical School in Nashville, Tennessee, meeting his tuition there by teaching pharmacy. Both a man's man and a lady's man in his youth, he was naturally gregarious, a great mixer, and a captivating storyteller. Somehow he managed to juggle teaching, studying, and partying with minimum effort and maximum results; he was an excellent teacher, superb student, and much-chased bachelor.

While in school a classmate invited him to visit Petersburg, Virginia. He liked the town so much that he decided to settle there after marrying his Nashville sweetheart, Lillian Allen. As a doctor in a small town, he was dedicated to his work, put in unusually long hours, and brightened the lives of his patients, but he also always found time to play cards and go to the races and his luck was sensational! Money never seemed important to him, yet he attracted it from many directions. Once, he thought one of his elderly patients couldn't afford to pay for his services, so he refused to accept any money from her. When this seemingly destitute senior citizen passed on, she willed him a considerable sum!

He appreciated a good joke (especially the racy kind), a good cigar, a drink or two, and keeping up with sports. When there was a major boxing bout or ball game he was either glued to his radio or was there if he possibly could be. He saw Jack Johnson fight, and loved to tell about the time he was in New York when Joe Louis knocked out Max Schmeling, the German champion. During that fight, fans like J.B. were almost prostrate with prayer for Joe, and all of Harlem turned out with soaring spirits and pride to celebrate the Brown Bomber's victory. There was dancing at Small's Paradise, the Hotel Theresa, the Savoy Ballroom, and in the streets. Our Uncle J.B. never would have missed that kind of excitement— not for all the tea in China.

Thoughts of J.B. conjure up images of big shiny cars, polished two-toned shoes, straw hats tipped to the side, and the continual party that always seemed to be going on around him. He loved people, action, and a good time, and when he stepped into a room, it all showed.

As if all this were not enough, he was also a good cook and preferred to eat his "dinner" first thing in the morning. Uncle J.B. was a meat-and-potatoes man.

BEEF STEW

4 tablespoons butter
3 pounds lean beef cubes
2 medium-size onions,
  chopped
1 clove garlic, chopped fine
3 cups water
2 bay leaves
Pinch of thyme
1½ tablespoons salt
2-3 dashes pepper

5 good-sized white potatoes,
  peeled and halved
6 carrots, halved
10-12 small white boiling
  onions
3 stalks celery, cut in thirds
2 medium-size ripe tomatoes
  sliced in eighths
1 cup dry red wine
2 tablespoons flour
¼ cup cold water

Melt butter in a large Dutch oven. Add beef cubes and brown fairly rapidly. Remove beef cubes, lower heat, and add onion and garlic. Sauté until onion is limp. Return beef cubes and add water, bay leaf, thyme, salt, and pepper. Simmer, covered, for 1½ hours. Then add potatoes, vegetables, and wine. Cook for 1 more hour. Mix flour in ¼ cup cold water and add to thicken gravy to desired consistency.

Yield: 6 servings.

BAKED BEEFSTEAKS FOR TWO

When in doubt about the tenderness of steaks, bake!

1½-2 pounds steak, any of
  the less expensive cuts,
  cut into 2 pieces
Juice of ¼ or ½ lemon,
  depending upon amount
  of steak
Salt and pepper to taste

Garlic powder to taste
2 green frying peppers,
  sliced thin
1 medium-size onion,
  sliced thin
½ cup water

Rub steaks with lemon juice. Sprinkle both sides liberally with salt, pepper, and garlic powder. Place in shallow pan. Lay sliced peppers and onion on top of steaks. Add ½ cup water and cover with tin foil. Bake in a preheated 225° oven for 2 hours. Add more water in small amounts if necessary.

Yield: 2 tender-as-butter, mouth-watering steaks.

BEEF AND LIMA BEAN STEW

4 tablespoons butter
2½ pounds lean beef cubes
1 clove garlic, minced
1 large onion, diced
¼ teaspoon thyme

Salt and pepper to taste
1 12-ounce can beer
2 cups fresh raw baby lima
  beans, or 1 package frozen

Melt butter in a Dutch oven. Add beef cubes and brown. Add garlic, onion, and seasonings. Sauté for 5 minutes more. Add beer, cover, and simmer slowly for 2 hours, or until meat is just about tender. Add water if necessary, but only small amounts at a time, since a fairly concentrated essence is desired. After the 2 hours, add lima beans and continue cooking for ½ hour. Serve over steaming hot rice.

Yield: 4 servings.

LEMON ROASTED LEG OF LAMB

3-pound leg or shoulder of
  lamb
½ cup vinegar
½ cup water
Juice of 1 lemon

Rind of ½ lemon, chopped
1½ teaspoons dried mustard
1 teaspoon salt
¼ teaspoon pepper

Prepare lamb by making inch-deep slices, spaced 1 inch apart. In a small saucepan, place vinegar, ½ cup water, lemon juice, rind, mustard, salt, and pepper. Bring to a boil and pour over lamb. Bake in a preheated 300° oven for 1½ hours, basting frequently. When serving, slice thinly and spoon pan juices over meat.

Yield: 4 servings.

SMITHFIELD HAM

Uncle J.B. used to mail us these hams from Virginia.

10-pound Smithfield ham
½ cup vinegar
½ cup brown sugar
1 cup apple cider
2 bay leaves

½ cup brown sugar
Whole cloves
1 can sliced pineapple, syrup
  reserved
Maraschino cherries

Using a vessel large enough for the ham to float freely, cover ham with water and soak for 2 hours. Pour off water and scrub ham with a stiff brush under running water. Cover again with cold water and let soak for 18–24 hours, changing the water periodically. Drain off water, rinse off any residue from vessel, and cover with clean water. Then add vinegar, brown sugar, cider, and bay leaves, bring to a boil (it may be necessary to use 2 burners). Lower heat and cook slowly, uncovered, just barely simmering, for about 4–4½ hours, allowing 25–30 minutes per pound. Remove ham from liquid and cool. Slice skin off, leaving a thin layer of fat. Place ham fat side up in a shallow roasting pan. For topping, spread with brown sugar that has been moistened with enough pineapple syrup to make a paste. Stud with whole cloves. Lay pineapple slices across with a cherry in each center. Bake in a preheated 375° oven for about 30 minutes or until brown. This is a deliciously salty ham which should be sliced thinly and served as a second meat. It is a particularly good complement to a turkey dinner. Use leftovers for sandwiches, as breakfast meat, or as a seasoning for vegetables.

ROAST PORK

1 4-pound pork roast, loin
  or center cut
2 cloves garlic, minced
Salt and pepper to taste

4 bay leaves
½ cup vinegar
½ teaspoon thyme

Pierce the roast in several places with a two-pronged fork. Force minced garlic into each hole, again with the aid of the fork. Sprinkle liberally with salt and pepper. Place the 4 bay leaves in the bottom of the roasting pan. Place the roast on top, fat side up. Combine vinegar and thyme, and pour evenly over the roast. Place in a preheated 325° oven, allowing 35 minutes baking time per pound. Baste occasionally.

Yield: 5–6 servings.

HOT POTATO SALAD

4 medium-size white
  potatoes
⅓ cup oil
¼ cup vinegar
½ teaspoon salt

¼ teaspoon pepper
½ teaspoon paprika
¼ teaspoon dry mustard
¼ teaspoon savory
¼ cup parsley, chopped

Peel and dice potatoes. Place in a saucepan and cover with salted water. Cook until tender, then drain off water. Mix oil, vinegar, and seasonings together and pour over potatoes. Sprinkle with parsley and serve hot.

Yield: 4 servings.

WHITE POTATO AND CHEESE CASSEROLE

8 medium-size potatoes
½ cup milk
½ pint heavy cream

2 eggs, lightly beaten
1½ cups grated Swiss or
  Cheddar cheese
Salt and pepper to taste

Peel and boil potatoes in salted water until tender. Drain and mash with a potato masher, adding milk as you do so. Stir in heavy cream, eggs, and cheese, reserving some of the cheese to be sprinkled on top. Season with salt and pepper. Place in an ungreased casserole dish. Bake in a preheated 450° oven for 15 minutes or until golden brown.

Yield: 6 servings.

HASHED BROWNED POTATOES

4 cups peeled, cubed raw
   white potatoes
Salt and pepper to taste
6 tablespoons bacon fat

1 medium-size onion, halved
   and sliced thin
2 teaspoons oregano
Worcestershire sauce

Sprinkle cubed potatoes with salt and pepper. Melt bacon fat in a heavy skillet. Add potato cubes, turning until well coated. Cook for 10 minutes over medium heat. Add onion, oregano, liberal squirts of Worcestershire sauce, and more salt and pepper if desired. Cook for 20–25 minutes more, or until potatoes are crusty brown and tender. Stir frequently. Add more bacon fat if potatoes stick.

Yield: 4–6 servings.

Aunt Lillian

If you think it's impossible to be a superstar at eighty-plus, you haven't met Aunt Lillian. A fireball of energy, she is always on the go and at a pace that would stagger many a twenty-year old. As the only survivor of her family of thirteen Allens, she jets from her home in Petersburg, Virginia, to Los Angeles, Cleveland, New York City, and Nashville to visit a host of grandnieces, nephews, and assorted friends. Wherever she goes, her fast and witty conversation makes her a welcomed and valued guest.

Aunt Lillian possesses an uncanny gift for presenting people in their best possible light and inspiring them to reach elusive goals—"quitters never win; winners never quit" is her motto. We have never known her to utter a disparaging word about anyone—unless, of course, that person fully deserved it. Like her late husband, J.B., she has a passion for cards, humorous anecdotes, and effortlessly takes center stage in any group.

She lives so intensely in the present that it's hard to get her to reminisce. "I never dwell on the past, I'm too busy moving into the future," she will say with a smile. "But let's see. Papa was a headwaiter at the old Tulane Hotel in Nashville, and that was thought to be a good job for a black man in those days. It was a time when your people seemed to do so much for you with so very little." Aunt Lil loathes cooking and admits it. "Sorry, dearie, I can't even remember how to cook." However, a trip to her "ice-box" reveals the secret of her flawless complexion: fresh fruits, vegetables, and homemade cold cream. She credits her sister Nell for introducing her to cosmetics. "I used to think what a vain old sister Nell is, but when she died at ninety, her skin was clear and beautiful." One of Nell's secrets, cerated violet vanishing cream, doesn't seem to be on the market anymore, but you can make it yourself if you follow Lil's formula.

Here are a few of Aunt Lil's beauty ideas. And she is truly a woman who knows how to keep her "Y & B"—Youth and Beauty!

BEAUTY FOODS

The garden is a woman's best source of cosmetic treasures. Aunt Lil says to eat plenty of fresh vegetables and fruits and use them externally, too.

Cucumber: Cucumbers are renowned for their beautifying abilities, so rub a slice over your face and neck. It will soften and smooth skin by refining pores. Also eat them raw with a little salt.

Watermelon: Watermelon rind has many of the same properties as cucumbers and is equally useful for beautifying skin. Rub the rind on face and neck. It is really refreshing on a hot summer day.

Tomato: Tomato juice is great for oily skin! Try swishing a slice of raw tomato over the face from time to time. It's so good for oily and pimply skin.

Potato: Peel and grate a little white potato and place under the eyes. Good for relieving swollen bags and dark circles if you've been crying or are just tired.

Eggs: Egg whites, beaten and applied to the face, work as a tightening mask to draw up wrinkles. Skin can use external sources of protein from the yolk too, as time marches on. Smear on either and rinse off with water after fifteen minutes.

Peaches, Cream, and Honey: Aunt Lil takes this one literally. Whip up a little heavy cream (¼ cup), mash ½ peach and mix with 1 tablespoon of honey. Apply to face and leave on for 15 minutes. Enjoy licking your lips! Stored in refrigerator, remainder will last for two weeks.

Lemon: To whiten nails, plunge them into the white part of a lemon rind for a minute or two. Also, to get an additional gloss, on nails, buff with an old-fashioned buffer.

Buttermilk: Drink it and use it as a mask. It aids the digestive system and acts as a cleanser and astringent for the face.

Lillian Allen Darden displaying her flawless complexion

The Allen family—little Lil, right corner, sister Nell behind mother Allen

VIOLET VANISHING CREAM

Aunt Lil gave us the recipe for sister Nell's own violet vanishing cream.

2 tablespoons white beeswax
2 tablespoons lanolin
9 tablespoons mineral oil

½ teaspoon Borax (sodium borate)
3 tablespoons rose water
¼ teaspoon essence of violet oil

Place beeswax, lanolin, and mineral oil in the top of an enamel, or glass double boiler. Heat until thoroughly melted. Dissolve Borax in warmed rose water and add this to beeswax mixture. Remove from heat. Stir vigorously with a wooden spoon while mixture cools and thickens. Then add essence of violet. Continue beating until well blended. Jar and store in refrigerator if you wish.

Aunt Lil's husband, J.B., was a pharmacist, and it wasn't difficult for her to obtain these supplies. If they are not available at your local drugstore, write for them at Kiehl Pharmacy, Inc., 109 Third Avenue, New York, New York 10003.

HOMEMADE PERFUME

Here is a simple way to make any essence. Steep a cupful of petals (violets, roses, honeysuckle, lilacs) or the skin of 1 orange or 2 limes in 1 cup of safflower or olive oil for a day or so. Then strain off and reserve oil. Discard petals or skins and replace with fresh ones every other day for at least 10 days or longer (about 5 times). When the scent is strong, discard petals, measure oil, and mix with an equal amount of ethanol rubbing alcohol. Keep tightly capped. Shake once or twice daily for 2 weeks. Now spoon off the alcohol (an eyedropper is useful). The remaining drops are your own precious essence oils. We have had the best luck with honeysuckle perfume, but without fixatives used in commercial perfumes, the scent does not last long once applied. Still, it's fun to do and you can mix your own essence with regular colognes to produce unique and exotic fragrances.

eeeeeeeeeeeeeeeeeeeeeeeeeeeeeeeeeeeeeeeeeeeeeeeeee

SACHET

Distinctive fragrance is a part of Aunt Lil's aura. When you think of her neat white house with its sky-blue trim and rows of pink petunias leading up the walk, the first thing that floods the mind is its sweet smell. Old homes always seem to smell best. Aunt Lil uses sachet to refreshen her rooms.

1 quart flower petals and buds	Dash of mace
½ tablespoon salt	Dash of allspice
1 cinnamon stick	Drop of essence of lemon oil
6 cloves	Drop of essence of violet oil
Dash of nutmeg	1 tablespoon orrisroot, chips or powder (optional)

Gather petals of rose, lilac, honeysuckle, lily of the valley, violets, and whatever smells good or adds color. Dry them in the hot sun or in a 250° oven on a cookie sheet until they are crisp (about 15 minutes). Then place them in a jar that has a tight lid, alternate layers of petals and buds with a sprinkling of salt, spices, and essences so that everything is well distributed to begin with. (Orrisroot helps fix the scent but is not essential.) Every day for a week shake the jar to toss the petals and spices to mingle the scents.

Keep the jar closed for 2 weeks. The opened jar will scent a room. Some of the contents crushed and tied in scraps of cloth can be used as a drawer sachet and will fill a linen or clothes closet with a delightful aroma.

Lillian A. Darden, Fisk University music student

BODY TIPS

Dry Hands: Before going to bed, rub hands vigorously with lanolin, and put on a pair of gloves to retain heat and protect the bed linen. Allow the lanolin and gloves to remain overnight. You may look odd, but your hands will soften.

Feet: If you have rough feet, Aunt Lil recommends rubbing them with a pumice stone, then applying castor oil.

Lines and Wrinkles:

ANTI-WRINKLE CREAM

(for under the eyes, neck, forehead, laugh lines, etc.)

2 teaspoons honey
1½ tablespoons lanolin
2 tablespoons cocoa butter.

Melt the above in a small enamel or glass pot. Apply a little bit while still warm. Cool and jar the rest. Pat gently onto the skin. Remove excess with soft tissue after 10 minutes.

Hair: For dry scalp, warm ½ cup olive oil. Part hair in small sections and apply with cotton balls. Leave on overnight, wrapping the head in a scarf to protect pillowcases.

Teeth: When we asked Aunt Lil what people did about dental care in her youth, she told us that they brushed with salt and the charcoal from fireplaces. Baking soda was used for mouthwash as well as for deodorant in those preaerosol times.

Face:

LEMON NOURISHING CREAM

1 egg yolk
½ cup olive oil

1 tablespoon fresh lemon juice
3 drops essence of lemon oil

Beat egg yolk with an electric beater at high speed until light and lemony. Add a few drops of olive oil at a time, beating vigorously until mixture becomes thick and creamy. Add lemon juice, then essence of lemon or a few drops of your favorite perfume. Blend well, jar, and keep this super-rich cream refrigerated. Massage into the skin as a night cream.

Two parting beauty secrets we received from Aunt Lil on our last visit:

"Peace of mind is radiated in one's countenance, and it's not so easy to come by in times of trouble unless you work at it every day. I begin and end my day by reading "The Daily Word" [a religious pamphlet with inspirational thoughts for each day]. And once a week I take a special, long, leisurely, floral-scented bath, preferably by candlelight.

"During my bath I sort out the weeds of the last week and sow the seeds for the coming one. In life you just have to keep moving—stepping higher all the time."

Uncles C.L., Arthur, Russell & Charlie

Uncle C. L.

To each of his children, Papa Darden seemed to have transmitted some of his many talents. This was clearly in evidence in C.L. (Camillus Lewis), the only son who elected to remain home and help in the family business. Mechanical things fascinated C.L. and he inherited his father's ability to repair anything. At age eight, he could take a clock apart and reassemble it. Even if he had never seen the "contraption" before, if he knew what it was supposed to do, it was a matter of minutes before he had it better than new. This mechanical talent brought him so much revenue as a teen-ager that C.L. refused to leave Wilson and attend high school, though he encouraged the others to pursue their educations and financially assisted them.

By 1914, motorcycles, phonographs, and records had been introduced to the world. Many people thought these inventions were passing fads, so C.L. managed to acquire the only franchises in Wilson County to sell RCA Victor phonographs and records and Harley-Davidson motorcycles. He would travel deep into the rural sections where records had never been heard playing Bessie Smith and Bert Williams, or Caruso, as the occasion warranted. Black or white, anyone in or around Wilson who wanted a motorcycle or record player had to buy it from C.L. Eventually, new dealers flooded the market, so after Papa Darden retired, C.L. abandoned his mechanical interests, attended Mortuary Science School and took over the funeral business with his younger brother, Arthur.

Opposite in every way to outgoing and outspoken C.L., Arthur in early life was a quiet, introspective soul who loved books and music. He derived great pleasure from playing the tuba with a local band and singing deep baritone in church and with a street corner quartet. Although he had shown promise as a medical student, World War I interrupted his studies. Contrary to Papa Darden's strong conviction that blacks should avoid the military, Arthur was caught in the vortex of war hysteria and felt that participation in the armed forces would break down the doors of racial prejudice at home. He cut quite a splendid figure in his officer's uniform as he marched off, determined "to make the world safe for democracy." His letters home were at first filled with the excitement of Paris and foreign shores, but his enthusiasm quickly soured as the reality of the torment and anguish of war set in. While overseas, he was the victim of a nerve gas attack and returned to Wilson a bitter and disabled man, utterly disillusioned by the bigotry he had experienced and by the cruelty and horror of war. Despite an enormous struggle to regain his strength and resume his position as a wheelwright with Papa Darden, his health was shattered and he never fully recuperated. Even so, Arthur was able to finish Eckles Mortuary School, marry, and have a son. However, as the years passed, the debilitating effects of the gassing increased, sapping his energy and spirit and causing his marriage and ability to work to fail. For the rest of his life, he would resent the fact that he had fought and suffered for what he termed "the barest trickle of democracy."

*Arthur Darden
during World War I*

Therefore C.L. became the dominant force in the funeral parlor. He took his profession seriously and had a passion for ritual and routine, which ideally suited him to it. Ironically, one of the first funerals under his and Arthur's direction was that of their younger brother, Russell, who was in his last year at Howard University Law School. Russell had gone to New York City to look for adventure during the Christmas vacation. While there, he caught pneumonia and died at Harlem Hospital before any of the family could reach him. Russell had been a daring, fun-loving, robust, athletic young man known for his prowess on the football field. Our father remembers that the last time he saw Russell play football was at Livingston College. The score was Livingston 3, Biddle 3. The ball was snapped and thrown to Russell. He was running hard. The opposition tried for a tackle but missed and tore off the seat of his pants instead. Oblivious to the cheers and laughter of the crowd, Russell kept running and won the game 9-3 with his rear end showing. He had an aggressive spirit and was the pride and joy of his family. His death left an aching gap in the family circle.

Charles, the second oldest son, who had left home many years before, returned for the funeral and delivered a heartfelt eulogy. Russell had been his favorite brother and both had looked forward to a partnership in legal and political careers, plus the development

81

of the resort for black vacationers that Charlie had started to build on Lake Elsinore near Los Angeles. After Russell's funeral, Charles corresponded but returned to the East only once. For this reason he remains somewhat of an enigma. What is known about him, however, is that he was a dapper, lifelong bachelor who was renowned for his elocution; that he eventually became a presiding judge; and that he was frugal and had what was then considered "peculiar dietary habits" in that he was a confirmed vegetarian.

Of all these uncles, C.L. was the only one we really knew. He was a man who courted the regard and respect of his constituents yet fussed about his overloaded duties. That was just his way. Not a day went by that he didn't confer with his cronies. We would see them sitting on straw-backed chairs in front of the funeral home or on his front porch, smoking cigars while discussing sports, world politics, and the local news. Every issue—from what color to paint the church vestibule to bail money or employment of someone in need—claimed Uncle C.L.'s equal attention and bluster. Once he took a stand on an issue, he was not easily budged, and during his long years in Wilson he stood in the thick of many controversies, large and small.

One of the first town crises that Uncle C.L. helped resolve and told us about was the slap-that-started-a-school incident. In 1918 a

Russell Darden

Russell Darden—front row, second from left, in his class at Biddle, now Johnson C. Smith

"colored" schoolteacher was slapped in the face by the white superintendent of schools for alleged insubordination. Eight teachers decided to strike, and the community backed them by boycotting the public school. Uncle C.L., along with other community leaders, organized an effort to collect money from churches, lodges, and interested people to create an independent school. A building was bought and, despite a climate of fear and uncertainty about whether the school would be allowed to exist, three hundred children were enrolled by parents who willingly paid tuition. At the end of the school year the students presented a play (directed by Georgia Burke, later a Broadway actress) that attracted so many town well-wishers that a vacant warehouse had to be rented. This became an annual event for all Wilson, and the community-run school became a model for black educators of the day during the ten years it lasted. Uncle C.L. was duly proud of the part he played in the school's long success.

How our uncle enjoyed all the activities and accolades that his little town offered! He was a member of the Masons, the Elks, the Odd Fellows, the Civic Club, the Knights of Pythias Lodge, and was the chairman of the church trustees as well. Every town needs its solid citizen and, one thing is for sure, C.L. personified that role.

No, Uncle C.L. could not cook. As far as we know, none of these uncles did much in the cooking department. It is said that Russell had a hearty appetite, Arthur ate like a bird, and Charlie was a devotee of health foods; but none of their favorite recipes survive. We do know, however, that Uncle C.L. loved good food, and his special delight was the excellent seafood prepared by his wife Norma and their friends throughout the South, and sometimes caught by C.L. himself.

BAKED STUFFED SHAD

STUFFING:

1 large green pepper,
    chopped
2 medium-size onions, diced
1 cup diced celery
2 small cloves garlic, minced
¼ cup bacon drippings
6 slices buttered toast,
    coarsely crumbled

An equal quantity of leftover
    corn bread, coarsely
    crumbled
½ cup hot water
2 eggs, beaten
Salt and pepper to taste

Sauté vegetables and garlic in bacon drippings until limp. Combine toast and corn bread crumbs. Pour hot water over them. Add the sautéed vegetables and the beaten eggs. Mix well. Season to taste. Mixture should be fairly dry.

SHAD:

1 5-pound shad, split for
    stuffing, head and tail
    intact

3 slices bacon

Clean fish. Make 3 shallow slits across the top side. Sprinkle salt in stuffing cavity and the slits. Stuff cavity and close it with a skewer. Place fish in a shallow baking pan. Top with 3 slices of bacon for basting purposes. Bake in a preheated 400° oven for approximately 45 minutes. Remove the bacon about 15 minutes before the end of baking time.

Yield: 4 generous servings.

SAUTÉED SHAD ROE

2 fairly large sacs of shad roe
2 cups boiling water
Salt and pepper to taste

2 tablespoons butter
3 eggs, beaten

Place roe in a sieve. Pour boiling water over the roe and remove as much of the skin or sac as possible. Season with salt and pepper. Melt butter in a skillet. When bubbly but not brown, add roe, stirring constantly to prevent lumping and sticking. Roe is done when no longer red in color. Texture should be grainy. Add the beaten egg to this and stir as in scrambling. Cook until eggs are done. Serve hot for breakfast with grits and bacon.

Yield: 4 servings.

———◆◆———

OYSTER STEW

From Ed Lloyd, a fellow fisherman.

½ cup diced celery
3 cups milk
1 cup light cream
1½ teaspoons salt

½ teaspoon pepper
½ teaspoon paprika
2 tablespoons butter
1 pint shucked oysters

In a small saucepan, cook the celery in a small amount of boiling water until it is tender. Combine milk, cream, and seasonings in the top of a double boiler. Heat thoroughly, taking care not to allow the mixture to boil. Add celery, butter, and oysters and their liquid. Cook for about 5 minutes or until the oysters curl around the edges.

Yield: 4–6 servings.

———◆◆———

OYSTER CASSEROLE

A specialty of Wilson's star caterer—Georgia Dupree.

1 quart oysters
Milk
2 cups cracker crumbs
½ cup butter

Salt and pepper to taste
1 cup grated sharp cheese
Paprika

Bachelor Uncle Charles and Hollywood throng

Drain oysters, reserving liquid. To this liquid, add enough milk to make 2 cups. Melt butter and add to crumbs. In a casserole place a layer of crumbs, then a layer of oysters. Season with salt and pepper, then sprinkle with cheese. Continue alternating, ending with a layer of crumbs. Pour reserved liquid over the top. Sprinkle with paprika. Bake in a preheated 350° oven for 20–30 minutes.

Yield: 6–8 servings.

FRIED OYSTERS

1 quart oysters	¾ cup cracker crumbs
Salt	¼ cup yellow cornmeal
2 eggs, beaten	

Drain oysters in a sieve. Lay them out on paper towels and sprinkle with salt. Dip several oysters at a time into the eggs. Mix cracker crumbs and cornmeal on wax paper. Roll oysters in this mixture and then drop into deep hot fat (450°), frying only 1 layer at a time until golden brown. Drain on paper towels. Serve immediately. Excellent for breakfast with grits, eggs, and bacon.

Yield: 4–6 servings.

FRIED SALT FISH

Salt herring, mullet, or
  mackerel (fish that has
  been soaked in brine),
  allow 1 fish per person

Yellow cornmeal
Fat for frying

Have fish prepared at fish market (head, tail, and fins removed and fish split). Cover fish with cold water and soak for 2 hours. Drain, add fresh water, and soak overnight. In the morning, pat off excess water with paper towels. On the skin side, make 2 or 3 shallow slits. Coat entire fish with cornmeal. Fry in hot fat until golden brown. Serve hot for breakfast with grits and eggs.

POTLUCK GUMBO

1 large slice (¼ pound)
  precooked ham, diced
1 pound shrimp, shelled to
  tail and deveined
1½ cups chicken giblets,
  parboiled and diced
1 pound fresh okra, cut in
  ¼-inch rounds
1 medium-size onion, diced
1 green pepper, diced
2 cloves garlic, minced

½ cup chopped parsley
½ cup scallion tops, sliced
  thin
Pepper to taste
5 cups water
2 crabs, cooked, meat
  removed from shells, or
  4 ounces frozen
Salt
1 tablespoon gumbo filé

Sauté ham in its own border of fat, adding oil if necessary. Set aside, discarding fat. Sauté shrimp in same pan until pink. Remove and set aside. Then sauté chicken giblets. Add okra, onion, green pepper, garlic, parsley, scallion tops, and pepper. Add the 5 cups of water. Simmer for 1 hour. Add ham, shrimp and crab meat. Continue cooking for another 15 minutes. During the last 5 minutes of cooking add salt to taste, then gumbo filé. Serve over hot rice. (Gumbo filé is powdered sassafras leaf. It was originally made by the Choctaw Indians and is most easily obtained in Louisiana, but can be bought in most shops specializing in seasonings.)

Yield: 6–8 servings.

Aunt Norma

Norma Duncan Darden began life in Montgomery, Alabama, at the turn of the century as the middle child and only girl in the family. On a recent trip to her home, we browsed through her many photographs as she told us who was who and how and when they had entered her life. "My father ("Papa" to us), as the last male Duncan, inherited the ancestral home and rental houses, and owned a number of business places in the downtown part of the city. He was also a bondsman. Papa was known for his choice horses, as that was the era of the horse and buggy and sporty 'runabouts.' We could always tell when he was nearing home by Flora-Dora's (the horse that I remember) gait and sound on the brick-paved street. My father was considered the sport of his family. He was a betting man who loved to travel: Flora-Dora was named for a popular musical Papa saw on Broadway, and Mid-Way, our pug dog, was his gift to us from the exposition he attended in Atlanta. Mardi Gras time found him in Mobile or New Orleans while we anxiously awaited his return. It seems like yesterday when Aunt Arizona and her friends returned from the world's fair in St. Louis in their lovely frocks—long, sweeping taffeta skirts, leg-o'-mutton sleeves (the Gibson Girl look)—bringing confetti, dolls, and playthings for Henry, Richard, and me. What merriment! The paving blocks in front of our house were blue and white octagon shapes, so we played hopscotch without drawing the customary patterns. In back there was a stable with a loft and a playing area. On the other side was the chicken house, from the top of which my brothers and friends launched scooters and raced them down to the trolley-car tracks on our street. Behind all was a garden and fruit trees.

"Against this idyllic childhood, tragedy struck. First, Aunt Norma's paternal grandmother Ellen died. Then, when Norma was seven, her mother Evangeline also died. The household was taken over by her Aunt Arizona, a young grade schoolteacher and friend of our Aunt Maude's. But two years later, she contracted pneumonia and also died.

"My earliest memory of my mother was going to Sunday school and church with her—that she was tall, gentle and beautifully dressed—and the pretty pinafores she made for me. She had attended Fisk University, and one of her best friends became Mrs. Booker T. Washington, who later escorted me in her car to my wedding. I still have the shocking pink ostrich fan, my wedding gift from her. The other memory of my mother still vivid is a ride in the train coach with her and my brother Henry to Savannah, Georgia. We traveled with a huge trunk of clothes, as it was the custom in those days when visiting faraway family members to spend a few weeks or even a couple of months. We were traveling to visit her uncle, R. R. Wright, then president of Georgia State College. As a ten-year-old, Wright had electrified General O. O. Howard of the Union Army and his party during their inspection of the Atlanta schools after the signing of the Emancipation Proclamation. At the end of his address, the general had asked the little black children

89

Arizona Duncan, Aunt Norma's aunt, at St. Louis World's Fair in 1904

who had assembled around an abandoned freightcar which served as their school, 'What message shall I take to the people in the North?' Wright's stirring reply from one so young—'Tell them, sir, that we are rising!'—was immortalized in a poem by John Greenleaf Whittier. It was with the Wright family that I'm told I started kindergarten; although I don't remember."

After the death of all the women in her immediate family, Aunt Norma and her older brother were sent to Tallahassee, Florida, to live with her mother's brother, Major Henry Howard, a mathematics professor, commandant of a military unit, and bandleader at Florida A. & M. College. They spent two school terms there. Then her father, fearing that he could not raise a daughter alone, begged the faculty at Talladega College in Alabama to admit her as a special student. At twelve, she became the youngest boarder to enter, and for the next eight years, from eighth grade through college, Talladega was her second home.

Having spent most of her young life in black educational institutions, Aunt Norma tells us that many of them were originally intended to meet the needs of both black and white Southerners, but became segregated only after laws were passed enforcing separation of the races. She fondly remembers the dedication of the integrated faculty at Talladega.

Shortly before graduation, the news of Mary McLeod Bethune's monumental struggle to increase the school she had started in 1904

Aunt Norma, top right, with Mrs. Bethune, second from left, at her college in Daytona Beach, Florida

with five students in a single room reached Aunt Norma. She proudly joined the faculty as an English teacher there, twelve years after its inception. For a while, Mrs. Bethune encouraged what appeared to be a budding romance between Norma and her only son, Bert Bethune. However, our own Aunt Maude stepped into the picture initiating correspondence between Norma and Uncle C.L., her husband's brother, and, after two years of letter writing, arranged a meeting of the two "pen pals" at her home in Opelika, Alabama. C.L., who had fallen in love with Aunt Norma's gracious personality and stately beauty via the mails and a photograph, proved to be an ardent suitor, courting her with flowers, candy, and watermelon. In 1922 he married her in John and Maude's flower garden under the grape arbor, and took her to Wilson, North Carolina.

On first arrival the newlyweds lived with Papa Darden, but C.L., not wanting to move far from his father or the business, purchased a vacant lot across the street, and Aunt Norma designed her own floor plans for their "dream house." Her brother-in-law, John Barnes, built it. In similar fashion, she designed and supervised the renovation of the Darden Memorial Funeral Home. So, from the earliest days of her arrival in Wilson, Aunt Norma's innate sense of style and taste have won extravagant and deserved praise. Accustomed to life in an academic setting, she filled her time with the cultural and social activities of the town and became "the hostess with the mostest." With over fifty years in her "dream house," she continues to give luster to the title "homemaker." We ought to know. A portion of nearly every summer of our childhood was spent in her home, and fresh are our memories of dusting the furniture, setting the table, putting the flowers out, and serving refreshments to the ladies from the Book and Garden Club; the Church Missionary Society; her sorority, the AKA; the Links; the Mary Bethune Civic Club; and the Merry Matrons' Bridge Club, to name a few . . . and not to mention the gentlemen from Uncle C.L.'s groups. With so many meetings, activities, and visits from friends and relatives throughout the years, Aunt Norma has collected a large repertoire of delicious dishes and party potpourri. And here are a few of her unique entertaining ideas.

Once, when we were very young, Aunt Norma gave a breakfast come-exactly-as-you-were-when-invited party. One guest came in a bathrobe and curlers. Sensing the mood of abandonment at play here, we went upstairs and returned completely nude. What possessed us we will never know. But should you want to give a breakfast come-as-you-are party, whatever your guests wear we know they'll love Aunt Norma's baked grits and brains.

BAKED GRITS

3 cups cooked grits
2 tablespoons melted butter
2 eggs, beaten
1½ cups evaporated milk

1¾ cups grated Cheddar
  cheese
Paprika to taste
Cayenne pepper to taste
  (usually no more than 1 or
  2 dashes)

Mash grits if they are leftovers. Add melted butter, eggs, and evaporated milk. Then add 1½ cups grated cheese, reserving ¼ cup for the topping. Combine thoroughly. Add paprika and cayenne. Pour mixture into a buttered casserole. Bake in a preheated 425° oven for 25 minutes or until brown. Sprinkle with remaining grated cheese and more paprika. Return to oven and cook until topping has melted.

Yield: About 6 servings.

SCRAMBLED BRAINS

1 pound pork brains
Salt and pepper to taste

3-4 tablespoons butter or
  bacon drippings
4 eggs, beaten

Place brains in a sieve. Pour boiling water over them and remove as much of the covering membrane as possible. Season with salt and pepper. Melt butter or bacon drippings in a skillet. When bubbling, add brains, stirring constantly to break them up and to prevent sticking and lumping. When nicely browned, stir in beaten eggs with a fork as in scrambling. Cook until eggs are done. Serve hot for breakfast with Baked Grits and bacon.

Yield: 4-6 servings.

One year one of Aunt Norma's clubs gave a hobo party to raise scholarship funds. Everyone came dressed as vagabonds, and the menu was baked beans, hot dogs, cole slaw, corn bread, and coffee.

BAKED BEANS

1 pound navy beans, soaked
   overnight
1 medium-size onion, diced
2½ cups stewed tomatoes

1½ cups brown sugar, loosely
   packed
¼ pound salt pork, streaked
   with lean

Drain beans, place in a saucepan, cover with fresh water, and parboil with onions until the beans are tender but still firm (about 1 hour). Drain, reserving liquid. Add stewed tomatoes and sugar to beans. Put in a covered, ungreased casserole or bean pot. Slice salt pork ⅓ inch thick and place in strips over beans. Bake in a preheated 325° oven for 4 hours, turning salt pork over occasionally. As moisture evaporates, add enough reserved liquid to the pot to cover beans and prevent them from drying out. Then uncover and raise the oven temperature to 375° to brown the salt pork on both sides. If necessary, add more liquid. Cook for at least another hour, or longer, depending upon the texture of the beans.

Yield: 6–8 servings.

Another year the Merry Matrons gave a gypsy party complete with a fortune-teller who read palms and cards. Red, purple, and green was the color scheme, so Aunt Norma contributed her magnificent eggplant.

MAGNIFICENT STUFFED EGGPLANT

2 large eggplants, halved
   lengthwise
2 medium-size onions, diced
3 medium-size green
   peppers, diced
3–4 tablespoons bacon
   drippings or vegetable oil

8 ripe tomatoes, peeled and
   chunked
Salt and pepper to taste
8 ounces Cheddar cheese,
   grated (keep a fistful in
   reserve)
½–¾ cup bread crumbs

Carefully scoop out the eggplant from the skin, taking care not to puncture what should be a thin shell, less than a quarter of an inch thick. Place the eggplant pieces in salted boiling water to cover and cook until very tender. Meanwhile, sauté the onions and peppers in the bacon drippings or oil until onions are translucent. Then add tomatoes, salt, and pepper. Simmer. When eggplant is done, drain well and return to saucepan. Add cheese, stirring to facilitate melting. Add enough bread crumbs so that the mixture is somewhat dry and very cheesy. Add the simmering tomato mixture to this, using a slotted spoon. Then add as much of the remaining juice as necessary to make a moist but not watery, reddish mixture. If overly moist, add more bread crumbs. Fill eggplant shells. Bake in a preheated 425° oven for 45 minutes to 1 hour. Toward the end of baking time, top generously with more grated cheese. Allow some extra time for the cheese to melt and brown.

Aunt Norma, in the tradition of true Southern cooks, serves her stuffed eggplant as one of at least two accompanying vegetables in a meal. But we have found that it makes an exceptional meal by itself, one large shell served per person. Hot muffins with peach preserves make a delicious accompaniment to this dish. The recipe is fairly simple but time-consuming because of all the chopping, slicing, and dicing. For this reason, it is best prepared in quantity, with 2 large eggplants as a minimum.

Recently, Aunt Norma gave a "round-the-world" party where guests were requested to come in the apparel from whatever country they chose and to prepare a stunt! A prize was given for the best display of talent, and an international buffet was served. She has also used this theme for a "historical character" party where guests presented a few facts about heroines of bygone eras. Good for a buffet or dinner anytime is her Hungarian Beef Goulash.

HUNGARIAN BEEF GOULASH

3 pounds beef stew meat in
   small cubes
¼ cup butter or oil
2 large onions, chopped
1 clove garlic, chopped
1 heaping tablespoon
   paprika
1½ teaspoons salt

1 cup beef stock or 2
   bouillon cubes in 1 cup
   water
3 tablespoons dry white wine
2 tablespoons flour
3 tablespoons water
1 cup sour cream
Black olives
Chopped parsley

Brown meat cubes in butter or oil in a Dutch oven. Remove meat and brown onions and garlic. Return meat, add paprika, and salt, and stir. Add stock and wine. Bring to a boil, then reduce heat and simmer covered for about 1 hour or until tender. Blend flour in 3 tablespoons water, add to pot, and cook for 10 minutes more. Remove from heat and gently stir in sour cream. Garnish with black olives and parsley. Wonderful over noodles, mashed potatoes, or rice.

Yield: 6–8 servings.

We remember an Aunt Norma party where everything was yellow, from the plates and flowers to the tablecloth. She served her chicken purlo over yellow rice, yellow summer squash, yellow string beans, and banana punch. For dessert there was Pineapple Ice Cream served in miniature yellow flowerpots, with real daisies standing in each pot, and Lemon Cookies.

CHICKEN PURLO (PILAU)

3 medium-size stalks of celery, diced
1 large onion, diced
1 medium-size green pepper, chopped
2 small cloves garlic, minced
3 tablespoons bacon drippings
1 stewing hen, 4 pounds, cut into serving pieces
Salt and pepper to taste
4 cups chicken broth from boiling chicken
Pinch of saffron
2 cups uncooked rice
2 tablespoons flour
¼ cup water
3 hard-cooked eggs, coarsely chopped

In a large kettle sauté vegetables and garlic with bacon drippings until tender. Add chicken pieces and 7 cups of water. Add salt and pepper. Bring to a boil, cover, and simmer slowly until fork tender (about 1½ hours). When done, remove 4 cups of chicken broth and in a separate pot bring this to a boil. Add salt to taste, the saffron and raw rice.

Cook, covered, until the grains are tender and the liquid is absorbed, about 25–30 minutes. Remove chicken from its pot and thicken remaining broth with a mixture of the flour and water. Boil until desired thickness is reached. Adjust the seasoning and return

he chicken to the pot. Heat thoroughly before serving. Chicken
hould be served nestled in piping-hot rice, with coarsely chopped
ard-cooked eggs on top and with the gravy passed in a separate
ish.

Yield: 6 servings.

SOUTHERN FRIED CORN

ears corn	1 tablespoon sugar
cup bacon fat	1 cup water
tablespoons flour	Salt and pepper to taste

huck corn. Wash and remove silk. After cutting the kernels in half
with a sharp knife, cut kernels off. (This is called cream style
utting.) Scrape juice out of corn cob into the corn. Pour bacon fat
nto a frying pan. Heat. Add corn. Stir in flour, sugar, and 1 cup
water. Let simmer at medium heat until kernels are tender. Then
aise heat. Stir at intervals, letting mixture brown slightly on the
ottom. Scrape the brown off bottom and mix this well into the rest
f the corn. Add salt and pepper and, if necessary, add a little hot
water. Mixture should be moist.

Yield: 4 servings.

AUNT NORMA'S BANANA FRUIT PUNCH

oranges	1 28-ounce bottle ginger ale
lemons	28 ounces water
scant cup sugar	1 peach, sliced
cloves	1 handful blueberries
cinnamon stick	2 firm bananas, sliced

Squeeze juice from citrus fruits and pour into punch bowl. Add
sugar and spices. Stir. Add 2 trays of ice.* Pour in ginger ale. Dilute
with an equal amount of water. Garnish with sliced peach and
blueberries. Top with sliced bananas.

Yield: 12 servings.

*For a decorative touch to tall glasses of lemonade or iced tea, Aunt Norma freezes maraschino
cherries, mandarin orange sections, strawberries, raspberries, or fresh mint sprigs in ice cubes.*

Automobiles were fairly novel machines when Aunt Norma arrived in Wilson, and one of the first parties she remembers was an auto-tour party. For these many young people would get together and drive from house to house, having a different course, from appetizer to dessert, at each home. Aunt Norma was noted for a wide assortment of desserts and the last stop was always at her house.

These little cupcakes are very dainty if baked in miniature muffin tins, but they can also be made in regular size muffin tins or in a 9-inch skillet, using 5 pineapple rings for an upside-down cake.

PINEAPPLE UPSIDE-DOWN CUPCAKES

TOPPING:

4 tablespoons butter
7 tablespoons dark brown
   sugar

½ cup crushed pineapple
6 maraschino cherries cut in
   slices

CAKE BATTER:

¼ cup butter
¼ cup sugar
1 egg, separated
1 cup sifted cake flour

1½ teaspoons baking powder
¼ teaspoon salt
½ cup pineapple juice
½ teaspoon vanilla

Melt butter in a saucepan and add brown sugar. Cook over low flames until well blended, then stir in crushed pineapple, reserving juice. Pour about a teaspoon of this topping into the bottom of each greased miniature muffin cup and add a sliver of a red cherry. To prepare batter: Cream the butter, add the sugar, and beat until fluffy. Beat the egg yolk and add. Sift the flour, baking powder, and salt together; add alternately with the pineapple juice. Add vanilla. Beat the egg white until stiff and fold into the batter. Pour this batter over the topping and bake in a preheated 350° oven for 25 minutes. Cool, then turn cupcakes carefully onto a cake plate, the pineapple side up.

Yield: 2 dozen miniature or 1 dozen regular cupcakes.

Can be poured into a 9-inch skillet, using 5 pineapple rings for cake.

ECAN TARTLETS WITH CREAM CHEESE PASTRY

ASTRY:

ounces cream cheese,
softened

½ cup butter
1 cup flour, sifted

ILLING:

egg, well beaten
cup light brown sugar
cup chopped pecan meats

1 teaspoon vanilla
Pinch of salt

or the pastry, cream butter and cream cheese together. Mix in
our and refrigerate for easy handling. For the filling, mix egg,
rown sugar, pecans, vanilla, and salt, blending well. Then shape
hilled pastry dough into 1-inch balls. Place in tartlet tins 2½ inches
1 diameter, press over bottoms and sides. Spoon filling into shells.
ake in a preheated 325° oven for 25 minutes. (Miniature muffin
ns may be used if you cannot find tartlet tins. Five-and-ten-cent
tores have tin-foil ones that will do in a pinch.)

ield: About 18 tartlets.

Aunt Norma with her nieces—us

EGGNOG PIE

9-inch graham cracker pie
  shell (see Index)

FILLING:

1 envelope (1 tablespoon)
  unflavored gelatin
¼ cup sugar
1⅓ cups milk
3 egg yolks, lightly beaten

3 egg whites
¼ cup sugar
2 tablespoons dark rum
½ cup heavy cream

In medium-size saucepan combine gelatin, sugar, milk, and egg
yolks. Cook over medium heat, stirring until mixture comes to a
boil. Remove from heat. Chill for 15–20 minutes, stirring
occasionally until mixture begins to thicken. Beat egg whites into
soft peaks. Gradually add ¼ cup sugar. Beat until thick. Add rum to
chilled egg yolk mixture. Whip cream and fold along with egg
whites into egg mixture. Pour into pie shell and chill for 3–4 hours.

Yield: About 8 servings.

Aunt Alice

Alice Foster is our adopted aunt. Actually, she was Aunt Norma's roommate in college. The two were inseparable friends, so we grew up feeling she was part of the family.

Aunt Alice was a "divorced woman" at a time when that label carried a hint of mystery and intrigue. She left her native Birmingham (although the accent never left her) in the late forties and went to New York to seek her fortune and a better education for her daughters Vicky and Leah. For many years she taught home economics in the public school system and ran an alteration shop evenings and Saturdays. After her girls began careers of their own, she decided to see a bit of the world, packed her bags, and toured Europe and Africa, sending us a postcard from nearly every port. From Spain she wrote that she had just left Morocco and had settled in a villa near Palma for the winter. That simply knocked us out!

Aunt Alice was unbelievably exotic to us—our own resident sophisticated world-traveled *femme fatale*. We loaded all our intimate adolescent problems on her and loved her visits to our home and our visits to her magical apartment in Brooklyn that was filled with the treasures of her travels. We would whisper secrets over fenugreek tea (her favorite infusion for preventing colds) in her parlor, which was filled with every green foliage imaginable. We would sit on giant sofas covered with vivid floral prints and lots of bright pillows while her two fluffy white cats (who matched her white throw rugs) stalked around and a pet bluebird (which she had discovered on her window sill one day) chimed in occasionally.

Besides the opportunity to reveal our souls to her, the added allure of our Brooklyn jaunts were the assorted health and figure tips Aunt Alice would give us. Long before yoga exercises and eating "health foods" and talking to house plants were popular, Aunt Alice had been advocating these practices. We never could keep up with her well-disciplined beauty and health routine, but she has religiously practiced what she's preached for the last forty years. Every morning she rises at 6:00 A.M., drinks the juice of half a lemon squeezed into a glass of warm water, and then does her morning exercises (much toe-touching, bicycling, stretching, and head-stands). Then she washes her face with uncooked oatmeal blended with a little water in the palm of her hand. She never uses soap on her face and when she has used make-up removes it with corn or olive oil, followed by witch hazel. For breakfast she has a vitamin cocktail and a slice of her homemade natural bread. During the day she sips herb teas (rose hips and camomile) and vegetable broths of parsley and watercress steeped in hot water, and lunches on a salad. For her large meal, she rarely eats meat, preferring fish or fowl. And what exciting, tasty, healthful compositions she can create from her natural staples! Aunt Alice feels that her dietary habits hold the secret to her extraordinary good health and high energy level. She is indeed the personification of vim and vigor. So are her plants, who are on a special diet as well.

PLANT FOOD

Aunt Alice takes such special care of her plants that one of them, a hastatum, which botanists have not known to bloom, surprised everyone with three blossoms. Aside from giving them love, light, water, attention, and conversation, she supplements their nitrogen and phosphate diets with fish and brew. Taking a tip from Indian farmers who, she read, put fish heads in their rows of corn seed for healthy crops, she feeds her plants the ground-up heads, entrails, and tails of fish. They receive about a teaspoon of this mixture added to their soil once a month, as well as this unusual potion:

AUNT ALICE'S PLANT BEVERAGE

½ teaspoon baking powder ¼ teaspoon clear ammonia
½ teaspoon Epsom salts ½ gallon warm water
½ teaspoon saltpeter

Mix all ingredients and shake well. Feed a teaspoonful to plants once a month. It will keep indefinitely.

Three Tips from Aunt Alice:

—Always prune plants on the new moon according to the *Farmer's Almanac.*

—For apartment dwellers, bean sprouts and chives, so good in salads, are easy to grow in a window box.

—An aloe vera plant is a first-aid must for every home. The gelatinous substance in each leaf miraculously heals minor cuts and burns.

103

VITAMIN COCKTAIL

(People Food)

1 cup skimmed milk
½ banana
2 strawberries (or other fresh berries)
1 egg yolk (save white for a facial)
1 tablespoon wheat germ

1 teaspoon honey
1 teaspoon brewer's yeast
1 teaspoon liquid Vitamin C
½ teaspoon liquid Vitamin E
Liquid from 1 Vitamin A and D capsule

Blend ingredients in a blender. This drink is loaded with energy.

+╍╋╣ ╠╪╍+

SUNSHINE SANDWICH

Cream cheese
1 slice freshly baked Health Bread (see next page)

Honey
Walnuts or sunflower seeds
Golden seedless raisins

Spread cream cheese on your homemade bread, trickle a little honey over the cheese, and top with nuts or seeds and raisins.

Yield: 1 serving.

※

FRESH HERB BUTTER

1 pint heavy cream
1 teaspoon combined chopped fresh chives, parsley, and dill

¼ teaspoon salt

Place cream in a mixing bowl and beat with electric beater until water separates from a solid mass. Pour off the liquid, season the butter with herbs and salt, and spoon into a decorative dish. Excellent served with fresh vegetables, potatoes, or rice.

HEALTH BREAD

1 tablespoon safflower or
corn oil
1 tablespoon butter
1 tablespoon honey
1 tablespoon molasses
1 tablespoon brown sugar
2¼ teaspoons salt
1 cup boiling water
1 cup scalded milk

1 (¼-ounce) package active
dry yeast
¼ cup warm water
3 cups whole-wheat flour
2 cups soy flour or
unbleached white flour
½ cup wheat germ
½ cup bran

Place oil, butter, honey, molasses, brown sugar, and salt in a large mixing bowl. Pour in the hot water and scalded milk, stir well, and let cool until lukewarm. Mix yeast in ¼ cup warm water and add to bowl of lukewarm liquids (hot liquid will kill the rising action of the yeast, so be forewarned). Stir in flours, wheat germ and bran blending well until dough is moist but not sticky. Turn it onto a floured board and let it rest for 10 minutes. Then knead, adding more of any flour if necessary, until it is an elastic and smooth ball. Place dough in a greased bowl and turn it so that the whole ball of dough is oiled, then cover bowl with a tea towel and let dough rise in a warm place, 70-80° (in direct sunshine, on the top of a TV, near the stove, etc.) until double in bulk. This usually takes from 1 to 2 hours depending on the available heat. After dough has risen, punch it down, sprinkle with flour, and knead slightly on the board, shaping it into 2 loaves. Place dough in 2 greased 8-inch bread pans, cover, and let rise until again doubled in size. This takes from 45 minutes to an hour. Bake in a preheated 350° oven for 45 minutes to 1 hour or until bread is nicely browned and the edges have shrunk from the pans. Remove from pans and cool. This bread, wrapped in heavy foil, will keep in the freezer for up to 3 months. There are few things in life as satisfying as making one's own bread, or as delicious to eat.

Yield: 2 loaves.

AUNT ALICE'S HEALTH SALAD

1 head romaine lettuce
1 carrot, shredded
8–10 fresh raw mushrooms,
  sliced thin
1 zucchini, sliced
1 cucumber, sliced in rounds,
  then quartered
1 medium-size avocado,
  peeled, pitted, and sliced

2 tomatoes, chopped
2 celery stalks, minced
½ pound shrimp, cooked
  and cleaned
1 handful sunflower seeds
1 red onion, sliced and
  opened into rings
Sea salt to taste.

Toss together all ingredients but the last 3. Sprinkle with sunflower seeds. Garnish with onion rings. Serve with a dressing of sunflower oil and apple cider vinegar (2 parts oil to 1 part vinegar). Season to taste.

Yield: 4 servings.

PARSLEY SALAD

1 good-size bunch parsley
5 cherry tomatoes, quartered
¼ cup wheat germ

¼ cup oil and vinegar
  dressing
Sea salt to taste

Wash parsley thoroughly and drain or pat dry. (If the leaves are wilted, freshen by placing them, stems first, in a glass of water in the refrigerator for an hour or longer.) Holding the parsley in a firm bunch, cut across an inch at a time, including stems. Place in a salad bowl. Add cherry tomatoes and sprinkle wheat germ over salad. Add dressing, sea salt, and toss.

Yield: 2 servings.

SAUTÉED VINE VEGETABLES

1 tablespoon butter
1 tablespoon olive oil
1 large onion, sliced
1 small eggplant, sliced and
  quartered
1 medium-size yellow
  squash, sliced

1 medium-size green squash,
  sliced
1 green pepper, diced
2 green tomatoes, chopped
1 red tomato, chopped
½ teaspoon savory
Sea salt and pepper to taste

In a large skillet heat butter and olive oil. Add onion and sauté until tender. Then add all of the vegetables and toss well. Season with salt and pepper. Sauté over low heat until all vegetables are tender.

Yield: 6 servings.

VEGETABLE CASSEROLE

1 cup thinly sliced carrots
1 cup fresh green beans, cut in halves
1 cup peeled, diced white potatoes
½ cup chopped celery
2 medium tomatoes, quartered
1 small yellow squash, sliced
½ small cauliflower, cut in flowerets
½ Bermuda onion, chopped
½ cup chopped sweet red pepper
½ cup frozen green peas
½ cup beef bouillon
⅓ cup olive oil
2 cloves garlic, minced
1 bay leaf
2 teaspoons salt
1 teaspoon fresh dill
½ teaspoon savory

Place vegetables in an ungreased large casserole, toss well. Heat bouillon in a saucepan with oil, garlic, bay leaf, salt, dill, and savory. Bring to a boil and pour over vegetables. Bake in a pre-heated 350° oven for 1 hour, stirring occasionally.

Yield: 12 servings.

CHILLED FRUIT SOUP

½ cup dried apricots
¼ cup seedless black raisins
¼ cup seedless golden raisins
2 cups water
1 cinnamon stick
4 cups apple juice
2 cups mixed fresh sliced mangoes, nectarines, purple plums, strawberries, blueberries, and seedless grapes

SPOONBREAD AND STRAWBERRY WINE

Place dried fruits in a saucepan with 2 cups water and cinnamon stick and simmer for ½ hour or until soft. Then place half of this mixture in a blender and purée. Return to saucepan, add apple juice, and reheat. When fully heated add mixed fruits. Cook for 5-8 minutes or until all fruits are soft, then remove from heat. This delicious nectar can be served hot or chilled as an appetizer.

Yield: 6 servings.

The Darden Sisters

Aunt Annie

John and Annie Darden Barnes in front of their home

Annie Darden was the second oldest child and the oldest daughter of Papa and Mama Darden. Much of the family responsibilities fell on her shoulders, and they couldn't have fallen on stronger or more loving shoulders. She was highly sensitive to the needs of others and treasured harmony and tranquillity above all things. The slightest argument would upset her, and her main concern was that everyone should love one another. She was the family peacemaker, and all the problems of the entire group came her way. She offered solutions and never betrayed a confidence—that's how she got her nickname, "Big Chief."

Annie was as mild mannered as her mother was fiery, yet the two remained exceptionally close. Even after Annie had left the nest—finished college, was working, married, and had children of her own—she lived right across the street from her parents, continuing to help with the dressmaking and the raising of the younger children. Instinctively she seemed to have realized the toll that continual childbearing and hard work had taken on Dianah, and gladly continued in her role as Big Chief.

Her daughters, Thelma and Artelia, tell us that mothering was so deeply ingrained in her that her tenderheartedness, compassion, and affection were not reserved for friends and family alone. For a while the local hospital was next door, creating great agony for Annie, who couldn't bear to hear the people in pain. She never became immune to it and was deeply concerned with each new case, taking flowers, soup, and comfort to the patients.

Annie's husband, John Barnes, was a striking contrast to her. She was plump, he was lean; she was talkative, he was a man of few words; she always had a smile on her face, he was known to cast a stern stare. She collected stray cats and dogs; he shooed them away but carefully cultivated prized Rhode Island Red chickens in his back yard. She was an indulgent mother, he is remembered as a strict disciplinarian. Yet this union was one of deep mutual devotion and respect.

John Barnes was a contractor-mason by trade, and he built Uncle C.L.'s and Aunt Norma's house and the A.M.E. Zion Church, which our whole family attended and where he was the violin soloist. These buildings, as well as banks, stores, and other homes in the east Carolina area, are still standing and are visible testimony to his splendid craftsmanship.

Most evenings, as the sun went down, he could be seen sitting on his front porch in his wicker rocker, chewing a little tobacco and giving passing neighbors a terse: "How do." Some may have found John Barnes a bit forbidding, but Annie knew how to please him. The one thing certain to bring a smile to his lips was her wonderful cooking. Meals were always prepared on time in her home, but the menu never failed to include the two items to which John Barnes attributed his stamina and strength—buckwheat pancakes for his early morning breakfast and sweet potatoes for his evening supper.

AUNT ANNIE'S BUCKWHEAT CAKES

½ cup buckwheat flour
½ cup whole-wheat or
   unbleached white flour
2 teaspoons baking powder
¼ teaspoon salt

1 egg
¾ cup milk
1½ teaspoons blackstrap
   molasses (we prefer sweet
   unsulfured molasses,
   though)

Sift separately and then measure buckwheat and whole-wheat or white flours. Then sift together with baking powder and salt. Beat egg until light and frothy. Add milk and molasses to egg, stirring until well blended. Pour over dry ingredients, blending well. Fry pancakes on a lightly greased hot griddle. When pancakes are puffed full of bubbles and cooked around the edges, turn and cook on the other side. Serve with butter and molasses or maple syrup.

Yield: 10 medium-size pancakes.

BAKED SWEET POTATOES

John Barnes ate a sweet potato in some form every day of his life. Goodness knows there is nothing tastier than a steaming hot sweet potato with a pat of melting butter.

Sweet potatoes, as desired
Vegetable shortening

Wash potatoes and pat dry. Rub skins with vegetable shortening. Bake in a preheated 425° oven for 45 minutes to an hour, depending on size. Test for doneness by squeezing, using a pot holder, or piercing with a fork. Serve with a pat of butter.

BAKED STUFFED SWEET POTATOES

For the sake of variety, Annie would sometimes stuff her baked sweet potatoes.

To stuff, remove insides. Add 1 teaspoon of orange or pineapple juice; 1 pat of butter; a dash of brown sugar, cinnamon, ginger, or nutmeg; a bit of crushed pineapple, mashed banana, canned peach slices, or applesauce. Restuff the potato shell or place in a half-orange shell and bake for 15 minutes more.

SWEET POTATO BISCUITS

2 cups sifted all-purpose
   flour
3 teaspoons baking powder
½ teaspoon baking soda
¾ teaspoon salt
3 tablespoons brown sugar
Dash of cinnamon
½ cup melted butter
1 cup boiled, peeled, mashed
   sweet potatoes
⅔ cup buttermilk

Sift flour, baking powder, baking soda, salt, brown sugar, and cinnamon and set aside. Using a medium-size bowl, beat melted butter into the sweet potatoes. Add dry ingredients, stirring in a little at a time, alternating with buttermilk. Mix just well enough to moisten through. Form into a ball, turn out onto lightly floured board. Lightly pat top side with flour as well, since it is rather sticky batter. Roll out to ½–¾-inch thickness with a floured rolling pin. Cut with a floured biscuit cutter. Bake in a preheated 450° oven for about 20–25 minutes.

Yield: 12–14 biscuits.

SWEET POTATO BREAD

⅓ cup solid shortening
¾ to 1¼ cups sugar, depending
   on sweetness of potatoes
2 eggs
½ cup molasses
1 cup cooked, peeled,
   mashed sweet potatoes
2 cups all-purpose flour
¼ teaspoon baking powder
1 teaspoon baking soda
½ teaspoon salt
½ teaspoon powdered
   cinnamon
½ teaspoon powdered
   nutmeg
½ teaspoon powdered
   allspice
¼ teaspoon ground cloves
¼ cup raisins
¾ cup chopped walnuts

Combine shortening, sugar, and eggs. Beat until light and fluffy. Stir in molasses and sweet potatoes. Sift dry ingredients and spices. Add to sweet potato mixture. Add raisins and chopped walnuts. Blend well. Turn into a greased loaf pan (9″ × 5″ × 3″). Bake in a preheated 350° oven for 1 hour. Turn out of pan and cool completely on baking rack.

Yield: 1 sweet potato loaf.

FRENCH FRIED SWEET POTATOES

Number of sweet potatoes desired
Salt or sugar to taste

Peel and cut sweet potatoes into thin strips. Fry in hot fat until crisp, brown, and tender on the inside. Drain on paper towels. Serve hot. Serve plain or sprinkled with salt or sugar. This is particularly excellent with breakfast as a substitute for grits or hashed brown potatoes.

Yield: 1 medium-size sweet potato serves 2 nicely.

SWEET POTATO PUFFS

Sweet potatoes
Brown sugar to taste
Butter to taste

Pecans or walnuts, ground
(a little less than ¼ cup
per potato)

Use as many sweet potatoes as you wish. Boil until tender. Peel and mash. Add brown sugar and butter. Form into balls. Roll each ball in ground nuts until entire surface is covered. Place in a warm oven until ready for use. Use as garnish for meat or poultry platter.

Yield: 2 puffs per medium-size potato.

SWEET POTATO CROQUETTES

4 medium-size sweet
  potatoes
3 tablespoons melted butter
1 teaspoon vanilla
½ cup chopped black
  walnuts

1 cup seedless raisins
2 tablespoons brown sugar
1 egg, beaten
1 cup crushed cornflakes

Wash potatoes well and boil them in their jackets until tender. Then peel and mash until lumps are removed. To this add melted butter, vanilla, black walnuts, seedless raisins, and brown sugar. Mold into 2-inch croquettes. Dip in beaten egg. Roll in crushed cereal. Place on buttered baking sheet in a preheated 350° oven for 25 minutes or until light brown. Remove croquettes from sheet with spatula and lift to platter. Delicious served around beef roast.

Yield: 8 croquettes.

SWEET POTATO SPOON CUSTARD

1 cup mashed, cooked sweet
  potatoes
2 small bananas, mashed
1 cup milk

2 tablespoons brown sugar
½ teaspoon salt
2 egg yolks, beaten
3 tablespoons seedless raisins

Combine mashed sweet potatoes and bananas. Add milk and blend. Add brown sugar, salt, egg yolks, and raisins. Mix well and pour into a well-greased 1-quart casserole. Bake in a preheated 300° oven for 45 minutes until custard is firm and golden brown. Wonderful as an accompanying dish for lamb or pork.

Yield: 6–8 servings.

CANDIED YAMS*

6 medium-size yams*
¾ cup brown sugar
1 teaspoon grated lemon
  rind
2 tablespoons flour

¼ teaspoon salt
¼ teaspoon cinnamon
¼ teaspoon nutmeg
4 tablespoons butter
1 cup orange juice

Boil yams in their jackets until tender but firm (about 10 minutes). When cool enough to handle, peel and slice. To the sugar, add grated lemon rind, flour, salt, cinnamon, and nutmeg. Place half of the sliced yams in a medium-size casserole dish. Sprinkle with the spiced sugar mixture. Dot with half the amount of butter. Add a second layer of yams, using the rest of the ingredients in the same order as above. Add orange juice. Bake in a preheated 350° oven for 45 minutes.

Yield: 4–6 servings.

* Large sweet potatoes are popularly called yams.

GLAZED SWEET POTATO AND APPLE CASSEROLE

4 medium-size sweet potatoes	3 tablespoons butter
2 large apples	⅓ cup molasses
½ teaspoon salt	¼ cup brown sugar
2 teaspoons lemon juice	¼ cup chopped nuts

Boil sweet potatoes until tender but still firm and allow them to cool. Then peel, slice, and place in a shallow baking dish. Core and slice the apples, then sprinkle salt and lemon juice over them. Bring butter to a slow sizzle and toss the apple slices around in the pan until slightly soft. Arrange the apples with the sweet potatoes. Then add the molasses to remaining butter in pan and bring to a boil. Pour over apples and sweet potatoes, coating well. Sprinkle brown sugar and nuts on top. Bake in a preheated 325° oven for 30 minutes or until brown and bubbly on top.

Yield: 4–6 servings.

HEAVENLY HASH SWEET POTATO SALAD

4 medium-size sweet potatoes, cooked and chilled	½ cup chopped pecans
	¼ cup diced celery
¾ cup crushed pineapple, drained	2 tablespoons orange juice
	½ cup mayonnaise
¾ cup marshmallows cut in small pieces or miniatures	Red cherries

Peel chilled sweet potatoes and cut into small cubes, add pineapple, pecans, marshmallows, and celery. Mix orange juice with mayonnaise, add to salad, and toss gently. Serve on bed of lettuce and top with red cherries.

Yield: 4-6 servings.

NORTH CAROLINA GRATED
SWEET POTATO PUDDING

5 cups coarsely grated raw
  sweet potatoes
¾ cup brown sugar, packed
1½ cups milk
½ cup melted butter
3 eggs, well beaten
¼ teaspoon powdered
  nutmeg
½ teaspoon powdered
  cinnamon

¼ teaspoon powdered
  allspice
¼ teaspoon ground cloves
½ cup seedless raisins
½ cup shredded coconut
½ cup chopped pecans
1 teaspoon grated orange
  rind

Mix all ingredients and pour into a buttered medium-size casserole dish or skillet. Bake in a preheated 400° oven for 50-60 minutes. As crust forms around edges, remove from oven and stir pudding well to mix the crust throughout. Do this several times until cooking is finished. Serve warm or cold, plain or topped with whipped cream or ice cream.

Yield: 8 servings.

SWEET POTATO PIE

3 large eggs
¾ to 1¼ cups sugar, depending on sweetness of the potatoes
Dash of salt
1 teaspoon powdered cinnamon
½ teaspoon powdered allspice
¼ teaspoon powdered nutmeg
1 cup heavy cream
3 cups cooked mashed sweet potatoes
1 unbaked 10-inch pie shell (see Index)

Beat eggs well, add sugar, salt, and spices, and mix thoroughly. Add cream and stir. Add mashed potatoes and mix thoroughly. Turn into pie shell and bake in a preheated 350° oven for 1 hour or until firm.

Yield: 8–10 servings.

Lizzie

Lizzie Darden, still wearing high-school graduation cap, with date, girl friend, and Brother C.L. (seated)

Every large family has its designated "beauty," and in the Darden household that distinction went to Lizzie. Of all the girls, she was the most impetuous, flirtatious, and popular with the boys. She was reputed to be one of the best dancers in the county, and Mama Darden saw to it that she was certainly one of the best dressed. Papa Darden and sons were very protective of Lizzie and discouraged potential gentlemen callers so that she would finish her education.

Lizzie's distinguishing talent was her dramatic recitation of poetry from memory. Her theatrical gestures and well-timed pauses kept her in demand with church groups and women's clubs in Wilson and neighboring towns who invited her to perform at their teas, testimonials, and concerts. However, Lizzie never contemplated the stage as a career; when it came time to pick an occupation, she chose nursing.

At the suggestion of her brother John, she enrolled in Tuskegee Institute near his home in Alabama. But shortly after graduation, without waiting for the family's stamp of approval, Lizzie eloped. She had lost her heart to the school's star athlete, Mr. Randall James, a soft-spoken, well-mannered Texan, and the two set out to seek their fortune. Mr. James tried making a living at several occupations in several towns before settling in his native Texas as a mortician. Both he and Lizzie were working for a local undertaker in his hometown when they discovered oil on their land. Thoughts of great wealth dazzled them, but large companies had tight control of oil fields, and the several court battles they engaged in only served to deplete their meager savings.

After a long sickness and many crushed dreams, Mr. James died, leaving Lizzie with two young sons, Randall and Charles, and a daughter, Johnnie K. Learning of her plight, Uncle C.L. sent for her to return to Wilson, where she settled in Papa Darden's house and worked in the funeral parlor as a female attendant. Also, she and her children sang at funerals.

But Lizzie was never the same. Old Wilsonians barely recognized the lively beauty who had kicked up her heels just twelve years earlier. Eventually she married Mr. Allen Morgan, and again her dreams were dimmed when old World War I injuries caused him to be confined to a wheelchair. When we knew her, Lizzie had turned the old family home into a boardinghouse where she took the best possible care of her Mr. Morgan and her boarders, all of whom she championed as the finest, most sterling citizens Wilson had ever produced (even the ones who were months behind in their rent and the few who left without paying at all). She was always willing to share—perhaps a bit too generously—what little she had.

As Lizzie grew older, the church became the dominant pillar of her life. In the evenings we would see her, hymnal tucked under her arm, rushing off to choir practice (always a little late). She derived great comfort and strength from religion, and even though her life had never matched her hopes and expectations, she remained loving, gentle, and, above all, tolerant of human frailty.

BRUNCH AT AUNT LIZZIE'S

At least once during the summer Aunt Lizzie would have the family over for brunch after church. She was perhaps the slowest cook in the history of the South. Her after-church Sunday brunches took hours to prepare, but this never seemed to disturb Lizzie's serenity. Humming to herself, she'd float around the kitchen, unaware of time. But, once she got it all together, a fabulous meal was put on the table and, miracle of miracles, everything was hot!

MENU
Fried Chicken or Broiled Chops
*Homemade Sausage
*Fried Apples
Eggs Scrambled with Green Pepper and Onions
Bacon
*Fluffy Grits
*Soda Biscuits
Compote of Peaches and Figs (direct
from her back yard) with Cream

* *Recipe appears in this chapter.*

FRIED APPLES

4 apples, preferably green   2 tablespoons butter or
                                    bacon fat

Core the unpeeled apples, then cut into circles or slices. Cook in the butter or bacon fat until soft. Then, *if you have a sweet tooth* or if the apples are bland in flavor, stir in ⅓ cup brown sugar and 2 tablespoons water. Continue cooking until apples are coated with syrup.

Yield: About 4 servings.

HOMEMADE SAUSAGE

2 pounds fresh ground pork
   butt
1 teaspoon powdered sage
1½ teaspoons salt

1 teaspoon black pepper
1 red pepper, minced, or
   ¼ teaspoon cayenne

Mix and blend everything together, using your fingers. Shape into 2-inch patties. Fry until crisp and brown on both sides.

Yield: 16–18 patties.

FLUFFY GRITS

2 cups cold cooked grits
1¾ cups milk, heated
4 tablespoons butter

Pinch of salt
4 egg yolks, beaten
4 egg whites, beaten stiff

Mash grits with a masher and add heated milk. Blend well, leaving no lumps. Add butter, salt, and egg yolks. Fold in stiff egg whites. Pour into a medium-size, greased soufflé dish or casserole. Bake in a preheated 350° oven for about 45 minutes.

Yield: 8 servings.

SODA BISCUITS

2 cups all-purpose flour
½ teaspoon baking soda
½ teaspoon salt

4 tablespoons shortening
¾ cup buttermilk or sour
   milk

Sift flour. Measure 2 cups. Sift again with dry ingredients. Cut shortening into flour mixture until fine. Add enough milk to make a soft dough. Turn onto a floured board. Knead slightly. Roll ½ inch thick. Cut with a small floured biscuit cutter. Place on an ungreased baking sheet. Bake in a preheated 475° oven for 12–14 minutes.

Yield: 12–15 biscuits.

SAUSAGE BISCUITS

Soda biscuit dough (see
   above)

½ pound soft pork sausage
   meat

Roll out biscuit dough in 1 piece to ¼-inch thickness. Spread on a
thin layer of sausage. Roll as you would for a jelly roll. Slice ½ inch
thick. Place on a lightly greased pan and bake in preheated 450°
oven for 15 minutes.

Yield: Approximately 15–18 biscuits.

❖✲

MORE BRUNCH FAVORITES FROM
AUNT LIZZIE'S KITCHEN

SWEET MILK GRIDDLE CAKES

3 cups all-purpose flour
3 teaspoons baking powder
½ teaspoon salt
¼ cup sugar

¼ teaspoon ground
   cinnamon
3 eggs
2 cups milk
3 tablespoons melted butter

Sift flour, measure 3 cups, then sift 3 times together with the baking
powder, salt, sugar, and cinnamon. Beat eggs, add milk, and pour
slowly into the dry ingredients. Beat thoroughly and add butter.
Drop by spoonfuls onto a lightly greased hot griddle. When puffed
full of bubbles and cooked on edges, turn and cook on other side.

Yield: 24 small or 12 large griddle cakes.

PECAN WAFFLES

2 cups sifted all-purpose
   flour
3 teaspoons baking powder
2 teaspoons sugar
½ teaspoon salt

3 egg yolks, lightly beaten
1¼ cups milk
4 tablespoons melted butter
3 egg whites, beaten stiff
¼ cup finely chopped pecans

Sift the dry ingredients. Beat the egg yolks and mix with the milk. Add to flour mixture. Beat until smooth. Stir in melted butter, gently fold in the stiffly beaten egg whites. Add pecans. Bake in a hot waffle iron. The lightest, tastiest waffles you've ever had.

Yield: 6 waffles.

~~~~~~

BANANA DOUGHNUTS

2 cups all-purpose flour
2 teaspoons baking powder
½ teaspoon baking soda
½ teaspoon salt
2 tablespoons shortening
⅓ cup sugar
1 egg

¼ cup buttermilk
1 medium-size banana,
  mashed
⅛ teaspoon each of nutmeg,
  and cinnamon, or mace and
  cloves
½ teaspoon vanilla

Sift together flour, baking powder, soda, and salt. Beat shortening until creamy, then add sugar and beat until light. Add egg and beat in well. Then add buttermilk, banana, spices, and vanilla. Blend in dry ingredients. Put onto floured board, knead lightly, and roll to ½ inch thickness. Cut with doughnut cutter. Fry in hot deep fat until nicely browned, drain on paper towels, and dust with powdered sugar.

Yield: 2 dozen doughnuts.

FRUIT FRITTERS

1 cup all-purpose flour
1½ teaspoons baking
  powder
2 tablespoons sugar
½ teaspoon salt
1 egg
½ cup milk
1 tart apple, pared, cored,
  and cut in 6 sections

1 peach, peeled and sliced
1 orange, sectioned
1 banana, sliced
Handful of pitted cherries,
  grapes, or prunes
1 pear, peeled and sliced
Powdered sugar
Nutmeg

Mix and sift dry ingredients. Beat egg with milk, add dry ingredients, and mix well. Then dip individual pieces of fruit into the batter and coat evenly. Fry in deep hot fat until brown. Drain and sprinkle with powdered sugar and nutmeg. Best served as a dessert for brunch or dinner.

Yield: 6–8 servings.

♩ ♩ ♪   ♪

Lizzie's little nieces loved "short'nin', short'nin'," Lizzie's little little nieces loved short'nin' cakes.

SHORTCAKES

2 cups all-purpose flour
4 teaspoons baking powder
1 teaspoon salt
2½ tablespoons soft brown sugar
⅓ cup shortening or butter

⅔ cup light cream
1 tablespoon melted butter
1½ quarts combined strawberries or raspberries mixed with blueberries and sliced peaches
Sugar to taste

Mix and sift flour, baking powder, salt, and brown sugar. Cut in shortening with a knife or rub with fingertips. Add light cream gradually, mix to a soft dough. Roll out on a lightly floured board to slightly over ½-inch thickness. Cut 12 circles with a large biscuit cutter. Place 6 circles in a lightly buttered pan or cookie sheet. Brush with melted butter and top with remaining 6 circles. Bake in a preheated 425° oven for 15 minutes. Then let the shortcakes cool slightly, remove the top half, and put the sweetened fruit in any combination of your choice between halves and on top of cakes. Make sure fruit has lots of juice. Add a little orange juice if it doesn't. Top with a dot of whipped cream. (Note: The same shortcakes can be used with creamed meat or fish filling, omitting the brown sugar.)

Yield: 6 shortcakes.

Artelia

Artelia Darden Tennessee with husband Jessie

Artelia was the youngest Darden girl and the spunkiest. Independence and individuality were always important to her. As a child, she was considered a tomboy since she favored male companionship, enjoyed playing games, and was especially good at baseball.

Always eager to keep up with her brothers, she bravely accepted all their challenges. Once she smoked ten of Arthur's cigarettes in a row, silently suffering the resulting headaches and dizziness for the sake of the backslapping and congratulations she won. Uncle J.B.

taught her how to play cards, and she played casino and whist with gusto and abandon, usually winning. Of course these were secret activities which took place in the back of the shed, for not even Artelia would have dared to smoke or play cards in Papa Darden's house!

Artelia inherited her mother's staunch pride. When she was seven, a new minister in town stopped by her father's store and requested that she deliver some string beans to his home at a later time. However, when she arrived he refused to let her in the front door and ordered her to go around to the back door. Many seven-year-olds would have been intimidated into obeying this order from a man of the cloth, but Artelia never cared much about public opinion. She knew she'd been insulted, and marched home, taking the beans with her.

Like her mother and sisters, Artelia was an excellent seamstress and milliner, but, unlike them, she was never fond of studying. She valiantly struggled through college to please the family and went on to teach elementary school, but she was quite relieved to marry Jessie Tennessee, a blacksmith, and move to Phoebus, Virginia. Everyone held their breath waiting to see if the former tomboy would be able to cook and keep house. And Artelia had quite a surprise for them—she was not only a housekeeper, but a most inventive cook who had a knack for making anything taste good.

Some years later Artelia "surprised" the Darden family once again. She announced her decision to divorce Jessie and remain in Phoebus. At a time when widowed or divorced women took their children and moved back to their parents' home, Artelia characteristically chose to remain where she was. Her romance had been stormy, but after their marital rift, Artelia and Jessie became good friends. Neither remarried and when both were in advanced years he was still known to accompany her to her lodge meetings and Friday-night card games. Throughout her life, Artelia remained very close to her children, Butch, Eugene and little Artelia and they remember that she loved to bake and would sing and hum in the kitchen. When they heard her sing out, "Take two and butter them while they're hot," they knew it meant that she, an accomplished baker, had prepared one of her best breads. Muffins, biscuits, and fruit loaves were her specialties, and one thing is for sure—no one could stop at just two.

TEA BISCUITS

3 medium-size Irish potatoes,
  peeled and cut up
2 tablespoons melted lard
½ cup melted butter
⅓ cup sugar
1½ teaspoons salt

1¼ cups sweet milk
1 yeast cake or 1(¼-ounce)
  package active dry yeast
1 whole egg plus 1 egg yolk,
  beaten
6–7 cups all-purpose flour

Boil and finely mash potatoes. Add melted lard, butter, sugar, and salt. Scald milk, then cool to tepid. Dissolve yeast in milk. Add the whole egg and extra yolk. Stir into potato mixture. Then gradually add the flour. Knead 8 to 10 minutes and place in a greased large bowl to rise. When doubled in bulk, remove to a floured board and work into a smooth dough. Roll out about ½ inch thick, cut with a small biscuit cutter. Brush each biscuit with additional melted butter and put in buttered pans. Let rise until doubled in bulk. Bake in a preheated 425° oven for 12 to 15 minutes. These are delicious. Take two and butter them while they're hot!

Yield: About 36 biscuits.

ARTELIA'S PLAIN BISCUITS

2 cups sifted all-purpose
  flour
4 teaspoons baking powder
1 tablespoon sugar

¾ teaspoon salt
¼ cup shortening
Approximately ¼ cup milk

Sift dry ingredients together, then cut in shortening. Slowly add milk until mixture is wet enough to hold together. Turn onto a floured board. Roll to ½-inch thickness. Cut with a biscuit cutter. Bake in a preheated 450° oven for 10–12 minutes.

Yield: About 12 biscuits.

"SURE NUFF DOWN HOME CRACKLIN" BREAD

2 cups cornmeal
½ teaspoon salt

1 cup water
1 cup diced cracklings

SPOONBREAD AND STRAWBERRY WINE

Cracklings are made from the crisp brown skin of ham rind or pork fat. To make your own cracklings, cut rind or fat into small pieces. Place them in a skillet and fry as you would bacon, until all the fat is removed and the remaining pieces are brown and crisp. The same can be done with the skin of a chicken.

Sift the dry ingredients together and add water and cracklings. Shape into 8 round or oblong loaves and put on a greased baking sheet. Bake in a preheated 450° oven for 30 minutes. Serve hot.

Yield: 8 small loaves.

HUSH PUPPIES

2 cups white cornmeal
1 teaspoon baking powder
1 medium-size onion, chopped fine
1 cup milk, more if needed
4 tablespoons shortening, melted
½ teaspoon salt
2 eggs, well beaten

Mix all ingredients to the consistency of a very thick pancake batter. Drop by rounded teaspoonfuls into deep hot fat. Fry until golden brown. Serve hot with fried fish or chicken.

Yield: 8–10 hush puppies.

BLUEBERRY MUFFINS

2 cups all-purpose flour
4 tablespoons sugar
3 teaspoons baking powder
½ teaspoon salt
⅓ cup melted butter
1 egg, slightly beaten
1 cup milk
1 cup fresh blueberries

Sift flour, then measure 2 cups. Add sugar, baking powder, and salt and sift twice again.* Stir melted butter and beaten egg into milk. Add to the flour mixture along with the blueberries, stirring just enough to moisten mixture. Batter should look lumpy. Fill greased muffin cups ⅔ full. Bake in a preheated 400° oven for 25 minutes or until golden brown.

Yield: 10–12 muffins.

*Most of today's sifters, sift 3 times in one use, thank goodness.

❖✿❖✿❖✿❖✿❖✿❖✿❖✿❖✿❖✿❖✿❖✿❖✿❖✿❖✿❖✿❖✿❖✿❖

PEACH OR APRICOT MUFFINS

2 cups all-purpose flour
⅓ cup brown sugar,
   firmly packed
3 teaspoons baking powder
¼ teaspoon baking soda
⅛ teaspoon powdered
   allspice

⅓ cup melted butter
1 egg, beaten
1 cup milk or 1 cup sour
   cream
⅔ cup chopped fresh
   peaches or apricots

Sift flour and then measure 2 cups. Add brown sugar, baking powder, baking soda, and allspice. Sift twice more. Stir melted butter and beaten egg into milk or sour cream. Add to the flour mixture, stirring just enough to moisten. Add chopped peaches or apricots. Stir only until mixed. Batter should look lumpy. Fill greased muffins cups ⅔ full. Bake in a preheated 400° oven for 25 minutes or until golden brown.

Yield: 10–12 muffins.

PECAN MUFFINS

1 cup whole-wheat flour
1 cup all-purpose white
   flour
4 teaspoons baking powder
½ teaspoon salt

1 cup milk
⅓ cup honey
2 eggs, beaten
⅓ cup melted butter
½ cup chopped pecans

Sift each flour, then measure 1 cup of each. Add baking powder and salt and sift twice more. Scald milk. Stir in honey. Let cool to room temperature. Stir in beaten eggs and melted butter. Add to the flour mixture, stirring just enough to moisten. Add chopped pecans. Stir only until mixed. Mixture should look lumpy. Fill greased muffin cups ⅔ full. Bake in a preheated 400° oven for 25 minutes or until golden brown.

Yield: 10–12 muffins.

RAISIN BREAD

1 cup applesauce
¼ cup melted butter
1 egg, beaten
½ cup sugar
¼ cup brown sugar, packed
2 cups all-purpose flour
2 teaspoons baking powder
¾ teaspoon salt

½ teaspoon baking soda
½ teaspoon powdered cinnamon
1 teaspoon powdered nutmeg
¾ cup seedless raisins
¾ cup chopped walnuts

Combine applesauce, butter, egg, and the 2 kinds of sugar in a bowl. Blend well. Sift other dry ingredients (including cinnamon and nutmeg) together and stir into applesauce mixture until smooth. Add raisins and chopped nuts. Turn into a well-greased 9″ × 5″ × 3″ loaf pan. Bake in a preheated 350° oven for 1 hour. Serve plain or toasted with butter or cream cheese.

Yield: 1 loaf of bread.

BANANA NUT BREAD

2½ cups sifted all-purpose flour
1 tablespoon baking powder
½ teaspoon salt
¼ cup soft butter
1 cup sugar

1 egg, beaten
1 cup mashed ripe bananas
1 tablespoon grated lemon rind
½ cup milk
1 cup chopped walnuts

Sift flour, baking powder, and salt together. Cream butter, gradually adding sugar, then add the egg. Beat until smooth. Add bananas, lemon rind, and milk. Add flour mixture. Stir until blended. Then add nuts. Pour into a greased 9″ × 5″ × 3″ loaf pan. Bake in a preheated 350° oven for 1 hour. Let cool for 10 minutes in the loaf pan, then remove and cool completely on a wire rack. This bread is even better on the second day.

Yield: 1 loaf of bread.

♥

CRANBERRY NUT TEA CAKE

1½ cups halved fresh cranberries	1 teaspoon salt
¾ cup powdered sugar	⅓ cup brown sugar, packed
3 cups all-purpose flour, sifted	¼ cup softened butter
3 teaspoons baking powder	2 eggs, slightly beaten
	1¼ cups milk
	½ cup chopped walnuts

Combine halved cranberries and powdered sugar in a small bowl and let stand. Sift flour, baking powder, and salt together. Then cream sugar and butter until smooth, and beat in eggs. Gradually add flour mixture, alternating with milk. Blend until smooth. Add cranberry mixture and nuts. Place in a lightly greased 9″ × 5″ × 3″ loaf pan and bake in a preheated 350° oven for 1 hour. When done, remove from pan and brush with melted butter.

Yield: 1 teacake.

"Bud"
Walter T. Darden

Our father, Walter Theodore Darden (affectionately called Bud), like the song says, has been a lot of places and seen a lot of things, and has the gift of knowing how to share his experiences. He is a consummate teller of tales (tall and real). His one-man dramas, told in a deep, sonorous voice, and replete with the facial expressions, body gestures, and vocal mannerisms of all the characters, have unfolded on the screens of our minds and kept us laughing ever since we've known him. Primarily, Bud's is the story of four towns: Wilson, North Carolina, and Opelika, Alabama, where he grew up; Tuskegee, Alabama, where he tried to settle; and Newark, New Jersey, where he did settle.

CULTURE AND HIGH DRAMA IN WILSON

That Bud was a busy kid. As the youngest child in his large family, he was practically smothered with attention, errands, and jobs. He claims that Mama Darden kept him too dressed up for his taste and that his sisters babied him, while Papa Darden kept him hopping—trimming caskets, selling items in their store, and peddling records and sheet music for his older brother C.L. Perhaps this is why the Chautauqua stands out in his memories. Every summer he was excused from chores when this variety show from far-off New York City came to town. He remembers the high spirits and excitement in small-town Wilson when a large striped tent was erected to house the prominent personalities who participated in the plays, operas, lectures, and acts which comprised each week-long Chautauqua. "Even the most offensive bigots lost their diabolical sting at that time of year when the town got 'culture,'" he says. Once John Philip Sousa's Marching Band appeared. Bud left that show vowing to become a famous bandleader.

The good feelings that the traveling Chautauqua generated were short-lived in 1911. For off a freight train and into Wilson came the well-known and feared black outlaw, Louis West, and his band of desperadoes. They had pulled many daring robberies and, although their actions were deplored by some, they had become underground black folk heroes, on the order of Jesse James and Robin Hood. Word leaked out to the sheriff that Louie was resting up in Wilson, so he and a posse rushed over to their hideout. Louie demanded to see a search warrant, and a shoot-out ensued. When the smoke cleared, the sheriff was mortally wounded. While making their getaway, Louie and his gang were apprehended and jailed. Most Wilson blacks stayed off the streets, fearing reprisals. Bud didn't. He even skipped school to hear Louie's lawyer give an impassioned plea for mercy, to see Louie stoically stand to hear himself sentenced to the electric chair, and Shorty, his sidekick, and the rest of the gang get life. Mama Darden told him to forget the saga of Louie West's defiance and get back to school. She packed his favorite sweet potato biscuits in his lunch pail, but schoolboy Bud was pondering justice and courtroom drama and had decided to become a lawyer instead of a bandleader.

Bud Darden and friend Bud Vick in front of family business

DIVERSIONS IN OPELIKA

After the death of his mother, Bud was sent to live for a while with his oldest brother John and his wife Maude in Opelika, Alabama. From then on, he divided his time between those two towns. He says that Opelika, a rural town, was more spread out and less populated than Wilson. His routine consisted of a ride by pony to Miss Parish's one-room schoolhouse, and then on to John's drugstore for his soda-jerking duties. Excitement was rare; there was no Chautauqua to look forward to. The only annual event Bud remembers at all was Sheriff Moon's Bar-B-Que. It was a two-day

134

affair. The first day for the whites, the second for the "coloreds." Sheriff Moon, he says, was known for his ten-gallon yellow Stetson hat, his red neck, a colorful, long, glistening pearl-handled pistol on each hip, and his general meanness. But his picnic was always a big hit. He served enough food to last the average person a week. Every meat that could be barbecued—squirrel, deer, bird, raccoon, opossum, bear, fish—in short, anything that could swim, fly, or crawl was dumped into barbecue sauce. Bud claims that bicarbonate of soda actually saved his life after such an outing.

Saturday night was Opelika's one time to come alive. All the farmers came to town to get supplies, exchange news, let off steam, and live it up. Bud's arms would be tired at the end of the day from scooping out tutti-frutti ice-cream cones. (That was the most popular flavor for those who were not knocked out from moonshine, which flowed freely from Mason's Shoeshine Parlour around the corner.) Sometimes things got rough. One summer evening when Bud was fourteen, a very beautiful and voluptuous woman many years his senior requested that he deliver some ice

Bud during his Atlantic City bellboy days

135

cream to her home. Once there, she suggested that he stay and play the phonograph for some guests that she was expecting. The guests never arrived, so Bud left. Later it was discovered that a paramour of the lady in question had seen Bud's entrance, clocked the time of his exit, and was plotting his demise. This was his first brush with the intense and often irrational passion that pervaded those hot Saturday nights.

Fortunately, it was time for him to return to high school at Livingston in North Carolina, so the incident blew over.

Like his brothers John and J.B., Bud decided to become a physician and, like them, he held a bevy of jobs to get himself through school, which for him was Howard University, in Washington, D.C.

ARTISANS AND THE KLAN IN TUSKEGEE, ALABAMA

Degree in hand, Bud returned to Alabama. "For the grand sum of eight dollars a month, I accepted an internship at John Andrews Hospital in Tuskegee, which was an oasis of black self-sufficiency. One could purchase anything from a house to a pair of shoes that had been made by the hands of black artisans."

Bud might have stayed in Tuskegee had it not been for a local white doctor who, as fate would have it, was a Klan leader. The Klan doctor had wrongly diagnosed a child's fractured arm and sent the child away with only a bandage. Bud put a cast on the child's arm. "Professional pride" forced the Klansman to demand Dr. Darden's immediate departure from town. At first our father rejected the idea, but Brother John, with his sixth sense, encouraged him to go north. It was arranged for him to join Dr. John A. Kenney, who had left under similar forced circumstances and who had opened a hospital in Newark, New Jersey.

WORK, MARRIAGE, AND OTHER PURSUITS IN NEWARK, NEW JERSEY

In a two-toned Nash (yes, his style as well as his skills was too flamboyant for the Klan!) Dr. Bud arrived in Newark to establish his career. His salary at the hospital was $1,800 a year; the days began at 7:00 A.M., often ending after 11:00 P.M. He learned a lot from Dr. Kenney, and then decided to open his own office. Among his first patients was a woman who had not walked for years because of a crippling arthritic condition. Four hefty men brought her to his office. She had a fear of needles and began thrashing around, nearly crushing Bud when he tried to give her an injection. To quiet her, and perhaps to protect himself, he said inadvertently, "Be still so you'll get well and walk." She took him at his word and walked into the waiting room, shocking the four hefty fellows. The power of suggestion might have been at play here, but the story spread and certainly didn't harm his beginning practice.

Bud felt that he didn't have time for marriage and swore he would remain a bachelor like his debonair brother Charles in Los Angeles. However, his brother J.B. in Petersburg, Virginia, introduced him to a lovely schoolteacher, Mamie Jean Sampson. Shortly after they met, she took a job as a community worker in

Strolling on the boardwalk in Atlantic City, Bud and Mamie Jean with friends Charlotte Kyle and Marie Kellar

Buffalo, New York, so weekends found Walter T., the confirmed bachelor, taking a long train ride to visit her. They married and, after honeymooning in Cuba, settled in on the floor above his office, and eventually had us.

Life with Father has never been dull. He has attained some of his boyhood ambitions. He didn't become a bandleader, but for a while he was quite an impresario, bringing to Newark the big bands of Count Basie and Benny Goodman, presenting fashion shows, entertainers, and celebrities for the benefit of various educational, civic, and civil rights groups. He didn't become a lawyer, but he appeared in court as a medical consultant and added a dash of drama to the courtroom scene. Lately new talents have surfaced. Cosmopolitan Bud has given way to a tug back to his southern heritage and created a garden in his back yard. On weekends one can find him preparing unique concoctions from his homegrown produce or old-time family favorites, such as his version of Papa Darden's Grape Wine, using grapes from his own vines. Every Fourth of July when the garden is in full swing, he gives a picnic for friends, neighbors, and relatives, usually totaling over fifty people. Everyone pitches in, either bringing a dish or setting up the games, picnic tables and lawn umbrellas. At the end of the day everyone is well fed and exhausted. Bud's chapter is therefore divided into his picnic menus, weekend concoctions, and old-time favorites.

Bud and Jean vacationing in the Caribbean

BUD'S FOURTH-OF-JULY BASH

*Suckling pig
*Fried chicken
*Barbecued spareribs
*Charcoal-broiled flank or
  shell steak
*Corn on the cob
*Greens (collard or mixed)
  String beans (see Index)
*Potato salad or macaroni
  and shrimp salad
*Jubilee salad

*Deviled eggs
*Buttered garlic French
  bread
  Ice-cold watermelon
  Homemade tutti-frutti ice
  cream (see Index)
  Coconut cake (see Index)
*Strawberry wine punch
  Assorted sodas and cold
  beer

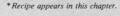

Recipe appears in this chapter.

TIPS FOR PICNIC

Steaks: sprinkle on garlic powder, salt, pepper, and onion salt. Squeeze fresh lemon juice on both sides; this is an excellent tenderizer. Grill over slow-burning coals for 5 to 10 minutes on each side to make a nice medium steak.

Corn on the cob: cover with cold salted water. Add a little milk, to sweeten corn. When water boils corn is done.

Garlic bread: make deep slits across loaves of French bread. Butter each side of slits with softened butter and sprinkle with garlic powder. Wrap in tinfoil and heat on top of grill or in moderate oven for 15 minutes.

Jubilee salad: add fresh-cooked or canned corn kernels, sliced cucumbers, and shoestring beets to mixed salad greens and toss with oil and vinegar dressing and seasonings (count on 8–10 heads of lettuce for 50 people).

Strawberry wine punch: pour 2 bottles of Strawberry Wine (see Index) over a chunk of ice in a large punch bowl. Add a bottle of club soda and whole strawberries as a garnish.

ROAST SUCKLING PIG (OUTDOOR)

This is a recipe that does not lend itself to strict directions and will require some experimentation on your part. Much depends upon the size of your grilling equipment and what size pig it can accommodate. With the help of a good friend, we made our own grill out of a fifty-gallon metal oil drum. The drum was cut in half, hinged together, punctured with air holes, and mounted on a sturdy stand. Coals were placed in the bottom, a grating placed in the middle, and the pig placed on it.

Another method for roasting a pig is to dig a hole in the ground to accommodate hot coals, to cover the hole with some kind of metal grating, and to place the pig on top of that.

Now for preparation of the pig itself!

INGREDIENTS:

| 1 suckling pig (allow 1 pound per person) | Salt and pepper |
| Vinegar | Barbecue sauce |

Have the pig split in half for faster cooking time. Wash thoroughly and pat dry. Using your hands, rub the outside and the inside cavity with vinegar, and a liberal amount of salt, and pepper. Let stand for 12 hours in the refrigerator. Begin heating coals about one half hour before placing pig on the grill. For added flavor, mix hickory chips with the coals. Place the grill at least 10–12 inches from burning coals. Place pig on the grill so that it is opened flat, skin side down. Turn pig every 20–25 minutes for even cooking. In terms of cooking time, allow not less than 25 minutes to the pound. In the last two hours of cooking, baste with barbecue sauce. Basting before hand can cause the pig to burn. The best way to test for doneness is to explore the pig's inner cavity for any pink spots. The pig must be served well done. Fortunately, it is almost impossible to overcook a

pig. We found this out the hard way when our first attempt, a 35-pound pig caught on fire when placed too near the coals and cooked in 4 hours instead of 10. It appeared to be a disaster, but much to our surprise turned out to be delicious anyhow. So give it a try! There's enough room to make mistakes and still produce a success. Garnish the pig by placing an apple in its mouth and cherries in the eyes.

FRIED CHICKEN FOR FOUR

(Norma Jean's Specialty)

In a brown paper or plastic bag place:

1 cup flour	¾ teaspoon nutmeg
1 teaspoon paprika	½ teaspoon garlic powder
1 teaspoon dry mustard	

Cut a chicken into serving pieces and wash in warm water, leaving some moisture. Sprinkle with salt and pepper. Place a few pieces of chicken at a time in bag and shake until evenly coated. In a Dutch oven or large skillet, melt a 3-pound can of vegetable fat. If fat sizzles when a drop of water hits it, drop in the coated pieces. Fry until golden brown, then drain on paper towels. Fat can be strained and used again.

FRIED CHICKEN GRAVY

Place 2 tablespoons fat used to fry chicken in a skillet. Add 2 tablespoons flour. Stir over medium heat until brown. Add salt and pepper to taste and ¾ cup milk or cream. Pour over chicken, rice, or potatoes.

FRIED CHICKEN FOR FIFTY

When frying chicken for 50, use 12 chickens. Be sure to change the frying grease at least 3 times, since the crumbs at the bottom of the kettle will burn and eventually affect the flavor. Mix the flour coating in the small amount indicated in the above recipe so that it won't become gummy. Use 2 large kettles, so that you can fry several pieces at a time.

COUSINS KELLY AND ARTELIA BRYANTS' BARBECUED SPARERIBS

We allow 3 ribs per person, since we serve other meats as well.

4–6 PEOPLE		50 PEOPLE
4 pounds	spareribs	30 pounds
¼ cup	vinegar	1½ cups
½ cup	water	3 cups
2 tablespoons	brown sugar	¾ cup
1 tablespoon	prepared mustard	6 tablespoons
1½ teaspoons	salt	3 tablespoons
½ teaspoon	black pepper	1 tablespoon
¼ teaspoon	cayenne pepper	1½ teaspoons
1	lemon, juiced, or 2 tablespoons lemon juice concentrate	6 lemons or ¾ cup concentrate
1	onion, chopped	6
½ cup	ketchup	3 cups
2 tablespoons	Worcestershire sauce	¾ cup
2 tablespoons	butter (optional)	1 stick
1½ teaspoons	liquid smoke (optional)	3 tablespoons
½ cup	crushed pineapple, drained (optional)	3 cups
Splash of	beer	1 can

Grill on pit or in the oven

Mix vinegar, water, brown sugar, mustard, salt, pepper, cayenne, lemon juice, onion, and ketchup, and bring to a boil. Lower heat and simmer for 20 minutes in an uncovered pan. Add Worcestershire sauce and any of the optional items you wish. Place spareribs in a roasting pan, cover with tin foil, and bake in a preheated 425° oven for 45 minutes. Pour off excess grease, pour on half of barbecue sauce and reduce heat to 350°. Baste with additional sauce and bake for 1 hour longer or until ribs are nicely browned and fork tender. To grill, marinate the ribs for 1 hour or longer in the sauce, place on grill, and turn frequently over slow coals until fork tender, basting occasionally.

MIXED GREENS

Bud eats greens every day, so he always makes them in quantity and reheats them during the week. For the picnic he doubles the proportions.

2 ham hocks or 1½ pounds
    salt pork
2 quarts water
5 pounds mustard greens

5 pounds turnip greens (and
    small turnips attached to
    turnip greens, peeled and
    quartered)
Salt and pepper to taste

Boil meat in 2 quarts of water for about 1 hour. In the meantime, prepare greens, removing damaged parts and stems. Wash 3 or 4 times or until rinse water is clear. The leaves of mustard and turnips are fairly small and do not require cutting before cooking. Instead, add whole leaves, turnips, and seasoning to the boiling water; cover and cook rapidly about 25 minutes or until tender. When done, cut greens with a knife and two-pronged fork while still in pot.

Yield: 12–15 servings.

COLLARD GREENS

1½ quarts water
1 teaspoon crushed red
    pepper
1½ pounds pork neck bones
    or 2 ham hocks
About 8 pounds collards

2 teaspoons sugar
½ cup cider or white
    vinegar
Salt and pepper to taste

Place 1½ quarts water in a large pot. Add red pepper and meat and boil for about 1 hour while preparing greens. To prepare greens, discard damaged or yellow parts of leaves. Cut away tough stems

143

from each leaf and wash collards thoroughly until rinse water is clear of dirt and grit. Collard leaves are large and usually require cutting before cooking. To do so, fold leaf in half at its center vein, fold over once or twice, then cut them in half with scissors or a knife. Add remaining ingredients to meat in boiling water, then the greens. Cover and cook rapidly for about ½ hour or until greens are tender but firm. Serve with diced raw onions and vinegar.

Yield: 16 servings.

"POT LIKKER"

The liquid in which greens have been cooked is called pot likker. It is renowned for its nutritional value and can be used as an excellent vegetable stock for soups, as a soup in its own right, or traditionally to dunk corn bread. Pot likker can be enriched by tying several mustard and turnip stems in a bunch and cooking them with the greens. Discard stems when the greens are done.

COUSIN JOHNNIE K.'S MACARONI AND SHRIMP SALAD

FOR 6		FOR 50
8 ounces	macaroni	3 16-ounce packages
½ cup	diced celery	3 cups
½ cup	chopped onion	3 cups
¼ cup	chopped green pepper	1½ cups
1 pound	small shrimp, cooked and shelled	6 pounds
½ cup	mayonnaise	3 cups or more
	Salt and pepper to taste	

Add 1 tablespoon salt to 4 quarts rapidly boiling water for each pound of macaroni. Add macaroni and cook, uncovered, until tender, stirring occasionally. Drain, rinse in cold water. Toss all ingredients thoroughly with macaroni. Season with salt and pepper, and garnish with pimentos and paprika.

POTATO SALAD

Carole makes a glorious potato salad.

FOR 6		FOR 50
6	potatoes	4, 5 lb. bags
2 teaspoons	salt	5½ tablespoons
¼ teaspoon	paprika	2 tablespoons
¼ teaspoon	dry mustard	2 tablespoons
5 tablespoons	salad oil	2½ cups
2 tablespoons	vinegar	1¾ cups
2	hard-cooked eggs, chopped	20
1 small	onion, coarsely chopped or grated	5 medium
½ cup	diced celery	4 cups
½ cup	mayonnaise	3½ cups
1 tablespoon	prepared mustard	½ cup
1 teaspoon or more	celery salt	3 tablespoons or more

Boil potatoes in their jackets until tender. Cool, peel, and cut into coarse chunks. In a small bowl, mix the salt, paprika, dry mustard, salad oil, and vinegar. Stir this into potatoes, mixing lightly. Chill for several hours. Then add the chopped eggs, grated onion, and celery. Stir in mayonnaise and prepared mustard. Season liberally with celery salt. Garnish with pimento, stuffed olives, and green pepper rings.

∽∽∽∽∽∽∽∽∽∽∽∽∽∽∽∽∽∽∽∽∽∽∽∽∽∽∽∽∽∽∽∽∽

CAROLE'S DEVILED EGGS

FOR 4		FOR 50
5	eggs, hard-cooked	30
2 tablespoons	mayonnaise	¾ cup
1½ teaspoons	prepared mustard	3 tablespoons
1½ teaspoons	vinegar	3 tablespoons
1 teaspoon	lemon juice	2 tablespoons
	salt and pepper to taste	

Peel hard-cooked eggs and cut in half lengthwise.

Remove yolks and mash them with a fork. Briskly stir in mayonnaise, mustard, vinegar, and lemon juice until mixture forms a smooth paste. Add salt and a few grains of pepper to taste. Fill egg whites with yolk mixture and dust with paprika. Refrigerate for at least ½ hour before serving.

WEEKEND CONCOCTIONS

BUD'S SUNDAY ROAST CHICKEN

2 2½–3-pound roasting chickens

2 tablespoons prepared mustard

Salt and pepper
Juice of 2 lemons

Rinse chickens thoroughly and pat dry. Rub chickens with prepared mustard. Sprinkle with salt and pepper, then stuff with Chestnut and Rice Stuffing (see recipe following). If you don't have time for a stuffing, a stalk of celery and a whole onion placed in each cavity give a nice flavor. Place chickens on a rack in a roasting pan. Cover with lemon juice. Bake in a preheated 375° oven for about 1½ hours, basting from time to time and adding a little water if need be.

Yield: 8 servings.

CHESTNUT AND RICE STUFFING

Hester White, Bud's wonder secretary, sometimes makes this fantastic stuffing for his roast chickens.

1 cup chopped onion
½ cup chopped celery, including leaves
2 tablespoons melted butter
1½ teaspoons poultry seasoning
1 teaspoon salt

2 tablespoons chopped parsley
½ cup chopped canned chestnuts
½ cup chopped cooked giblets (from chicken in recipe above)
2 cups cooked rice

Sauté onion and celery in melted butter until tender. Remove from heat and add poultry seasoning, salt, and parsley. In a bowl, blend together chestnuts, giblets, and rice. Add sautéed mixture and blend well. (Double this recipe to stuff a 12–14-pound turkey.)

Yield: Stuffing for 2 chickens.

BUD'S SATURDAY SEAFOOD STEW

This dish is a family affair with everyone chopping, and Daddy supervising the results.

4 unshelled lobster tails,
   cut in thirds
1 pound raw shrimp
½ cup vegetable oil
2 onions, chopped fine
2 cloves garlic, minced
3 cups clam juice
6 ripe tomatoes, peeled
   and quartered
2 cups peeled and cubed
   potatoes

Salt and pepper to taste
1 bay leaf
1 teaspoon basil
2¾ teaspoons parsley
1½ cups white wine
1 pound haddock fillets,
   quartered
1 dozen clams, washed
   and scrubbed

Shell shrimp, leaving the tails intact. Wash and devein shrimp and set aside. Place vegetable oil in a large pot. Add onions and garlic, and sauté until tender. Add lobster and sauté until pieces turn red. Remove lobsters and reserve. Add clam juice, tomatoes, potatoes, salt, pepper, bay leaf, basil, and oregano. Bring to a boil, lower heat, and simmer, covered, for 25 minutes. Then add wine, shrimp, haddock, and lobster. Simmer for 5 minutes longer. Add clams and continue simmering until they open. Serve as a main dish in large soup bowls.

Yield: 5–6 servings.

BUD'S STEWED FRUIT COMPOTE

1 dozen fresh kumquats if
   in season, or 1 whole
   orange, unpeeled, chopped
Juice of 1 lime
Juice of 1 lemon
Rind of half a lime, chopped
Rind of half a lemon,
   chopped

1½ cups water
2 cups unpitted dried prunes
2 cups dried apricots
1 cup dried peaches
Sugar to taste (about 4
   heaping teaspoons—
   optional)

Combine kumquats and the lime and lemon juices and rinds. Cover with water. Bring to a boil, lower heat and simmer, covered, for 30 minutes. Add prunes, apricots, and sugar if you like. (Bud never uses sugar, preferring a very tart mixture.) Continue cooking until all fruits are tender (about 1 hour). Served hot or cold as a breakfast fruit, a dessert or as a bedtime snack.

Yield: 6 servings.

OLD-TIME FAVORITES

TIPSY CAKE

4 eggs
2 cups sugar
⅛ teaspoon salt
1 quart milk
1 pint dark rum or whiskey
1 pint heavy cream

¼ pound almonds, blanched
   and toasted
1 very large, stale
   spongecake
1 small jar each of red and
   green maraschino cherries

Beat eggs one at a time until they are light and fluffy. Add sugar and salt and beat thoroughly. Scald milk and stir into mixture. Return to the pot and cook until thick but not long enough to curdle mixture. Remove from stove and cool. Then add 1¾ cups rum or whiskey to the custard.

Cut nuts coarsely. Break cake into coarse pieces and line bottom of a large bowl with a layer of cake. Cover with a layer of custard and continue alternating until all the cake and custard are used. Whip cream until it forms stiff peaks; add ¼ cup more rum or whiskey and additional sugar to taste.

Cover cake with whipped cream and decorate with chopped almonds and maraschino cherries.

Place in the refrigerator for about 2 hours to ripen. It is even better the second day.

Yield: 12 servings.

SYLLABUB

2 cups heavy cream	4 tablespoons rum or brandy
½ cup sugar	Nutmeg

Whip the cream until stiff. Fold in sugar and rum or brandy. Cover and chill in the refrigerator for 1 hour or so. Serve in sherbet glasses or punch cups with a faint dusting of nutmeg.

Yield: 6 servings.

THE SAMPSONS

16 Noble Street in Delaware, Ohio—the house Granddad built for his family

Granddad Sampson

Granddad Sampson was the only grandparent we ever met, and although he died when we were young we remember him well. He was a strikingly handsome man with a long white flowing beard which in later years reached almost to his waist. He had six fingers on each hand, which might have made a lesser man self-conscious. But Granddaddy would say that this only made his hands more powerful, and what a powerful man he was! His incredible physical strength, which lasted until his death at nearly 100 years of age, made an indelible impression on all who knew him. He was a man of few words, but his presence carried more weight than words ever could. His was not the silence of diffidence but of many weathered storms and deep inner reserves, rooted in a tortuous childhood and the constant struggle to ensure the survival of his family in adulthood. Somewhat eccentric in later years, he once replied when chided for talking to himself, "I can't think of a more interesting person to talk to."

William Sampson was born in Kentucky in approximately 1865. He lived with the Percivals, a wealthy white family who had taken him into their home to be raised as a houseboy. He had no knowledge of his own family except a vague memory of being part of a large family. He was told that he had been given away by his mother to a stranger who appeared at their door when he was three years old. Granddaddy assumed that he was given away in this manner because his family could not afford to care for him. But he was never able to gather any information from the Percivals about his true origins, nor the identity of the stranger who brought him to their home, or even if William Sampson was his true name. These factors were to haunt him all of his life. As a young boy, he was aware of unconfirmed rumors among the townsfolk that he was actually the son of one of the Percivals and a servant. The day before the will of old Mr. Percival was to be read, the courthouse mysteriously burned down, destroying the document and intensifying rumors that William Sampson, who had been summoned to the dying man's bedside, may have indeed been an heir.

As a boy, "Pony," as he was called, was raised with a mixture of affection and abuse that characterized such master-servant relationships. In the summer he was forced to go barefoot, and in the winter he was given the same shoes to wear for four years. As a result, his feet were stunted and pained him all his life. He was not allowed to go to school but learned whatever he could through his duties as a playmate for the Percival children, who shared their school lessons with him until he was ten. Then it was decided that he had received enough education and he was given the work load of a man. He had to work from sunrise to sunset, had no contact with other children, and was frequently beaten if he became fatigued or made a mistake. He received no medical care. Once he fell from a horse and, though in excruciating pain, he was still required to work. It was not discovered that his hip had been fractured until he was hospitalized after a fall from his apple tree at the age of eighty. Though he suffered a second fracture from this fall, miraculously he recovered.

Dad Sampson was an amazingly tough, resilient, and self-reliant man. He could make his own clothes and prepare his own food. He built most of the homes in which his family lived, as well as the furniture, and he also made some of his own farming tools. At different times throughout his life, he was a migrant farm worker, a butcher, manager of a dairy farm, railroad construction worker, and was for the latter part of his life the boiler man as well as night chef at a hospital in Delaware, Ohio, where he finally settled with his family. But Granddaddy's first love remained farming. He was profoundly rooted to the earth, was happiest when working with his hands, and often seemed in closer harmony with things of nature than with people. Yet he was a deep and loving man. He taught us that when doves coo mournfully, it will rain within hours; when maple leaves turn upward, it will rain in a day; and when the barks of trees are thicker than usual, it will be a bad winter. He could look at the sky and predict the weather, feel soil and tell you what it would and would not yield. Plant and animal life thrived under his care. He raised bees, cows, rabbits, chickens, vegetables, and fruits. From his beehives, Granddad Sampson would extract the most delicious honey. It was one of his favorite foods and he used it for everything from home remedies to baking his favorite cakes. Frequently he would send our family honey in the comb with advice on how to use it. The following recipes were inspired by his suggestions.

FRUITED HONEY CHICKEN

1 3-pound chicken, salted
    and peppered and cut
    for frying
¾ cup apple cider or juice
½ cup orange juice
¼ cup lemon juice
1 onion, chopped
½ cup oil

1 fresh unpeeled apple,
    sliced (or a handful
    of dried apples)
1 handful seedless raisins
1 handful dried apricots
1 handful pitted uncooked
    prunes
2 tablespoons honey

Marinate chicken in fruit juices and onion for 1 hour or so (reserve marinade), then brown both sides of all pieces in oil. Place chicken in a covered casserole and cover with marinating juices plus the apple, raisins, apricots, prunes, and honey. Bake in a preheated 350° oven for 45 minutes, basting occasionally with marinade and pan juices.

Yield: 4–5 servings.

HONEY DUCK

1 4-pound duck
1 clove garlic
1 teaspoon salt
1 orange, peeled, sliced, and
    quartered or sectioned
¼ teaspoon powdered ginger

¼ cup lemon juice
2 tablespoons honey
½ cup seedless grapes (if
    not in season use 1 small
    can black cherries)

Quarter duck, place it skin side up on a rack in a baking dish. Bake in a preheated 325° oven for 1 hour. Drain off the fat and arrange the duck in a casserole. Add garlic, salt, orange, ginger, lemon juice, and honey. Cover and bake for 30 minutes more. Add grapes (or canned cherries) and bake, uncovered, for 10 minutes more.

Yield: 4 servings.

HONEY CUSTARD

3 eggs
½ cup honey
⅛ teaspoon salt
2¾ cups milk

½ teaspoon lemon extract
½ teaspoon grated orange
    rind
Nutmeg

Beat eggs until light. Add honey and salt. Continue beating until well blended. Scald milk. Slowly pour milk over egg mixture, stirring constantly. Add lemon extract and orange rind. Pour into buttered custard cups. Sprinkle nutmeg on top. Set in a shallow pan filled with an inch of hot water. Bake in a preheated 350° oven for 45 minutes or until set.

Yield: 5–6 servings.

OLD-FASHIONED HONEY SPONGECAKE

1 heaping cup of sifted
    cake flour
¼ teaspoon salt
5 large eggs, separated
½ cup sugar

½ cup honey
¼ cup hot water
1½ teaspoons vanilla
1 teaspoon grated lemon rind
¾ teaspoon cream of tartar

Sift flour and salt together and set aside. Beat egg yolks until frothy, stir in sugar, honey, hot water, vanilla, and lemon rind until well blended. Add flour mixture. In a separate bowl, beat egg whites until foamy. Add cream of tartar. Continue beating until stiff peaks form. Fold into batter mixture. Pour batter into a lightly greased 9-inch tube cake pan and bake in a preheated 325° oven for 50 minutes. When cool, dust with powdered sugar or frost with Honey Icing (see recipe following).

P.S. Stale honey cake can be used for Tipsy Cake (see Index).

Yield: Makes 10–12 slices.

HONEY ICING

2 tablespoons softened
  butter
2 tablespoons honey
2 cups confectioner's sugar

A drop of vanilla
A pinch of salt
1 egg white (unbeaten)

Cream the butter and honey together, adding ½ cup of the sugar, a drop of vanilla, and the salt. Stir well, add egg white and remainder of sugar. Beat until smooth and ice honey cake (preceding).

HONEY PUNCH

1½ quarts water
1 cup honey
Juice of 3 lemons
Juice of 3 oranges
3 cups pineapple juice

1 cup unsweetened
  grape juice
1 cup crushed pineapple
Fresh mint sprigs

Heat 2 cups of the water so that it is warm enough to blend honey into it easily. Cool. Then mix in remaining water, juices, and crushed pineapple. Pour into tall glasses filled with ice. Garnish with mint sprigs.

Yield: About 3 quarts of punch.

HONEY REMEDIES

A doctor was a luxury to Granddad Sampson, and he was suspicious of them anyway, so he blended his own cold preventives. He believed in the curative health-giving properties of honey, and even advocated warm beeswax for relieving stiff joints.

Dad Sampson making soap in his back yard

GARGLE

Blend equal parts of honey, glycerin, and vinegar. Use as needed.

❦ ❦

COUGH SYRUP

His children don't remember the proportions but do know the ingredients.

Honey	Onions
Tea brewed from horehound	Vinegar
leaves and stems	Few drops of turpentine
Lemons	

LYE SOAP

When we were children, we used to watch Granddad making soap in a big black pot in his back yard.

1 gallon old leftover grease
Water, about 4 gallons
3 boxes Red Devil lye

Strain crumbs from grease and place it in a large iron kettle or washpot. To start, add 2 gallons of water. Add lye. Boil for about ½ hour, stirring constantly until lye "eats" up grease (mixture will become lighter and lighter). Then add 2 more gallons of water. Continue boiling, stirring constantly until mixture is the consistency of molasses or honey. Remove from fire and let harden in pot for 2-3 days. Then cut out of pot in usable blocks. It is an economical, all-purpose soap that can be used for almost anything in life that ever needs washing—laundry, floors, hair, and in a pinch the body. It even soothes insects bites.

Grandmother Corine Johnson Sampson

Corine Sampson with husband William and sons William and Glenn in Elizabethtown, Kentucky, around 1908

Grandmother Corine was known for her religious zeal. One church was not enough for her. She was an active member of two—the Baptist Church and the Holiness Church. For the Baptist, she taught Sunday school and for the Holy Tride Stone Church, she was a "home missionary," which meant that she traveled to neighboring towns to "save souls" and recruit members. She saw no conflict between the two faiths but adopted what she considered the more Christ-like approach of the Holiness members: conservative dress (long sleeves and skirts), no personal adornment (make-up or jewelry), no body defilement (smoking or drinking), and strict observance of the Sabbath at all costs (no working or cooking on Sunday). Mom Sampson was literally in church on Sunday from dawn to midnight, yet she led by example rather than decree, allowing religious freedom. Therefore, some of her children remained Baptist even after the Holiness Church finally absorbed her full attention.

Without any doubt, Mom Sampson was the most vocal personality in her household. She held strong opinions about most things and led her family in an austere life where cleanliness was next to godliness, where the rod was not spared for fear of spoiling the child, where children were expected to be seen and not heard, and where hard, honest work was the order of the day.

She was an excellent manager, and when Dad Sampson brought in his salary, she gave him thirty-five cents for chewing tobacco and proceeded with the weekly budget. This was in no way meant to demean him, but she had a strong sense of herself and her capabilities, and they both recognized her uncanny ability to stretch a dollar as far as it could go—and then some. Pursuit of worldly goods did not interest Corine, but she was concerned that her family have proper food, good shelter, and adequate clothing. The one luxury that she possessed was a piano. Dad Sampson traded a cow for it, and she patiently gave each of her children music lessons and taught them hymns.

Little is known about Corine's early days. She was born in Camden, Alabama, and was one of five brothers and sisters, graduated from Tuskegee Institute, and was a schoolteacher by profession. She went to Elizabethtown, Kentucky, to live with her sister Rutelia and to teach. There she met and married William Sampson. He was quite a few years her senior, but this did not bother her. She said that she would rather be "an old man's darling than a young man's slave."

Early in their married life, Corine's mother died, leaving two small children, Clyde, nine, and Mamie Jean, our mother, four. Corine and Mr. Sampson took them in and raised them as their own children, never telling William and Glenn, who were infants at the time, or Asa, who came later, that they were not their natural siblings. It was her feeling that this would make the family "more harmonious."

Corine felt strongly that a woman's role should not be limited to the home, and was very appreciative of the support and understanding she got from Dad Sampson concerning her religious convictions, even though he was less active in the church. Without his co-operation she couldn't have functioned as actively as she did in her religious pursuits and evangelistic missions. For while she was doing God's work, he was often called upon to run the household and cook the meals. They held each other in high esteem and were never known to utter one harsh word between them.

Corine advised her only daughter to be self-sufficient, not to marry early, and to find a man who would encourage her to pursue her own individual interests. With this in mind, she would greet all of her daughter's suitors at the door with a lecture (sometimes lasting for an hour) on the importance of education before romance, and religion above all.

Grandmother Corine pricked herself while sewing and died of blood poisoning before we were born. But the most vivid image in our minds in the description our mother used to give us of Corine's annual Christmas celebration. Her memory also came through to us in the many so-called "wholesome foods" that we were required to eat, such as liver and creamed spinach and, in our favorites, spoonbread and tapioca. Our mother explained to us that since the Sampsons had lived on a dairy farm many of their dishes utilized milk and cream, which were fresh and plentiful. We have therefore divided this chapter into two quite different sections—Corine's Christmas preparations and our favorite "dairy" dishes inherited from her.

THE SAMPSON CHRISTMAS

Every year Corine organized the Christmas celebration. Granddaddy Sampson would chop the Christmas tree and the whole family made the decorations. It was a very big event. For many days everyone would string cranberries to make long chains, and pop and string popcorn. Large red apples were shined and hung. Oranges were punctured with cloves until no skin showed, and they were suspended from ribbons on the tree. Peppermint sticks and painted cookies dangled tantalizingly from the branches. Granddaddy could whittle wood so there were miniature wooden toys hanging along with paper angels and snowflakes, but the crowning glory of the Sampson Christmas tree was a sprinkling of little brass candleholders filled with white candles made from the beeswax from Granddaddy's hives.

Mom and Dad Sampson on their way to church in Delaware, Ohio

The family did not exchange gifts with one another but invited the two Sunday-school classes that Corine taught to share their Christmas spirit. Corine would lead in the caroling while her son William played the piano. Punch and frosted cake were served, then each child was given a treat from the tree to take home.

PAINTED CHRISTMAS COOKIES

1 cup butter
1 cup sugar
1 egg
3 cups sifted all-purpose
  flour
Pinch of salt

1 teaspoon rose water*
1 teaspoon orange flower
  water*
½ teaspoon almond extract
½ teaspoon lemon extract
Food coloring

Cream butter and sugar well, then add egg. Stir in flour and salt. Divide dough into 4 parts. To first part add rose water, to the second orange flower water, to the third almond extract, and to the last lemon extract. A drop of red food coloring in the rose, orange in the orange flower, green in the almond, and yellow in the lemon will differentiate the flavors. Chill dough for 1 hour. Then roll each section separately on a well-floured board. Dough should be ¼ inch thick. Cut with Christmas tree, star, animal, Santa Claus, or snowflake cookie cutters and place on an ungreased cookie sheet. Prick a hole in the top of each cookie if you plan to string them on the tree. Bake in a preheated 375° oven for about 10 minutes.

Yield: 5 dozen cookies.

Rose water and orange flower water, favorite flavorings at the turn of the century, can still be purchased in some drugstores and gourmet shops.

COATING

2 cups confectioner's sugar
1 teaspoon vanilla
3 tablespoons heavy cream

Blend all together and divide into sections. Using food coloring, tint each section a different hue and paint cooled cookies with a small paintbrush. Use granulated sugar, also tinted, for accent, as well as small bits of nuts, citron, slivered red cherries, and raisins. Have fun.

CORINE'S "DAIRY" DISHES

KIDNEY STEW

2 large beef kidneys
2 tablespoons vinegar
2 tablespoons butter
1 medium-size onion, chopped
4 tablespoons flour

1½ cups beef stock (or 2 cubes beef bouillon in 1½ cups water)
Juice of 1 lemon
1 cup sour cream
Salt and pepper to taste
Parsley as a garnish

Soak kidneys for 1 hour in a bowl of water to which 2 tablespoons of vinegar has been added. Rinse well and place in a saucepan with fresh water to cover. Parboil for 5–10 minutes. Remove from pan, cool a bit, then chop into small pieces. In a frying pan heat butter. Add onion, sauté until tender, then add kidney pieces. Sprinkle the flour over this and brown the mixture well, stirring frequently. Add beef stock and lemon juice. Simmer for 10 minutes. Add sour cream, stir, and simmer for 1 minute more. Season to taste. Serve over steaming rice and garnish with parsley.

Yield: 4 servings.

CREAMED SWEETBREADS

4 pairs sweetbreads
3 tablespoons butter
4 teaspoons grated onion
1 tablespoon flour
2 cups light cream

1 dozen small mushrooms, sliced
Salt and pepper to taste
Paprika

Soak sweetbreads in cold water for 1 hour. Parboil for 5 minutes. Let cool. Remove skin and cut into small pieces. Put butter in a frying pan and heat until hot and bubbly. Add sweetbreads and grated onion. Fry until sweetbreads are slightly brown, stirring frequently. Sprinkle flour over mixture and blend. Then add cream and mushrooms, mixing thoroughly. Cook over low heat for about 10 minutes. Season with salt and pepper. Dust with paprika. Serve over hot toast or in heated patty shells.

Yield: 6 servings.

LIVER WITH CREAMED GRAVY

4 strips bacon
4 slices beef or calf's liver
¼ cup flour
¼ teaspoon salt
⅛ teaspoon pepper

1 medium-size onion, chopped
½ cup sweet or sour cream

Fry bacon to a crisp and drain on paper towels. Dredge liver in flour, salt, and pepper mixture and fry for 5 minutes on each side or until nicely browned. Add onions to pan for last 5 minutes. Remove liver when done and add crumpled bacon and sweet or sour cream to pan juices and onion. This makes a nice gravy for hominy grits (breakfast) or rice (dinner).

Yield: 3–4 servings.

TONGUE WITH HORSERADISH SAUCE

1 4–5-pound beef tongue
1 medium-size onion, quartered
2 celery tops

1 clove garlic
¼ teaspoon salt
6–8 peppercorns

Cover tongue with water, add onion, celery tops, garlic clove, salt, and peppercorns. Cook for 20 minutes per pound or until a fork pierces the tongue easily. Remove skin carefully, slice thinly, and serve with the following sauce.

167

HORSERADISH SAUCE

1 tablespoon grated onion
1 tablespoon butter
1 tablespoon flour

1 cup light cream
4 tablespoons prepared
  horseradish

Sauté onion in butter until slightly browned. Add flour and blend
well. Slowly add cream, stirring constantly. Add horseradish and
heat thoroughly. Serve with tongue. Excellent with corned beef or
boiled beef also.

Yield: 6 servings.

MOM SAMPSON'S SPOONBREAD—
OUR FAVORITE

1 cup yellow cornmeal
2 cups boiling water
3 tablespoons butter

1 teaspoon salt
3 large eggs, well beaten
1 cup milk

Slowly add cornmeal to the boiling water, stirring constantly until
thick and smooth. Add butter and salt and cool to lukewarm. Then
add eggs and milk. Beat for 2 minutes, pour into a greased casserole
and bake in a preheated 375° oven for 35 minutes or until golden
brown. Spoon out while piping hot and pass more butter!

Yield: 8 servings.

PINEAPPLE SYLLABUB

2 tablespoons sugar
1 teaspoon vanilla
3 egg whites, stiffly beaten

1 cup heavy cream, whipped
1 cup drained crushed
  pineapple

Add the sugar and vanilla to stiffly beaten egg whites. Fold in the
whipped cream and crushed pineapple. Chill and serve in punch
cups.

Yield: 4–6 servings.

ORANGE TAPIOCA

¼ cup tapioca
¼ cup sugar
⅛ teaspoon salt
2⅓ cups milk
1 egg yolk, slightly beaten
1 egg white

1 tablespoon sugar
1 teaspoon orange extract
6 fresh orange sections, peeled (or canned mandarin)

Add tapioca, sugar, and salt to the milk. Stir in egg yolk. Cook over low heat, stirring occasionally until thick. Remove from heat. Beat egg white until soft peaks form. Add sugar and continue beating until stiff and glossy. Fold into tapioca mixture. Add orange extract. Pour tapioca into sherbet glasses. Garnish with orange sections. Serve warm or chilled.

Yield: 4–6 servings.

The Sampson Brothers

Clyde

On a recent visit to Cincinnati, we asked our mother's brother, Uncle Clyde, to share some of his childhood reminiscences with us, but he found it difficult to talk about the past. We left, disappointed, but a few days later we received this letter telling us about his life.

My earliest memories are of being in a log cabin with my mother, older half brother, Sam; and your mother, in Camden, Alabama. We had no stove, in fact, no conveniences. Out back was a garden though, where we grew vegetables, and a spring where we drew water. I had a little job delivering groceries to two old maids who had a turkey farm on the edge of town. Every Sunday we had fried chicken and rice for breakfast and that was considered a very good breakfast. Fireworks were exploded at Christmas time in those days. Then, one Christmas, I remember the neighbors telling me not to play; that it wasn't appropriate because our mother was very ill. Soon after that, she died. The church women laid her out and since there was no funeral parlor in those days, we purchased a simple casket in the furniture store. Our sister, Tiny, came from Kentucky and packed us up to go with her. The white man who ran the grocery store in Camden asked her to leave me with him to work but she said "no," that we wouldn't split up the family. We took the train from Camden to Birmingham, Alabama, and when I looked out the window I saw a man with a wagon selling milk. He had a white horse and every time he would go into a home the horse would walk to the next house and wait for him. It's funny the things you remember. When we reached our destination, Elizabethtown, Kentucky, we had trouble locating the house where Rutelia and Corine, our older sisters lived. We knocked on the wrong door and a man answered. I thought he said his name was "Jesus" and I ran back and told Mamie that we had moved to a town where "Jesus" lived. At the time I was about eight or nine years old. It was decided that since Rutelia and Tiny were not married, and Corine was, we would stay with her and her husband, Dad Sampson. Corine said to cut down on confusion, we would all be called Sampson and from then on we were just like any other family.

I don't remember the reason for it, but we left Elizabethtown a couple of years later and stopped on a farm where we all picked strawberries and weeded the onions for a farmer. They did not have proper living conditions there and we were housed in an abandoned chicken coop. Mom Sampsom saved every penny and from there we went to Xenia, Ohio where Dad opened a small meat market. A competitor up the street lowered his prices drastically and we soon went broke. Mother, anxious to settle where good schools were, decided

Clyde Sampson after a good day's shooting

to locate on a dairy farm in Wilberforce, Ohio. We worked for Farmer Brice and I never will forget the day he installed indoor plumbing. I had never seen anything like that before, and I said to Mamie, "One day we're going to have it too." It was here that Mamie and I started grade school. I had to get up at 4 A.M. to milk the cows and check the traps and go through deep snow to do it sometimes. Then I'd have my breakfast and Mamie and I would walk to school. We carried our lunch pails and Mamie, being liberal and generous, many times allowed me to eat most of her lunch before we reached school. We had to walk a mile and a half each way. Mother used to make cracklin' bread and bran bread for us to carry. After school we had to work then do our lessons. When I finished grade school, that was considered a very good education. Mother had a revelation that we should re-settle in Delaware, Ohio. This we did. It was a small college town, Ohio Wesleyan is there, and work opportunities were good. We had chores to do in the house and jobs in the community. Mamie did not like to clean the lamp chimneys, so she paid me ten cents a week to clean them and not to tell. I would pull her braids if we had a scrap. I always regretted when the church had its annual hayride as mother insisted that I chaperone Mamie. This I disliked. Mamie earned her first monies from the sale of ice cream cones. She and another girl, Elsie Austin, who was my first girl friend, had a pony and a cart which they drove from door to door. She also shucked corn for tuition money. William was a clerk in a novelty store, Glenn did everything, but mainly dug for fresh water clams and oysters. He once found a pearl that he sold for $42.00—big money in those days. Asa cleaned out the movie house. I used to hunt and trap fur-bearing animals—mink, muskrats, coons, polecats, etc. The money saved went for my tuition at Tuskegee Institute where I studied plumbing and incidentally happened to install new fixtures for Maude Darden in Opelika, long before anyone knew there would be a connection between the Sampson and Darden families. William graduated from Wilberforce; Glenn, Ohio State; Mamie from Ohio University; and Asa attended Fisk. I think our family did all right, considering our beginnings as migrant workers and the hard times we saw. It has taken me all this time to see the power of our mother's religious convictions.

Until his retirement, Uncle Clyde worked for an insurance company in Cincinnati. Hunting was his main pastime then, and he

Clyde's son Lowell, with prey

173

took his son Lowell as well as the boys to whom he was a "big brother" on camping and hunting trips. Often he cooked in the "bush," but sometimes brought his game home for his wife Marie to prepare. He emphasizes that one must be inventive and use the accompaniments and garnishes that the seasons provide and employ common sense in the proportions given, as they will vary according to the size of the catch. Here, then, are a few of the recipes from Uncle Clyde's "wild" days.

BRUNSWICK STEW

1 medium-size rabbit
1 squirrel
2 quarts water
1½ tablespoons salt
1 large onion, chopped
1½ cups fresh baby lima
   beans or 1 package
   frozen
2 slices bacon, diced

4 medium-size potatoes,
   peeled and cubed
3 cups chopped fresh
   tomatoes
½ teaspoon pepper
1 teaspoon sugar
2 cups fresh corn
2 tablespoons flour
2 tablespoons butter

Skin and clean the rabbit and squirrel and wash in several changes of water. Cut in desired pieces for servings. Bring the 2 quarts water to a boil and add rabbit and squirrel. Boil for 1 hour. Add salt, onion, lima beans, bacon, potatoes, tomatoes, and pepper. Cover and cook slowly for another hour or until tender. Then add sugar and corn. Continue cooking for 15 minutes. Mix flour and butter to a paste and add to stew. Adjust seasoning. Cook for about 15 minutes longer. Serve hot. (This dish can be made with a 4–4½-pound stewing chicken as a substitute for rabbit and squirrel.)

Yield: 4–6 servings.

FRICASSEED RABBIT OR SQUIRREL

1 medium-size rabbit or 2
   squirrels
1 teaspoon salt
½ teaspoon pepper

1 cup flour
¾ cup bacon fat
2 cups boiling water

Skin, clean, and cut up rabbit into 6 parts. Roll the pieces in salt, pepper, and flour. Place bacon fat in a large, heavy skillet and heat. Fry rabbit until it is brown on all sides. Pour off most of the fat and add the 2 cups boiling water, then cover and simmer for 20–30 minutes. Serve with gravy from the pan.

Yield: 2–3 servings.

ROAST RABBIT

1 rabbit	4 bay leaves
Vinegar	3 tablespoons bacon fat
Ground cloves or sage	2 teaspoons grape or mint
Salt and pepper	jelly (optional)
1 onion, sliced	

Skin and clean the rabbit and wash in cold water. Pat dry and rub with vinegar. Rub rabbit with ground cloves or sage, salt, and pepper. Place in a shallow pan and lay sliced onion and bay leaves on top. Drizzle the 3 tablespoons bacon fat over meat, then cover with aluminum foil. Cook slowly (30 minutes to the pound) in a preheated 300° oven until tender. Grape or mint jelly may be added and stirred into the pan juices before serving.

Yield: 2–3 servings.

DEER STEAKS

Venison steaks—allow 1 per person	1 bay leaf
½ cup vinegar	½ teaspoon prepared mustard
½ cup vegetable oil	¼ teaspoon black pepper
1 clove garlic, minced	Butter

175

Cut venison into slices about 1 inch thick. Combine the rest of the ingredients except butter and marinate steaks in this sauce for 3 hours. Then remove from marinade, rub with butter, and broil under a hot fire for roughly 8 minutes on each side.

Leftover venison makes a good hash, says Uncle Clyde.

ROAST OPOSSUM

with Yams

1 opossum	4 bay leaves
Salt and pepper	2 cups boiling water
Powdered sage	6 yams
Juice of 1 lemon	Butter

Skin and clean the opossum. Take out the intestines, etc., being careful to remove musk glands from the small of the back and beneath front legs. Rinse well. Rub inside and out with salt, pepper, sage, and lemon juice. Place in a roasting pan on top of bay leaves and pour boiling water over it. Cover and cook in a preheated 350° oven for 45 minutes. Turn meat and add peeled and cut yams dotted with butter. Continue cooking for 45 minutes more or until tender, removing cover for final 10 minutes of browning.

Yield: 3–6 servings, depending on size of opossum.

ROAST QUAILS

6 quails	1 onion, chopped
½ cup cider vinegar	1 clove garlic, minced
4 tablespoons butter	2 cups chicken broth
½ pound chicken livers, quartered	1 cup port wine
	1½ cups rice (uncooked)
	½ teaspoon salt

Cover quails with cold water to which vinegar has been added. Soak overnight. Then rinse in cold water. Pat dry. Melt butter in a large pan and brown quails on all sides. Remove from pan. Sauté chicken livers in same pan. Add onions, garlic, and sauté until brown. Pour in chicken broth and return quails to pan. Add wine and stir in rice and salt. Cover and bake for 30 minutes in a preheated 375° oven.

Yield: 6 servings.

PHEASANT WITH PECAN STUFFING

1 good-size pheasant	2 tablespoons butter
Salt and pepper	½ cup sherry
1 clove garlic, halved	Blueberries (optional)

Pluck and clean pheasant. Rub inside cavity with salt, pepper, and garlic, then stuff with Pecan Stuffing (recipe given below). Place bird in a roasting pan, rub with butter, pour over sherry, and roast in a preheated 350° oven, allowing 25 minutes per pound. Baste often with pan juices, adding more sherry, if necessary. Wild blueberries swirled around in the natural gravy make a nice garnish.

Yield: 2–3 servings.

PECAN STUFFING

¼ cup honey	¼ cup minced celery
¼ cup melted butter	¼ cup minced onion
1 egg, well beaten	½ cup seedless raisins
¼ cup heavy cream	2½ cups bread crumbs
¼ cup water	1 cup chopped pecan meats

Mix honey, butter, egg, cream, and water together and pour into a bowl containing the celery, onion, raisins, bread crumbs, and pecans. Combine well. Use to stuff pheasant or any other fowl.

Yield: 4 cups stuffing.

ROAST GOOSE

A Sampson Christmas treat.

1 8–10-pound goose

STUFFING:
½ pound prunes
Apple cider
5 medium-size tart apples,
   peeled and sliced
½ cup slivered almonds
1 teaspoon grated orange
   rind

For the stuffing, soak prunes in enough apple cider to cover for several hours. Remove prunes from cider and combine with apples, almonds, and grated orange rind. Reserve cider. Wash goose well, removing any extra fat from the inside. Place in a roasting pan and stuff with fruits. Roast goose in a preheated 350° oven for 3 hours. Baste with reserved apple cider.

Yield: 8 servings.

JEANIE'S BRAN BREAD

Uncle Clyde's daughter, Jean Marie, has learned to bake this much-loved bread from her father's school-pail days.

1 egg
1⅔ cups buttermilk
½ cup honey
2 cups coarse bran
2 cups unbleached white or
   whole-wheat flour
2 teaspoons baking powder
1 teaspoon salt
1 teaspoon baking soda
½ cup seedless raisins or
   chopped dates (optional)

In a large bowl, beat egg until light. Add buttermilk and honey. Mix dry ingredients and add to egg mixture, blending well. Add raisins or dates (if you like them) and pour batter into a greased 9½″ × 5½″ loaf pan or 12 muffin cups. Bake in a preheated 350° oven for 50–60 minutes.

Yield: 1 loaf or 12 large muffins.

William

Unfortunately, we never got to know Uncle Bill as well as we would have liked to before he died. Our mother had always told us about her brother in Chicago who was an accountant for the Government, and one hot summer she took us to visit him and his wife Ruth. Beside the intense Chicago heat, the standout of the trip for us, was Uncle Bill's ham radio set. He told us that he had started out in 1916 at the age of twelve with a crude crystal set and little by little had advanced to the sophisticated equipment that then monopolized his entire den. Right after dinner he checked his watch and invited us to join him for a call from Hamburg, Germany. We told a thick German accent that we were Uncle Bill's nieces from New Jersey and told the same to a ham radio buff in Alaska.

We made only one other trip to his home but were again impressed by the many friends Uncle Bill, a somewhat reserved man, had made through his radio.

Recently his brother Asa told us that, as a boy, William played the organ for his mother's religious gatherings and served as choir director for the Baptist church, but quite unbeknown to puritanical Mom Sampson, moonlighted with a local dance band. And though the churchgoers were always tattling on the "sinners," lucky for him the news never traveled home!

William's widow, Ruth, related to us that their romance actually started in the dining room at Wilberforce University in Ohio, where they were both students. She had a part-time job in the cafeteria and caught his attention by giving him extra portions at suppertime.

Shortly after their marriage, Ruth's sister died, leaving two orphaned sons. Just as his father and mother had done with Clyde and Mamie, he took the children in and happily raised them as his own. The two boys, Gerald and Thomas, tell us that their father got a big kick out of being a Boy Scout leader and commissioner of the Maywood, Illinois, Civil Defense Unit and that for recreation he loved to bowl and taught them the game. The family bowled often, and after an invigorating game Billy Sampson's favorite and most requested meal was Aunt Ruth's pot roast dinner with bread pudding for dessert.

AUNT RUTH'S POT ROAST

2- to 3-pound round roast	¼ teaspoon powdered cloves
Salt and pepper	1 cup water
1 tablespoon brown sugar	4 medium-size white
2 tablespoons butter	potatoes, peeled and cubed
2 tablespoons oil	8 tiny white onions
1 large onion, chopped	4 carrots, sliced
1 tablespoon tomato ketchup	

Uncle Bill and Aunt Ruth at Wilberforce in the Roaring Twenties.

Season meat with salt and pepper and rub with brown sugar. Melt butter and oil in a heavy pot. Add meat and brown quickly on all sides. Add onions and brown them also. Stir in ketchup, cloves, and 1 cup water. Cover tightly. Cook over a very low flame for 1½ hours. Then put in potatoes, white onions, and carrots, and continue cooking for 30 minutes. To serve, slice thinly and spoon pan juices and vegetables over the meat.

Yield: 4 man-size servings.

MAMA JENNY'S BREAD PUDDING

Ruth inherited this recipe from her mother.

CUSTARD:
3 egg yolks
A pinch of salt
¼ cup sugar
1¾ cups milk, scalded
¼ teaspoon vanilla extract

Approximately 8 slices
  white bread
¼ cup apple jelly
⅓ cup seedless raisins

TOPPING:
3 egg whites
⅛ teaspoon cream of tartar

¼ cup sugar
¾ teaspoon vanilla extract

For the custard, beat egg yolks slightly and combine with salt and sugar. Add milk slowly and cook in the top of a double boiler until mixture coats a spoon. Add vanilla. Butter bread on both sides and toast each side under the broiler until brown. Cut into ½-inch cubes and line the bottom of an 8-inch-square pan with ⅓ of the toast cubes. Dot with apple jelly and sprinkle with raisins. Add a layer of custard, then alternate layers of toast, apple jelly, raisins, and custard until pan is full. Bake in a preheated 325° oven for 30 minutes or until almost firm. For the topping, beat egg whites until foamy, add cream of tartar, and beat until stiff but not dry. Add sugar and vanilla, and beat until well blended. Pile the meringue lightly over pudding and bake for about 8 minutes or until meringue is golden brown.

Yield: About 9 servings.

Glenn

Members of our family have told us that when Glenn was a grade school boy in Delaware, Ohio, doing odd jobs—mainly tending lawns and caring for the elderly who couldn't get about—someone requested that he change a tire. The Sampsons had never owned a car, so Glenn replied that it was a little out of his line and he didn't know how. Dad Sampson, who was standing nearby, took him aside and advised him to remove "can't" and "don't know how" from his vocabulary and replace them with "I will do it tomorrow." Dad Sampson reasoned that, given time, one can master almost anything. This was a lesson that Glenn took to heart. He has always been a jack-of-all-trades and a master of many.

Glenn's savings just barely got him through Ohio State, where he graduated as a pharmacist. He was practically down to his last quarter when in Buffalo his sister heard about a long-ailing banker who was looking for a man Friday who was a dietitian, masseur, and landscaper. She put in a word for Glenn, who brushed up on nutrition on the train ride, improvised the massage, already knew landscaping, and was hired. The banker's health took an upward spiral so he put Glenn in charge of supervising the meals for sixty people (staff and family) who lived and ate on the family compound. More fish, fresh vegetables, fruits, and no rich sauces was Glenn's simple idea.

At night Glenn took on a full-time position at the post office and he maintained these two jobs until retirement. Through the banker, he gained access to rare coins, and, through his post office career, access to rare stamps, and that's how he began two collections that are highly prized today. He knows the complete history of every coin and stamp in his collection—where they were minted or printed, as well as their origins and political implications, and on occasion has testified as an expert in cases of fraud.

Uncle Glenn has a quiet manner that can be deceptive. The family remembers that when a man demanding a bill got carried away and pushed Dad Sampson, fifteen-year-old Glenn, who happened to witness the incident, jumped out of the second-floor window and landed on his feet with fists up ready to defend his father. The ferocity of his approach—to say nothing of the velocity or uniqueness—startled the bill collector so much that he hotfooted it down the street, never to return.

Glenn tells us that even he doesn't know how he accomplished this Superman flight and that most of his Delaware days were far less dramatic. Pure heaven for him were Mom Sampson's orange and lemon peel candies and Dad Sampson's sun-dried fruits. But unfortunately these recipes were not handed down and none of the Sampsons can remember how they were done. The old family custom that Uncle Glenn does continue today is fruitcake baking. He and his wife Cassie always have different kinds on hand at Christmas, and we can testify that all of his cakes will have you jumping for joy and flying for more.

UNCLE GLENN'S EIGHT-YEAR
BLACK FRUITCAKE

1 pound butter
1 pound brown sugar
10 eggs
1 teaspoon ground cinnamon
1 teaspoon ground nutmeg
1 teaspoon ground cloves
1½ teaspoons mace
1 wineglass (½ cup) red
   wine
1 wineglass (½ cup) brandy

1 cup rose water
1 pound all-purpose flour,
   sifted
2 pounds seedless black
   raisins
2 pounds currants
¾ pound citron and candied
   fruit
1 cup chopped black walnuts

Cream the butter and brown sugar, then add eggs, one at a time, beating each before adding. Mix in spices, wine, brandy, and rose water. Sift in half the flour, blending well. Mix the other half of the flour with the raisins, currants, citron, and nuts. Add this mixture last. Pour into 3 9-inch loaf pans or 2 10-inch funnel pans, lightly greased, and bake in a preheated 350° oven for 20 minutes. Then turn oven down to 275° and bake for 2½ to 3 hours until firm. Cool to room temperature and place individual cakes in rustproof lidded cake tins. Pour 5–6 tablespoons of dark rum evenly over each cake, seal tightly, and store in a cool, dark place. Every 3 months,

*Glenn Sampson posed
on the lawn he designed
in Buffalo*

continue to add 5–6 tablespoons of rum for the next 2 to 4 years, depending upon your patience. Then thoroughly wash and dry cake tin. Wrap cakes securely in wax paper, replace in cake tins, and seal. The cake can be eaten at any time but improves with age. The longest Uncle Glenn waited to serve this holiday treat was 8 years.

ORA WHITE'S WHITE FRUITCAKE

Glenn's wife Cassie got this unspiked recipe from a friend.

1 cup butter
2 cups sugar
1 teaspoon lemon extract
2½ cups cake flour, sifted
2 teaspoons baking powder
½ teaspoon salt
1 cup milk
1 pound white raisins
1 pound candied citron, pineapple, and orange and lemon peel
½ pound dried light figs
1 pound almonds, blanched and chopped
1 cup grated coconut
7 egg whites, stiffly beaten
½ pound candied cherries

Cream butter and sugar together and add the lemon extract. Sift and measure flour, reserving ½ cup. Sift remaining 2 cups of flour with baking powder and salt. Add to creamed butter and sugar, alternating with milk. Mix reserved ½ cup of flour with fruits, almonds, and coconut, and blend into the batter. Lastly, gently fold in beaten egg whites. Decorate the top with candied red cherries and bake in a well-greased and floured 10-inch tubular pan in a preheated 275° oven for 2½ hours.

NO BAKE FRUITCAKE

1 cup assorted candied fruits (pineapple, lemon, orange, citron, red cherries)
1 cup golden raisins
½ cup chopped dates
¼ teaspoon ground nutmeg
⅛ teaspoon ground cloves
1 cup miniature marshmallows, packed
1 tablespoon lemon juice

¾ cup chopped walnuts
3½ cups graham cracker
   crumbs (1 pound of
   crackers)
½ teaspoon ground
   cinnamon

3 tablespoons orange juice
⅔ cup evaporated milk
2 tablespoons honey
Whipped cream for topping

Mix candied fruits, raisins, dates, nuts, cracker crumbs, and spices. Mix marshmallows, citrus juices, milk, and honey, and stir well. Blend everything together until crumbs are moist then press into an 8-inch loaf pan. Chill for several days before slicing, and top each slice with a dollop of whipped cream. (Rum can be used in place of citrus juices or sprinkled on top.)

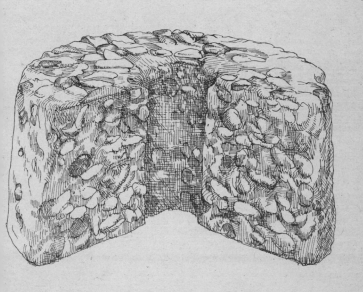

Asa

Asa was "the baby" of the Sampson family. In fact, he was ten years younger than his nearest brother, Glenn. Although quite loquacious now, Asa tells us that the motto of the house when he was growing up was "Silence is golden," and, in dealing with the community, "Stick to your own business." That meant that you were in no way to keep up with the Joneses or do what they were doing. This was a point Corine made crystal clear to Asa on Sunday. When some playmates, who knew he couldn't play on the Sabbath, asked to borrow his baseball gear, Asa readily lent them his bat, ball, and mitt. But when they were returned, Corine made Asa burn them up in the backyard. Moral: Thinking about or betting an act is as damning as participating in it.

Cards were considered the Bible of the devil, and movies and dancing were equally taboo. But Asa's curiosity got the better of him once. He found a partner and, with two other couples, learned to dance by listening to Arthur Murray's instructions over the radio. After Corine accelerated her Sunday-school activities by presenting Easter pageants with the neighborhood children, Asa began to feel that his dancing was a poor reflection on her and eliminated it from his agenda. He has been a serious member of his mother's Holiness Church ever since.

Asa says that although Mom Sampson was strict, she had a lovely smile and a teasing sense of humor. He recalls with a chuckle that after he had sold nine piglets and had come home from a shopping spree wearing a new shirt, she had inquired the price. When told it cost seventy-five cents, she laughingly shook her head and said, "Seventy-five cents! Imagine that, a seventy-five-cent shirt on a twenty-five-cent boy!" and gave him a hug.

Although Asa remembers more toil than pleasure in his childhood, there were happy days. During the spring, street carnivals came to town; in summer there was boating or swimming in the stone quarry; and then there were birthdays to anticipate. Dad and Mom Sampson gave each child a large apple or orange and a penny for every year.

Asa literally married the girl next door, Gertrude. They raised four children in the house that Dad Sampson built, and now play host to visiting grands. Everyday Asa walks three and three-quarter miles to the telephone company where he works and back. "Neighbors used to set their clocks by Dad's walk to work along the railroad," Asa told us, "but I now have to vary my route, because I've been robbed twice. That's one difference between today and yesterday. Folks didn't have to lock anything and no one was afraid to feed a stranger."

Asa is a photography buff and, while rummaging through some old negatives, discovered a quaint recipe for Devil's Food Cake in Corine's handwriting. Gertrude has added her own touch to another dish Mom Sampson used to prepare on Saturday for Sunday supper—Chicken in the Pot. Chicken and cake are still their favorite Sunday-night fare.

GERTRUDE'S CHICKEN IN THE POT

We have tried this using three Rock Cornish game hens with fine results.

1 4-5 pound stewing hen, or
  2 2½ pound chickens
Salt
2 slices lemon
8 small potatoes, unpeeled
4 carrots, scraped and diced
2 stalks celery, chopped

1 medium-size onion,
  chopped
½ pound string beans, cut in
  thirds
1 bunch parsley, chopped
¼ teaspoon thyme
Salt and pepper

Place chicken or game hens in a big pot (a Dutch oven will do nicely). Cover with water. Add a dash of salt and bring to a full boil. Skim the surface and reduce flame. Add lemon slices, cover, and simmer for ½ hour (1 hour for stewing hen). Add vegetables, herbs, salt, and pepper, to suit taste, and simmer for another 30 minutes or until fork tender. Serve in soup bowls with plenty of broth.

Yield: Will serve 4-5 ravenous people.

DEVIL'S FOOD CAKE

¾ cup cocoa
1⅓ cups sugar
⅔ cup shortening
1 teaspoon salt
1 teaspoon vanilla extract

1 cup buttermilk
3 eggs
1¾ cups sifted cake flour
1¼ teaspoons baking soda

Combine cocoa and sugar. Place shortening, salt, and vanilla in a mixing bowl. Add sugar-cocoa mixture in fifths, creaming 100 strokes* after each addition and adding 2 tablespoons of the buttermilk after the third addition of the sugar-cocoa mixture. Add eggs, one at a time, beating 100 strokes after each addition. Sift flour and baking soda together 3 times. Add flour in fourths alternately with remaining milk in thirds, beating 50 strokes for each addition of flour and 25 strokes for each addition of milk. Pour into 2 greased and floured 9-inch layer pans and bake in a preheated 350° oven for 25-35 minutes. Prepare White Mountain Cream Icing (recipe follows) and spread on each layer and sides of cake.

Yield: 8-10 servings.

*We estimate about 2 minutes in an electric mixer.

WHITE MOUNTAIN CREAM ICING

cup sugar
½ teaspoon cream of tartar
¼ cup water

1 egg white
½ teaspoon vanilla extract

Boil the sugar, cream of tartar, and ¼ cup water together. Beat egg white until stiff. Remove sugar syrup from fire when little threads spin off a spoon, and pour over beaten egg white. Beat vigorously with sweeping strokes until cool. Add vanilla extract and spread on cake.

Asa and all the Sampsons at a family reunion—Glenn, Clyde, William, Mamie Jean, and Marie, Clyde's wife

Mamie Jean
Sampson Darden

Our mother was a rare combination of femininity and strength. Sh
admired beauty in art and in nature and radiated a special beauty o
her own. She was fond of poetry, of harp and organ music, and
would sing in the oddest little light voice. Yet, if the lights went out
if a pipe burst or a tire went flat, she could fix them. Flowers grew in
profusion in her matchless flower garden, and she always gathered

them around her and gave them generously as gifts. So at home with nature was she that we can remember bees flying in and out of her hair without her fearing a sting. She had been the only girl growing up with four brothers on a farm, and could ride a horse, swim, bicycle, and play an aggressive game of tennis. In appearance, she was unassuming and modest, but if she thought she was right, we never knew her to back down on any issue. When she held a little girl's hand the universe seemed safe and secure.

Mamie Jean loved nothing better than giving or receiving a surprise. She was always embroidering or crocheting a gift for someone and always cooked a little something extra in the pot for any unexpected guest. We remember how surprised she was when we drew a mural all over her bedroom wall for her birthday present. It took her a moment to regain her composure, but she kept our scrawlings a week before calling in the painters. And how proud she was when we loaded strawberries from our garden into our red wagon and sold them door to door, earning our first money.

Mother never ever forgot her family's early struggles to survive, and shared her time and knowledge unselfishly. After graduation from Ohio University, she immediately went to where the greatest educational challenges at that time were—the rural South. There she taught elementary school in West Virginia, North Carolina, and Petersburg, Virginia, where she met her future husband—Bud, our father. A new job in Buffalo, New York, as a social worker for the Urban League brought her closer to him and to the altar.

Out of a concern for the quality of life for all people, she became a devoted community worker after her marriage. She was a member of the New Jersey Emergency Relief Administration, a YWCA board member, worked with voter registration, planned parenthood, and served on the board for youth consultation at the Friendly Neighborhood House. We remember the countless PTA and Town Hall meetings she attended and the many camping expeditions she led with her Girl Scout troop, but most of all we remember the annual skit she and her friends put on at Christmas time at the old folks' home. None of the ladies could sing, but that didn't put a dent in their spirits or the amusement of the senior citizens.

Many of Mother's friends and relatives depended on her advice because her keen insight always got to the heart of the problem and because her sense of justice and logic was unfailing. In her youth she had been her family's inspiration, smoothing all rumpled feathers and charting everyone's course. We called her "the answer woman" because our phone was always ringing with someone wanting a consultation on a problem—personal or financial. It seemed so

Mother's first class in the rural South

incongruous that little ex-schoolmarm Mamie Jean was quite a businesswoman, but she read the *Wall Street Journal*, studied economics with zeal, and attended many classes and lectures on real estate and investment. In her later years she regretted not having used her financial acumen in a professional manner, yet we still hear praise for the sound tips and business knowledge she gave to others. Her theory was that poverty and war were like weeds in a garden, enemies that must be removed from our world. The last task she completed before her death was, appropriately, plucking weeds from around her prized rose tree.

We are so grateful that she was our mother and that she taught us to live adventurously, to love rain, to suck the nectar from honeysuckle, to make a garden, to fashion dolls from corn silk, to color Easter eggs with plant dyes, and to recognize birds, flowers, leaves, and trees. She instilled in us a spirit of independence and taught us to stand firm in whatever we thought was right, and to pursue our own dreams until they became realities, without losing sight of the fact that how the struggle is waged is as important as the victory. In the best sense of the word, she was the most "liberated" woman we ever knew.

For many years she had been childless, so when we finally arrived she liked nothing better than feeding us. We were poor eaters, so she had to be creative with food, and she was. Surprises, sherbets, soups and basics—oh, what lovely treats we remember from Ms. Mamie Jean!

Mother and us

OUR FAVORITE SURPRISES

EGG SURPRISE

1 slice whole-wheat bread
1 pat butter

1 egg
Salt and pepper to taste

Take a slice of whole-wheat bread and, using a small teacup, hollow out the center. In a frying pan put a generous pat of butter and let it sizzle. Add the hollowed slice of bread over the melting butter and crack an egg into the hole over the butter. Fry until egg is firm and turn over. Toast the circle part of the bread on both sides in the pan, then place it over the egg section on a plate. It will delight a child.

Yield: 1 egg surprise.

SNOW ICE CREAM

On the first big snow of the year, our mother would collect some freshly fallen snow in a big pan. Then she would add a little sugar and some heavy cream, along with a few drops of vanilla extract, and stir it up. You had to eat fast before it melted. We called it Nature's Ice Cream and loved it.

ROSE PETAL JELLY

1 cup rose petals
¼ cup rose water flavoring
   or 1 teaspoon rose extract
¾ cup water

1⅓ cups sugar
1 tablespoon honey
1 teaspoon lemon juice

Pick tender rose petals until you have 1 well-packed cup. Cut into fine pieces and wash in a colander or large strainer. Place petals, rose water flavoring, and ¾ cup water in a saucepan and simmer for 5 minutes or until petals are soft. Strain petals and measure ½ cup of remaining liquid (add water if you have less). Return liquid to saucepan. Add sugar and honey and bring to rapid boil. Return petals to saucepan and reduce heat. Simmer very slowly for 20 minutes, stirring constantly, then add lemon juice and cook for 5 minutes more. Pour into heated jars and seal with paraffin (see Index for Strawberry Jam).

Once we accidently overcooked this recipe and made a delicious discovery. The mixture had become too stiff to make a jelly, so we dropped it by spoonfuls on a greased cookie sheet and enjoyed rose petal candy instead!

Yield: 2 small glasses.

LOLLIPOPS or HARD CANDY

2 cups sugar
¼ cup clear corn syrup
1 cup water
⅛ teaspoon salt
2 teaspoons cherry, lemon, or orange, etc., extract
¼ teaspoon food coloring
Lollipop sticks

Grease a cookie sheet, then combine the sugar, corn syrup, 1 cup water, and salt in a medium-size saucepan. Cook over medium heat, stirring constantly, until the hard crack point of 300° is reached on a candy thermometer or a drop of candy placed in a cup of cold water turns into a brittle ball.

Them promptly remove from fire and stir in the extract and drops of food coloring of your choice. Work fast, as candy hardens quickly. Pour little circles of candy on the cookie sheet and leave a bit of room for the sticks which you push in immediately, making sure that a ¼ inch of the end is well covered. When lollipops are cool, jiggle loose from cookie sheet and wrap in wax paper. If lollipop sticks are unavailable, Dixie cup spoons split in two work well. Without a stick, you will still have delicious hard candy. (You can put popsicle sticks into 4 large apples, dip them in this mixture, and make candied apples too.)

Yield: 2 dozen lollipops.

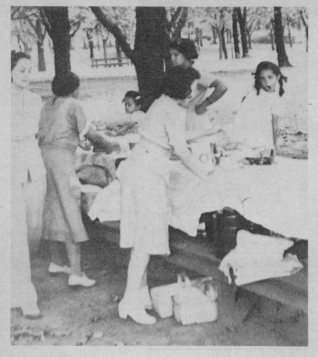

Mamie Jean at family reunion picnic in Delaware—Jean Marie, Gertrude (back row), Cassie (foreground)

WATERMELON CAKE

3 cups all-purpose flour, sifted
3 teaspoons baking powder
¼ teaspoon salt
4 egg whites, stiffly beaten
1 stick butter
1½ cups sugar
1 cup milk
1 teaspoon vanilla extract
¾ teaspoon red food coloring
⅓ cup seedless black raisins, floured

Sift flour, baking powder, and salt together. Beat egg whites until stiff, then set aside. Cream butter and sugar until fluffy and add flour, alternating with the milk. When well blended, add vanilla and carefully fold in the beaten egg whites. Pour half of the batter into another bowl, add red food coloring and raisins that have been tossed in a little flour. Grease and flour a 9-inch spring-form or tube pan and pour half of the white batter on the bottom of the pan. Gently spread the red batter on top (the raisins will look like watermelon seeds). Then cover with the last half of white batter (the rind). Bake in a preheated 350° oven for 45-50 minutes. When cool, frost with Dark Green Frosting (recipe follows).

DARK GREEN FROSTING

2 tablespoons butter
2 cups confectioner's sugar
2 tablespoons heavy cream

1 teaspoon green food
  coloring

Cream butter, add sugar, and cream. Add green food coloring. Mix until smooth and spread on watermelon cake (recipe above).

As kids, we were so thrilled with this recipe that we added 2 tablespoons of real watermelon juice to the red batter for authenticity and even attempted a cantaloupe cake by using an orange center with gold raisins for the seeds and Honey Icing (see Index) for the rind.

PEACH TEA

A refreshing twist on regular iced tea.

3 cups chilled tea
6 tablespoons sugar
½ cup lemon juice
2 12-ounce cans peach nectar

2 7-ounce bottles ginger ale
Ice, orange slices, cloves, and
  fresh mint sprigs

Combine first 5 ingredients in a large pitcher. Pour into ice-filled tall glasses. Decorate each glass with an orange slice studded with cloves and a sprig of mint.

Yield: 8 servings.

GINGER ALE SALAD

The name always intrigued us.

1 cup mixed fresh peaches, grapefruit, and cherries, sliced
½ cup canned crushed pineapple
¼ cup seedless grapes
¼ cup slivered almonds
2 tablespoons lemon juice
2 tablespoons unflavored gelatin

¾ cup drained juice from fruit
½ teaspoon powdered ginger
Pinch of salt
Pinch of paprika
½ cup mayonnaise
2 cups ginger ale

Combine fruits in a mixing bowl. Measure ¾ cup of the juice that has accumulated and place it in a saucepan. Sprinkle gelatin over the juice and let sit for 2 minutes, then simmer, until dissolved. Add lemon juice, ginger, salt, paprika, mayonnaise, and ginger ale. Blend well, and chill until mixture is the consistency of egg whites. Then stir in fruit and nuts. Mix well and turn into a 1½ quart circular mold or individual ones. Chill until set and serve on a bed of lettuce.

Yield: 6–8 servings.

CHOCOLATE PUNCH

We enjoyed serving this to the neighborhood gang.

4 1-ounce squares semisweet chocolate
½ cup sugar
¼ teaspoon salt
2 cups hot water
2 quarts milk

1½ teaspoons vanilla extract
1 quart vanilla ice cream
1 quart club soda
½ pint heavy cream, whipped
Cinnamon

In a large saucepan, combine chocolate, sugar, and salt with 2 cups hot water. Bring to a boil, stirring for 2 minutes. Add milk, continue heating. When hot, beat in vanilla with a rotary egg beater. Remove from heat. Chill, then pour into a punch bowl over ice cream. For sparkle, add the large bottle of club soda. Top with whipped cream dusted with cinnamon.

Yield: 12 servings.

Camping out with friends Clara, Bea, and Olivia in Buffalo

Who could ever forget Mother's favorite Girl Scout classics?

JUNGLE STEW

2 large onions, chopped
1 green pepper, chopped
1 clove garlic, minced
4 tablespoons oil
2 pounds ground beef

1 cup elbow macaroni,
    uncooked
2 15-ounce cans red beans
2 1-pound cans stewed
    tomatoes
Salt and pepper to taste

Sauté onions, pepper, and garlic in the oil in a pot. Add meat and brown. Then add all other ingredients and simmer until macaroni is tender.

Yield: 8 servings for hungry campers.

SOME MORES

1 milk chocolate bar
2 graham crackers
2 marshmallows

Toast marshmallows over the campfire. Then place them on top of a graham cracker. Add milk chocolate bar and top with the second graham cracker and press down to form a sandwich.

Mother enjoying ice cream she sold with friend Elsie

SHERBET

ORANGE JACK-o-LANTERNS

Sherbet was one of Mother's favorite snacks, and she loved making her own.

At Halloween, she would cut off the tops and scoop out the insides of oranges, make a little mouth, eyes, and nose, and fill them with homemade refrigerator orange sherbet.

ORANGE CREAM SHERBET

1 teaspoon unflavored gelatin	½ cup heavy cream
1 cup orange juice	Juice of 1 lemon
½ cup milk	½ cup sugar

Soak gelatin in 2 tablespoons cold water, then heat until dissolved. Combine all other ingredients and add cooled gelatin. Pour into an ice tray, cover with waxed paper, and put in freezer. When frozen put into a mixing bowl and beat until light. Return to ice tray and refreeze.

Yield: 1 ice tray or filling for 4 oranges.

EASY GRAPE SHERBET

1 cup unsweetened grape juice
½ cup sugar
2 cups milk

Warm grape juice. Dissolve sugar into it. Add cold milk.* Pour into 2 ice trays and freeze. When solid, remove from trays and beat briskly with an egg beater. Return to trays, cover with tin foil or wax paper and refreeze. For some reason this sherbet tastes like violets.

Yield: 6–8 servings.

Mixture may curdle but will become smooth during the freezing process.

MINT LIME ICE

1½ cups boiling water
1 8-ounce glass mint jelly
1 pint ginger ale

Juice of 3 limes
½ cup honey
2 egg whites, stiffly beaten

Pour boiling water over jelly in a bowl. Stir until dissolved. Let cool. Add ginger ale, lime juice, and honey. Pour into 2 ice trays, cover with wax paper or aluminum foil, and put in freezer. Chill to the semisolid stage. Remove from freezer and mix in beaten egg whites. Replace in freezer until solid.

Yield: 6–8 servings.

WATERMELON SHERBET

2 cups watermelon purée
(either mash through a
sieve or use a blender)
2 teaspoons unflavored
gelatin

¼ cup water
½ cup sugar
½ teaspoon lemon juice
⅓ cup milk
¼ cup heavy cream

Place watermelon purée in a large bowl. Soak gelatin in ½ cup water for about 5 minutes. Place in a small saucepan over medium heat, and stir until completely dissolved. Let cool. Stir into watermelon purée. Add sugar, lemon juice, milk, and cream. Blend well. Pour into 2 ice trays, cover with wax paper or aluminum foil, and freeze. When frozen remove from trays, beat briskly with an egg beater, return to trays, and freeze.

Yield: 6–8 servings.

CRANBERRY ORANGE SHERBET

1 cup heavy cream
1-pound can jellied
cranberry sauce
1 6-ounce can frozen
orange juice

¼ cup sugar
Dash of cinnamon
Dash of salt

205

Place heavy cream in a mixing bowl and beat with an egg beater until stiff peaks form. Gradually beat in cranberry sauce and frozen juice. Add sugar, cinnamon, and salt. Beat until well blended. Pour into 2 ice trays, put into refrigerator. Freeze until solid.

Yield: 6–8 servings.

SOUPS

Our winters were warmed and summers cooled with Mother's hearty soups.

VEGETABLE-BONE MARROW SOUP

- 2 1-inch-thick slices beef shinbone, meat and marrow intact
- 3–5 meaty beef neck bones
- 1 teaspoon pepper
- 5 quarts water (do not hesitate to use any vegetable stock available)
- 2 large onions, halved and sliced
- 2 (1-pound, 12-ounce) cans whole tomatoes
- ½ cup dried green split peas
- ½ cup dried yellow split peas
- ½ cup small dried lima beans
- ½ cup small-grain barley
- ½ pound okra, cut in ¼-inch rounds
- 3 carrots, scraped and cut in rounds
- 2 celery stalks, sliced
- 1 cup corn, fresh if possible, but 1 8-ounce can will suffice
- 1 cup string beans, uncooked, or 1 8-ounce can
- 2 medium-sized parsnips, peeled and cut into small rounds
- Salt to taste (about 3 tablespoons)

Add shinbone, neck bones, and pepper to 5 quarts boiling water. Simmer briskly for 1 hour, removing foam as it forms. Add onions and tomatoes. After an additional ½ hour, add peas, lima beans, and barley. Continue cooking for 1½ hours, stirring occasionally. Add prepared vegetables and salt to taste. Cook for a final 45 minutes to 1 hour, or until meat falls from the bones. Remove fat and unpalatable gristle. Total cooking time should be 3½–4 hours.

This soup is best when cooked in quantity, so if you don't have a 10- to 15-quart pot, now is the time to buy or borrow one.

This hearty soup, which is a meal in itself, can be refrigerated for 3 weeks or more, or frozen and used through the winter months.

Yield: Serves multitudes!

TURKEY SOUP

Turkey carcass
½ cup turkey stuffing if
   you have some left over
2 fairly large onions,
   chopped

2 bay leaves
Salt and pepper to taste
3 carrots, sliced in rounds
5 large celery stalks, halved
   (includes tops and leaves)

Since a turkey means a feast for our family and friends, this recipe is based on an 18-pound turkey or heavier. If you begin with a smaller bird, feel free to experiment and adjust proportions. At any rate, this is how ours is made.

Cut as much turkey as possible from the carcass, dice the meat, and set this aside. Place carcass, including wings, drumsticks, and stuffing in a large pot. Add water to cover, bring to a boil, lower heat. Add onions, bay leaves, and seasonings. Simmer for 2 hours. Then remove large bones and strain broth through a colander into a clean pot. Add carrots and celery and continue cooking for 45 minutes. Remove celery stalks with a slotted spoon and purée in a blender. Then stir purée into the soup to thicken it. Add diced turkey, adjust seasoning, and cook at a slow simmer for 15 minutes more.

Yield: About 10 servings.

TOMATO BISQUE

10 large ripe tomatoes
2 tablespoons butter
2 medium onions, chopped
1 cup chicken broth

1 bay leaf
A pinch of sugar
Salt and pepper to taste
1 cup light cream or milk

Reserve 1 tomato and coarsely chop the rest. Melt butter in a large saucepan and sauté onions until tender. Add chopped tomatoes and cook until tender. Purée vegetables in a blender (or food mill) and place back in saucepan. Add chicken broth and bring to a slow boil. Add bay leaf, sugar, salt, and pepper. Peel and chop reserved tomato into small bits. Place in saucepan along with milk. Simmer and serve.

Yield: 6 servings.

COLD BUTTERMILK SOUP

1 quart buttermilk
½ cucumber, peeled and diced fine
½ tomato, peeled and diced fine

1 small can baby shrimp (2½ oz.) or ½ cup cooked fresh shrimp, chopped
Fresh dill or parsley

Combine first 4 ingredients. Chill. Sprinkle with dill or parsley.

Yield: 4–6 servings.

Mother ready to serve

MOTHER'S BASICS

MAMIE JEAN'S CHICKEN FRICASSEE

1 4 4½ pound stewing
   chicken, cut in quarters
   or eighths
4 cups water
3 carrots, halved
2–3 celery stalks, cut in
   thirds
1 small onion, quartered

1 bay leaf
2 pinches rosemary
2 teaspoons salt
⅛ teaspoon pepper
2 cups elbow macaroni,
   uncooked, or batter for
   Drop Dumplings
   (recipe follows)

Wash chicken thoroughly, removing any visible pieces of fat. In a
Dutch oven, bring 4 cups water to a boil. Add carrots, celery, onion,
bay leaf, and rosemary. Drop the chicken, piece by piece, into this

so as not to lower the boiling point. Cover pot, lower heat, and simmer for 1 hour. Add salt and pepper and continue simmering ½ hour or until chicken is tender. Adjust seasoning, then add 2 cups of macaroni. If there is not enough broth to cover the macaroni, add more water. If making dumplings, ease teaspoonfuls of batter into the boiling liquid so that they rest partially on the chicken. Cover and continue cooking for 18 minutes. If you wish a fricassee with more liquid, cook noodles separately in 5 cups of chicken broth made from boiling the neck, gizzard, liver, and heart with a small onion, a celery stalk, salt, and pepper.

Yield: 5-6 servings.

DROP DUMPLINGS

1 cup flour	1½ tablespoons melted
½ teaspoon salt	butter
2 teaspoons baking powder	⅓ cup milk or chicken stock

Sift together dry ingredients. Add melted butter and milk, and mix. Batter should be moist but stiff. Drop by teaspoonfuls into boiling liquid. Cover and cook for about 18 minutes.

Yield: 1 dozen dumplings

TWO OF MOTHER'S HONEYMOON
DISHES UPDATED

∞∞∞∞∞∞∞∞∞∞∞∞∞∞∞∞∞∞∞∞∞∞∞∞∞∞∞

STUFFED RED SNAPPER (OR STRIPED BASS) WITH SHRIMP AND RAISIN STUFFING FOR TWO*

1 2-pound red snapper

STUFFING:
5 jumbo shrimp
1 tablespoon butter
2 tablespoons diced celery
2 tablespoons minced onion
⅛ teaspoon thyme
¼ teaspoon salt
¼ teaspoon garlic powder
2 dashes pepper
1¼ cups dried bread cubes
   or prepared stuffing mix

1 egg, slightly beaten
2 tablespoons milk
1 tablespoon raisins
1 tablespoon heavy cream,
   sour cream, or melted
   butter
1 tablespoon dried bread
   crumbs or dry stuffing
Paprika
⅓ cup white wine
Lemon slices

Have fish prepared for stuffing at the fish market. Request that the head and tail be left on so as to preserve fish juices. Wash fish thoroughly. Pat dry and place in a shallow baking dish. Salt fish liberally inside and out. Shell, wash, devein shrimp, and cut into ¼-inch slices. Set aside. In a small saucepan melt butter. Add celery and onion, sauté until tender. Add shrimp, sauté until slightly pink, and remove from heat. Stir in thyme, salt, garlic powder, and pepper. Mix the dried bread cubes or stuffing mix with the egg, milk, and raisins and add to the sautéed mixture. Mix thoroughly. Fill fish cavity, including the head area. Rub the top of the fish with the cream, sour cream, or melted butter. Sprinkle with dried bread crumbs and paprika. Pour wine into the baking dish but not over fish. Bake in a preheated 375° oven for 45 minutes. Garnish with lemon slices.

Yield: A filling meal for 2, served with only a salad.

Yield: About 1½ cups of stuffing.

* Shrimp and raisin stuffing is excellent for turkey and chicken as well. Adjust the quanity according to the size of the bird to be stuffed. Add one more ingredient—soft sausage that has been cooked in small lumps, about ¼ cup or less to every 1 ½–2 cups of stuffing.

SHRIMP STUFFED FILLET OF FLOUNDER
FOR TWO

5 jumbo shrimp, shelled,
    deveined, cut in small
    pieces
⅓ cup diced onion
⅓ cup finely chopped celery

1 tablespoon butter
¾ cup prepared stuffing mix
1 egg, lightly beaten
4 medium-size flounder fillets

SAUCE:

2 tablespoons butter
3 tablespoons flour
½ cup water
1 chicken bouillon cube
¼ teaspoon salt

½ cup white wine
¼ cup thinly sliced fresh
    mushrooms
Paprika

Sauté onion and celery in butter until tender. Add shrimp and continue cooking for 2 or 3 minutes until shrimp turns pinkish. Remove from heat. Add stuffing and beaten egg. Mix well. Spread equal amounts on top of fillets, and roll, starting with smaller end. Lay each rolled fillet on its flap so that it does not come apart. To prepare sauce: melt 2 tablespoons butter in a small saucepan. Stir in flour. Add ½ cup water and stir constantly over low heat until mixture thickens. Add the remaining ingredients and continue cooking for 3–4 minutes. Pour over fillets, sprinkle with paprika. Bake in a preheated 350° oven for about 25 minutes.

Yield: Stuffed fillets for 2.

~~~~~~

FRESH GREEN PEAS AT THEIR BEST*

2 pounds green peas in
    their pods
1½ tablespoons butter
1 medium-size onion, sliced

¼ teaspoon garlic powder
Salt and pepper to taste
1½ teaspoon butter
    (optional)

Shell peas, place in a saucepan and add just enough water to cover. Bring to a boil and cook rapidly, uncovered, for about 20 minutes or until peas are just tender. Drain and set aside. In a frying pan, melt 1½ tablespoons butter, add onion slices, and sauté until they are tender. Add peas and seasonings. Stirring frequently, sauté lightly for 6–8 minutes. Top with extra butter if you wish.

Yield: 4 servings.

Fresh green peas are also delicious as a raw vegetable served in salads.

~~~~~~

FRIED GREEN TOMATOES

2 large green tomatoes,
  unpeeled
3 tablespoons bacon fat

1 egg, beaten
Dry bread crumbs, lightly
  salted

Slice tomatoes a little over ¼ inch thick. Heat bacon fat in a heavy skillet. Dip tomato slices in egg. Coat with bread crumbs. Fry over medium heat until golden brown on both sides and tender throughout when pricked with a fork. Drain on paper towels. Serve hot as a dinner or breakfast vegetable.

Yield: 4 servings.

YELLOW SQUASH AND ONIONS

2 medium-size yellow squash
1 medium-size onion, sliced
  thin

2–3 tablespoons bacon fat
Salt and pepper to taste

Cut squash into ¼-inch slices. Place ¼ inch of water in a heavy skillet. When water boils, add squash. Lay onion slices on top. Cover and steam until all the water has evaporated, watching carefully so that squash doesn't burn. Add bacon fat, stirring so that squash is well coated. Add salt and pepper to taste, cover and cook over a low heat for about 30 minutes, or until tender, stirring occasionally.

Yield: 4 servings.

EXCELLENT SINGLE PIE SHELL

1½ cups flour
½ teaspoon salt

½ cup shortening
3 tablespoons ice water

Sift flour and salt into a bowl, reserving 4 tablespoons. Cut shortening into remaining dry ingredients until lumps the size of small peas form. Blend the reserved flour and ice water to form a paste. Add to flour and mix lightly and quickly until mixture can be formed into a somewhat flaky ball. Put dough on wax paper, placing a second sheet of wax paper over it. Roll, with short, light strokes of the rolling pin, to ⅛-inch thickness. Remove top layer of wax paper. Place in a pie plate 9″ or 10″ in diameter, using a knife to loosen dough gently from wax paper. Trim outer edge, leaving about ½ inch overlapping. Flute edges as desired. If pie shell is to be baked before being filled, prick dough in several spots over its surface with a fork. Bake in a preheated 475° oven for 8-10 minutes.

Yield: 1 pie shell.

❧ ❧

STRAWBERRY PIE

Carole's most requested dessert.

9-inch baked pie shell (see
   preceding recipe)
2 pint baskets of fresh
   strawberries
1 cup sugar
2 tablespoons cornstarch

1 cup water
2 tablespoons strawberry
   Jell-O powder
1 pint heavy cream, stiffly
   whipped
1 teaspoon vanilla extract

Prepare pie shell. Stem, wash, and drain the berries. Selecting a few of the riper berries, mash enough to make ⅓ cupful. Set aside. Combine sugar, cornstarch, and 1 cup of water. Cook over medium heat until thick and clear, about 15 minutes. Remove from heat and add Jell-O. Mix well. Cool slightly. Then add the mashed berries. Fill pie shell with whole berries. Pour mixture evenly over them. Chill for at least 4 hours. Just before serving, top with stiffly whipped cream, to which the vanilla has been added. Since this is a fairly sweet pie, we prefer unsweetened whipped cream, but you may like a little powdered sugar blended in. Delicious!

Yield: 6-8 servings.

APPLE BROWN BETTY

Carole's second-most requested dessert.

2 cups fresh whole-wheat
   bread crumbs
¼ cup melted butter
½ cup sugar
1 teaspoon cinnamon

Juice and grated rind of
   ½ lemon
5 or 6 tart apples, peeled,
   cored, and sliced
½ cup orange juice
Heavy or light cream

With a fork, lightly toss bread crumbs with melted butter. Combine sugar, cinnamon, lemon juice and rind to form a paste. Line the bottom of a buttered casserole dish with approximately ⅓ of the bread-crumb mixture. Spread half the apples over the crumbs, then half the paste over the apples. Repeat this process, with crumbs as final layer. Pour orange juice evenly over apple mixture. Cover and bake in a preheated 350° oven for ½ hour. Uncover and bake for another 15 minutes, or until apples are very tender. Serve hot or cold with whipped or plain cream.

Yield: 6 servings.

AUNT MARJORIE PALMER'S
EVERY-KIND-OF-COOKIE DOUGH

Aunt Marjorie, a close friend of Mother's, gave her this basic recipe and we have used it to make at least nine varieties of crunchy cookies.

¼ cup of half butter and
  half shortening
½ cup brown sugar
½ cup white sugar
1 egg

1 teaspoon vanilla extract
2 cups all-purpose flour,
  sifted
½ teaspoon baking soda
¼ teaspoon salt

Mix butter and shortening together to form ¾ cup. The butter is for flavor and the shortening adds crispness. Cream this with the sugars until fluffy, then add the egg and vanilla and blend well. Sift the flour with the soda and salt, then resift. Add to butter mixture, blending well. Divide dough in half and, using your hands, roll each half into a long roll about 2 inches in diameter. (One roll may be frozen for future use if you so choose.) Cut roll into ¼-inch slices or press through a cookie press. Bake on a greased cookie sheet in a preheated 400° oven for 8–10 minutes.

Yield: 5 dozen cookies.

———— ·•◦•· ————

VARIATIONS:

1. Peanut butter—combine ½ cup peanut butter with ½ cup butter, omitting shortening and use ½ cup less flour.
2. Chocolate chip—add ½ cup chocolate chips, ¼ cup chopped nuts, and 2 tablespoons milk.
3. Lemon wafers—add 1 tablespoon freshly grated lemon rind and replace vanilla with lemon extract.
4. Molasses spice—add 2 tablespoons molasses, 1½ teaspoons more soda, and replace vanilla with 1 teaspoon each ginger, cloves, and cinnamon.
5. Honey cookies—replace white sugar with ½ cup honey, add ½ cup more flour.
6. Pumpkin cookies—add 1 tablespoon pumpkin pie spice.
7. Apple cookies—add 1 tablespoon apple pie spice and 1 small apple, peeled, cored, and chopped.
8. Eggnog cookies—add 1 tablespoon rum and 1 teaspoon nutmeg.
9. Fruitcake cookies—add 1 tablespoon brandy and ½ cup chopped citron and nuts.

Mother and fellow teacher Marie

INDIAN PUDDING

Delicious, nutritious, makes you feel ambitious.

4 cups milk	1 teaspoon cinnamon
⅓ cup yellow cornmeal	¼ teaspoon ginger
2 tablespoons butter	2 eggs
½ cup molasses	1 cup cold milk
½ cup brown sugar	Light cream
½ teaspoon salt	

In the top of a double boiler scald the milk. Add cornmeal and cook for 15 minutes stirring frequently. Then add butter, molasses, sugar, salt, spices, and eggs. When well blended pour into a buttered medium-size casserole dish. Pour cold milk on top without stirring it in and bake in a preheated 350° oven for 1 hour. Serve hot, topped with cream.

Yield: 6 servings.

BROWNIES

2 1-ounce squares semisweet
  chocolate
⅔ cup butter
2 eggs, beaten
1 cup sugar
⅔ cup chopped walnut
  meats

½ cup flour, sifted
½ teaspoon baking powder
⅛ teaspoon salt
1 teaspoon vanilla extract

Melt chocolate and butter in top of a double boiler and let cool slightly. Then add all other ingredients in the given order. Mix well and pour into a greased 8-inch-square pan and bake in a preheated 375° oven for 25 minutes.

Yield: 16 brownies.

COCONUT CAKE

¾ cup coconut milk (see
  below)
¼ cup finely grated fresh
  coconut
3 cups cake flour, sifted
3 teaspoons baking powder
½ teaspoon salt

3 egg whites, stiffly beaten
1¾ cup sugar
1 cup butter
3 egg yolks
¼ cup milk (add more if
  coconut milk is scant)
1 teaspoon vanilla extract

Prepare the coconut by drilling a hole in the "eye" and draining the milk. Hammer it open, remove the white meat and grate it. Then sift the flour, baking powder, and salt together twice. Beat egg whites until stiff, then add ¼ cup of sugar and set aside. Cream butter until fluffy and add remaining sugar and egg yolks, mixing well. Add flour, alternating with milk and coconut milk, and blend until smooth. Add vanilla and the ¼ cup grated coconut. Last, fold in egg whites. Bake in 3 well-buttered 8-inch circular layer pans in a preheated 350° oven for 30 minutes. Cover with Seven-Minute Frosting (recipe follows):

SEVEN MINUTE FROSTING

2 egg whites, unbeaten
1½ cups sugar
5 tablespoons cold water
¼ teaspoon cream of tartar
   or 1½ teaspoons light corn
   syrup

¼ teaspoon salt
1 teaspoon vanilla extract
1½ cups finely shredded
   coconut

Place egg whites, sugar, cold water, cream of tartar or corn syrup, and salt in the top of a double boiler. Then place over rapidly boiling water, beating constantly with an egg beater, for 7 minutes or until icing will stand in peaks. Remove from heat, add vanilla, and continue to beat until thick enough to spread. When entire cake has been frosted, sprinkle coconut generously over the top and sides.

This huge production was Norma's birthday cake every year, and one year it somehow evolved into Ambrosia Cake when we ate too much of the coconut and had to stretch it with ¼ cup grated orange rind and decorate the top with mandarin orange sections.

Holiday Time with the Winner Sisters

When the holidays roll around, there is one event we look forward to with much anticipation—gorging ourselves silly at Mattie's house. She has our family over every Thanksgiving or Christmas for a dinner prepared with the help of her sisters, Waltine and Lucy, and her holiday feasts are so delectable that we hate to finish eating. The sisters have happily shared their entire menu, along with their thoughts on work, food, and fun in the thirties.

Mattie Winner was a nursing student at Tuskegee while our father was interning there. After he settled in Newark, he sent for Mattie from her native Texas to be his nurse. She joined him in New Jersey, and later arranged for Waltine and Lucy to follow suit.

In the early thirties, Newark was not ready for the sisters. Even though they arrived qualified to teach, black teachers were not being hired. So Waltine became Daddy's secretary, and Lucy took a job at Kellar's Drugstore in those preautomation days, taking photographs of people who posed in a little booth. Three for a dime and a dollar for a blowup were the prices.

"Newark was a doozie in the thirties," says Mattie. "The Southern migration brought a lot of people from the South here looking for a better life. But the Depression hit. People had to create their own jobs—and so the numbers racket and speakeasies were going strong. Contagious disease was common, and the increase of cases was alarming. We had to deliver babies at all hours of the night in the home, sometimes by candlelight. If hard work could kill you, we'd all be gone by now."

The sisters agree that World War II changed life for black people in Newark. Defense jobs opened up, the Army absorbed many jobless men, and new welfare systems were initiated. Waltine, who later worked for the Welfare Department, feels that relief did a lot of good for those in need at the time, but feels that after the war ended, much of the new-found employment disappeared, leaving only the welfare system for many.

Waltine and Lucy used to eat regularly at Father Divine's Restaurant. He was a colorful and controversial religious cult leader of the time. They remember his delicious and cheap (twenty-five cents for all you could eat) banquets and describe how steaming hot dishes flowed from the kitchen, all perfectly prepared in great abundance and served on long tables covered with white linen, sparkling silver, and bright and fragrant bouquets. No doubt these sumptuous affairs must have been the inspiration for their own holiday feasts in later years.

Lucy, who eventually did teach in the Newark school system, recalls her early years in Newark as "hard times," but feels that "somehow the town was jumping and we just had a lot of fun. All the big bands and top singers came here. Jimmy Lunceford and Billie Holiday were my favorites, along with Ella and Sarah. Plus, we had local revues and house parties. Rent parties were being given left and right. When the jitterbug hit, that was right up my alley, and don't forget the hukabuck."

Mattie married a dance promoter, Carl Jones, now a nightclub and restaurant owner. Lucy married a handsome undertaker,

221

Arthur Russell. And Waltine married a GI, Joe Thomas, now a printer. When we were children they were the most glamorous people in the world. And now that we are older, they still are.

HOLIDAY DINNER, TEXAS STYLE

For Twelve People

*Roast turkey with corn bread stuffing
*Turkey giblet gravy
*Barbecued ham
*Cranberry sauce
*Green string beans
　Mustard or turnip greens (see Index)
*Yellow turnips and carrots
*Creamed onions
*Sweet potato pudding topped with marshmallows
*Baked macaroni with cheese
*Tossed green salad with homemade mayonnaise
　Refrigerator rolls (see Index)
　Fruitcake (see Index)
*Mincemeat pie
*Ambrosia
*Eggnog
　Fresh fruit
　Nuts and mints

Asterisk indicates that recipe appears in this chapter.

MATTIE'S ROAST TURKEY

With Corn Bread Stuffing and Giblet Gravy

1 15-pound turkey (oven ready)
Salt and black or white pepper
Vegetable oil (approximately ½ cup)

Rub the inside of the turkey's cavity with salt and pepper. Rub skin with salt. Fill turkey loosely with Corn Bread Stuffing (recipe follows). Place turkey in a large brown paper bag. Pour vegetable oil freely on the bag and rub while pouring. Tie a cord loosely around open end of bag. Place in a roasting pan and do not cover with lid. Roast turkey in a preheated 350° oven for 4½ hours. Serve with Turkey Giblet Gravy (recipe follows Corn Bread Stuffing).

Yield: 10–12 servings.

CORN BREAD STUFFING

1 cup chopped onion
1 cup chopped celery
3 teaspoons poultry
   seasoning
½ cup margarine or
   vegetable oil
4 cups corn bread crumbs

4 cups bread crumbs or
   cubes
1 tablespoon chopped
   parsley
½ teaspoon salt
½–¾ cup water or turkey
   broth

Sauté onion, celery, and poultry seasoning in melted margarine or vegetable oil. Do not brown. Combine with corn bread crumbs, bread crumbs or cubes, and parsley. Add salt, ½–¾ cup water or turkey broth, and toss lightly with a fork until well mixed. If oyster stuffing is desired, 1 pint of shucked oysters, drained well and coarsely chopped, may be added.

Yield: 8 cups or enough stuffing for a 15-pound turkey.

TURKEY GIBLET GRAVY

Turkey neck, liver,
   gizzard, and heart
1 teaspoon salt

½ cup flour and enough
   water to make a watery
   paste
Salt and pepper to taste

Place turkey neck and giblets in a saucepan. Add 1 teaspoon salt and enough water to cover. Boil for 1 hour or until giblets are tender. Discard neck and cut giblets into small cubes. After turkey has cooked, puncture bag immediately, remove turkey, and place on a platter. Remove bag, leaving drippings in roasting pan. If there is not enough liquid for 3 cups, add enough water or stock to make that amount. Bring this to a rapid boil. Stir in flour and water paste for thickening. Add giblets and cook slowly for about 5 minutes. Adjust seasoning.

WALTINE'S BARBECUED HAM

1 5-pound precooked ham
1 bottle of your favorite barbecue sauce (we prefer
    Cousin Kelly Bryant's—see Index)

Preheat oven to 300°, place ham in a small roasting pan. With a small utensil mop or applicator, moisten the ham with sauce. Cook ham for 1½ hours, basting with sauce every 20 minutes. May be served hot or cold.

CRANBERRY SAUCE

1 pound (4 cups) fresh
    cranberries
1½ cups sugar
1 cup water
1 whole orange, unpeeled,
    chopped fine

¼ teaspoon cloves
½ cup crushed pineapple,
    drained
½ cup chopped walnuts
Sprinkle of cinnamon

Wash cranberries and set aside. Bring sugar and water to a boil. Add cranberries, orange, and cloves. Simmer over a high flame, stirring frequently, until the berries pop open. Add crushed pineapple, walnuts, and cinnamon, and blend. Cool and serve, or pack in hot jars and process for 15 minutes, according to canning directions in Chapter 2 (see Index).

Yield: About 2 pints.

MATTIE'S GREEN STRING BEANS

3 slices bacon
2 cups water
1 small onion, halved
½ teaspoon salt

2 pounds green beans, whole,
  with tips removed
1 small pimento

Place bacon in a quart saucepan, add 2 cups water. Bring to a boil, cook for 10 minutes. Add onion and salt. Cook for about 1½ minutes. Add string beans. Boil for 15–18 minutes. Chop pimento into small cubes and mix with beans for decoration.

Yield: About 8 servings.

WALTINE'S MASHED TURNIPS AND CARROTS

1 large yellow turnip
6 large carrots
¾ stick butter

1 medium-size onion,
  diced fine
2 tablespoons sugar
2–3 teaspoons salt

Peel and quarter the turnip. Pare and halve the carrots. Bring water to a rapid boil and toss in the vegetables. Cook rapidly until completely tender. Drain and mash with potato masher. In a second pan melt butter and add diced onion. Sauté until tender and translucent. Add the butter and onions, sugar and salt to the mashed vegetables, blending well. Reheat if necessary.

Yield: 8 servings.

LUCY'S CREAMED ONIONS

2 pounds small white onions
¾ cup water

½ teaspoon salt

Remove skins from onions. Place them in a small saucepan. Add ¾ cup water and ½ teaspoon salt. Simmer until tender. Don't overcook. Drain water. Prepare cream sauce:

CREAM SAUCE:

1 cup evaporated milk	1 bay leaf
1 tablespoon margarine	½ teaspoon salt
1 tablespoon flour	Paprika

Melt margarine in top of a double boiler, add flour and stir until smooth. Stir in evaporated milk. Cook until thickened, stirring constantly. Add bay leaf and ½ teaspoon salt. Cook for 5 minutes. Remove bay leaf. Add sauce to onions, simmer for 5 minutes. Sprinkle with paprika just before serving.

MATTIE'S SWEET POTATO PUDDING TOPPED WITH MARSHMALLOWS

2 pounds sweet potatoes	¾ cup evaporated milk
½ stick butter or margarine	2 teaspoons vanilla extract
¾ to 1¼ cups sugar, depending on sweetness of the potatoes	1 teaspoon powdered cinnamon
3 eggs	3 tablespoons dark rum (optional)
	1 pound marshmallows

Wash and boil sweet potatoes in their jackets until tender. Peel, then add butter or margarine while potatoes are still hot, and mash with a potato masher until mixture is smooth. Add sugar, stir until well mixed. Then add eggs one at a time, beating mixture well until all 3 eggs have been added. Stir in evaporated milk, vanilla, cinnamon, and rum if desired. Pour into a buttered 2-quart casserole and bake in a prehated 375° oven for 30 minutes. Top with whole marshmallows and continue baking until browned. Serve hot.

Yield: 8 servings.

226

MATTIE'S BAKED MACARONI WITH CHEESE

1 tablespoon salt
2 cups uncooked elbow
  macaroni
½ stick butter or
  margarine, melted

12 ounces sharp Cheddar
  cheese, grated
2 eggs, lightly beaten
1½ cups evaporated milk
Paprika

Fill a 3-quart saucepan with water and place over a high flame. When water comes to a rapid boil, add salt and elbow macaroni. Add the macaroni gradually so that the water does not stop boiling. Cook, uncovered, for 8–9 minutes. Remove from stove, pour into a colander to drain, then place colander with macaroni in it under cold running water for a few seconds. Put macaroni in a 2-quart casserole and add melted butter or margarine, 8 ounces of the grated cheese, eggs, and milk. Mix lightly. Sprinkle the remaining cheese over top and dust with paprika. Bake in a preheated 375° oven for 30 minutes.

Yield: 8 servings.

WINNER TOSSED GREEN SALAD

1 head iceberg lettuce
1 head romaine lettuce,
  chopped
3 stalks celery, chopped
1 cucumber, peeled and
  sliced

3 tomatoes, sliced
2 carrots, cut in strips
  (julienne)
12 radishes, cut in rounds
1 green pepper, cut in rings

In a large salad bowl place leaves of iceberg lettuce, which have been broken into pieces by hand, romaine lettuce, celery, cucumber, tomatoes, carrot strips, radishes, and green pepper rings. Toss and serve with your favorite dressing or with Mattie's homemade mayonnaise.

MATTIE'S MAYONNAISE

1 egg yolk
2 tablespoons white vinegar
¾ teaspoon salt

¼ teaspoon pepper
¼ teaspoon dry mustard
1 cup salad oil

Beat egg yolk and 1 tablespoon vinegar with salt, pepper, and mustard in an electric mixer at high speed. Add oil, 1 teaspoon at a time, for the first ¼ cup, then slowly add the remaining salad oil and vinegar, beating continuously throughout.

Yield: About 1 cup.

LUCY'S MINCEMEAT PIE

Lucy cans her mincemeat in the summer months, but you can of course make it for instant use.

FILLING:

8 cups chopped green
   tomatoes
8 cups chopped green apples
1 cup golden raisins
1 cup black raisins
1 cup chopped mixed dates,
   prunes, figs
1 orange, chop fruit and
   grate rind
2½ cups brown sugar
½ cup molasses

½ cup dark corn syrup
1 cup cider vinegar
1 tablespoon ground
   cinnamon
2 teaspoons salt
1 teaspoon ground cloves
½ teaspoon ground allspice
½ teaspoon ground ginger
½ teaspoon ground mace
½ teaspoon ground nutmeg
½ teaspoon pepper

Combine all ingredients in a large saucepan. Bring to a boil, then lower heat, and let simmer for 2 hours, stirring frequently. Pack in hot jars and process, as described in Chapter 2, for 20 minutes. Cool and let seal.

Yield: 3 quarts or filling for 4 9-inch pies.

HOT WATER DOUBLE PIECRUST
(for 1 9- or 10-inch pie):

1 cup shortening
⅓ cup hot water
1 tablespoon milk

2½ cups flour
½ teaspoon salt

Put the shortening in a bowl, pour the hot water over it, stir, adding milk till the mixture is thick and creamy. Sift the flour and salt and beat in till dough is formed. Pat into 2 balls, roll out 1 of them, and put into bottom of a 9-inch pie plate. Put in mincemeat filling (recipe preceding), and cover with rolled-out second ball of dough. Flute the edges and cut slits in the top.

WALTINE'S AMBROSIA

8 oranges, peeled and sliced
1 fresh coconut, grated
1 medium-size pineapple, peeled, cored, and cut into chunks

In a large crystal bowl, place a layer of sliced oranges, a layer of fresh grated coconut, a layer of pineapple chunks. Continue above routine until bowl is filled. Top with a layer of coconut. Pour extra orange juice, if desired, over mixture. Chill and serve.

Yield: 10–12 servings.

Waltine, Mattie, and Lucy with their father in their adopted town, Newark

MATTIE'S CHRISTMAS EGGNOG

12 eggs	1 cup brandy
1½ cups sugar	1 pint heavy cream
1 cup rye	Nutmeg
1 cup dark rum	

Separate egg whites from yolks. Beat yolks until light and frothy, adding ¾ cup of sugar while beating. To this mixture add rye whiskey, rum, and brandy. Beat egg whites until stiff, adding ½ cup sugar while beating. Whip heavy cream until light and fluffy, adding ¼ cup of sugar near the end of whipping. Fold egg whites and whipped cream into the egg yolk mixture. Pour mixture into a large punch bowl. Chill before serving if desired. If mixture has been allowed to set for a while beat with a rotary egg beater just before serving. Sprinkle nutmeg on top of each cup of eggnog when served. If a thinner consistency is desired, add 1 cup milk to mixture.

Yield: About 24 punch cups.

New Year's Day
Dinner At Our House

On New Year's Day we always have Open House at our fathers' home. It is a leisurely day, designed to give us an opportunity to unwind from the frenzy of New Year's Eve and time to reflect on the passing year, and make our resolutions for the coming one. As friends and family drop by we find it is the perfect time to rekindle old friendships, solidify new ones, reciprocate past hospitalities and draw our family together. What better way to bring in the New Year than with warm friends and hot food?

Black folklore has it that hoppin' john brings good luck in the coming year, so we always serve this traditionally southern meal with all the essential trimmings.

OUR MENU FOR TEN

*Pigs' Feet
Sliced Turkey and Ham Platter
*Hoppin' John (Black-Eyed Peas and Rice)
Mustard Greens (see Index)
*Stewed Tomatoes
Baked Sweet Potatoes (see Index)
*Apple-Walnut Salad
*Corn Bread
*Company Pies
Fruitcake (see Index)
*Eggnog
Champagne

Assorted Winter Fruits: Persimmons, Pomegranates, Pears, Apples, Tangerines, Tokay Grapes, and Kumquats

Asterisk indicates that recipe appears in this chapter.

PIGS' FEET

12 pigs' feet, halved
4 cups cider vinegar
4 celery stalks, cut in thirds
4 large onions, quartered
4 carrots, halved

4 bay leaves
12 peppercorns
3 teaspoons crushed red peppers
2 tablespoons salt

Carefully inspect pigs' feet and singe off any remaining hairs. Wash feet thoroughly. Place them in a large saucepan or kettle. Cover with water and add remaining ingredients. Bring to a boil, lower heat, cover, and simmer slowly for about 3 hours. When done, pigs' feet should be fork tender and no longer pinkish in color. Adjust seasoning and serve with additional vinegar and hot sauce.

Yield: 10 servings.

HOPPIN' JOHN
(BLACK-EYED PEAS AND RICE)

2 ham hocks
1 bay leaf
2 onions, chopped
1 celery stalk, diced
½ teaspoon crushed red pepper

Salt and pepper to taste
2 cups black-eyed peas
2 cups uncooked rice

Place ham hocks in a large saucepan. Add water to cover and simmer for about ½ hour. Add bay leaf, onions, celery, and seasonings. Sort out and discard any discolored or damaged peas, rinse remainder well, and add to the pot. If necessary, adjust water level so that the peas are well covered. Simmer slowly until tender and liquid level is low, about 2 hours. Cook rice separately according to package directions, steaming it until dry. Fluff into peas. Adjust seasoning and cook over low heat until all the liquid is absorbed. Even the most experienced cooks sometimes have difficulty estimating the exact level of liquid necessary to prevent the rice from becoming gummy. If in doubt, reverse the process and fluff the peas into the rice, adding a small amount of liquid.

Yield: 10 servings.

STEWED TOMATOES

4 tablespoons butter
2 medium-size onions,
  minced
12 large ripe tomatoes,
  peeled and cut in pieces

2 teaspoons salt
2 teaspoons brown sugar
¼ teaspoon pepper
1 teaspoon basil

In a large saucepan, melt butter and add onions. Sauté until tender. Add tomatoes, salt, brown sugar, pepper, and basil. Bring to a boil, lower heat, cover, and simmer slowly for about 25 minutes. Adjust seasoning if necessary.

Yield: 10 servings.

APPLE-WALNUT SALAD

12 apples
2 celery stalks, diced
1½ cups chopped walnuts
4 tablespoons seedless raisins
1½ cups mayonnaise

1 teaspoon lemon juice
½ teaspoon nutmeg
Lettuce
Purple grapes, halved and
  seeded, for garnish

Peel and core apples, and dice them into small cubes. Add celery, walnuts, and raisins. In a small bowl, blend mayonnaise, lemon juice, and nutmeg. Gently fold mayonnaise mixture into apples, coating evenly. Serve on a bed of lettuce and garnish with grape halves.

Yield: About 10 servings.

CORN BREAD

1 cup sifted all-purpose flour
1½ tablespoons sugar
2½ teaspoons baking powder
½ teaspoon baking soda
½ teaspoon salt

1 cup yellow cornmeal
2 eggs, beaten
1½ cups buttermilk
¼ cup melted butter

Sift together flour, sugar, baking powder, soda, and salt. Add cornmeal. In a medium-size bowl, mix eggs, buttermilk, and butter. Add flour mixture. Mix enough to moisten. Pour into a greased 8-inch-square baking pan or 12 muffin tins. Bake in a preheated 425° oven for 20–25 minutes, or 15–20 minutes if baking muffins. Cut corn bread into squares. (A small cooked sweet potato or banana, mashed and blended into corn bread batter, offers an interesting variation.)

Yield: 12 squares or muffins. Double recipe for 10–12 guests.

COMPANY PIES

We always serve one of Uncle Glenn's special fruitcakes, but not every one is a fruitcake enthusiast, so for abstainers we go into our store of recipes gathered from friends and prepare one of our special "company pies."

LEMON MERINGUE PIE
(SUZIE WALKER)
1 baked 9-inch pie shell (see Index)

FILLING:

4½ tablespoons cornstarch
1¼ cups sugar
¼ teaspoon salt
1½ cups water
4 egg yolks, lightly beaten

⅓ cup lemon juice
2 teaspoons grated lemon rind
2½ tablespoons butter

MERINGUE:

4 egg whites
¼ teaspoon cream of tartar
½ cup sugar

In the top of a double boiler combine cornstarch, sugar, and salt. Gradually add the water, stirring until smooth. Place directly over medium heat and bring mixture to a boil, stirring constantly until it thickens. Then place over the bottom of the double boiler, which should be filled with 1 inch of boiling water. Cook the mixture for 5 minutes longer. Place egg yolks in a bowl and beat with an egg beater. Working quickly, pour about half the cornstarch mixture into the yolks, beating well with a fork. Return the entire mixture to the double boiler top. Cook and stir for about 3 minutes over the boiling water. Stir in lemon juice, rind, and butter. Remove the custard from the heat and let cool.

Prepare the meringue by beating egg whites with cream of tartar until soft peaks form. Add the sugar, a couple of tablespoons at a time, beating after each addition. Continue beating until stiff peaks form. Pour custard into pie shell. Top with meringue, making peaks here and there. Bake in a preheated 400° oven for 8-10 minutes until meringue is a golden brown.

Yield: 8 servings.

LEMON CHIFFON PIE
(GRANDMA BOYD—OUR ADOPTED GRANDMOTHER)

1 baked 9-inch pie shell
  (see Index)
½ cup lemon juice
¼ cup orange juice
⅔ cup sugar
½ cup water
1 envelope unflavored gelatin

3 egg yolks, beaten
3 egg whites
1 tablespoon sugar
1½ cups heavy cream,
  whipped
Nutmeg

Prepare pie shell. Mix lemon juice, orange juice, and sugar in a saucepan and bring to a boil. Dissolve gelatin in ½ cup cold water and blend in. Lower heat, cook for 3 minutes, then pour over beaten yolks, stirring vigorously. Reheat entire mixture to the boiling point and strain into a bowl. Let it cool down a bit, then chill. When mixture begins to set, beat egg whites with 1 tablespoon sugar until stiff. Fold into gelatin mixture and pour into cooked shell and refrigerate. When ready to serve, cover with whipped cream and sprinkle with nutmeg.

Yield: 8 servings.

TRIPLE-DECKER BUTTERSCOTCH PIE
(COUSIN ALICE SCARBOROUGH)

CRUST:

2 cups flour
¾ teaspoon salt

⅔ cup shortening
6–8 tablespoons ice water

Sift flour and salt and cut in shortening. Add enough ice water to hold ingredients together. Divide dough into 3 parts and roll into 3 9-inch circles. Place separately on baking sheets, pricking each well. Bake in a 450° preheated oven until delicately browned. Cool.

FILLING:

2 cups milk scalded
1¼ cups brown sugar
⅓ cup flour
⅛ teaspoon salt

2 egg yolks, beaten
2 tablespoons butter
½ teaspoon vanilla extract

Scald milk in the top of a double boiler. Mix sugar, flour, and salt and add to milk, stirring constantly until thick. Add a little of the mixture to beaten egg yolks, then return to double boiler. Cook 4 minutes more. Stir in butter until melted, add vanilla, then cool. On a cookie sheet, put together 3 crusts like a layer cake, alternating with crust and filling, ending with filling on top. Prepare meringue:

MERINGUE:

2 egg whites
4 tablespoons sugar

½ teaspoon vanilla
Sprinkle of salt

Beat egg whites until stiff but not dry, adding sugar gradually, and vanilla and salt. Pile meringue lightly on top and sides of pie and bake in a preheated 325° oven for 15 minutes until light brown. Serve warm or chilled.

Yield: 8 servings.

ORANGE PIE
(SPAULDING BERRY)

1 9-inch graham cracker pie
  shell (see Rum Pie, recipe
  following)
1 tablespoon unflavored
  gelatin
1½ cups fresh orange juice

⅔ cup sugar
¼ teaspoon salt
¼ cup lemon juice
1 teaspoon grated
  orange rind
1 cup heavy cream

In the top of a double boiler, place the gelatin and ½ cup orange juice. Cook until dissolved, stirring frequently. Add sugar and salt. Remove from heat. Add the remaining orange juice, lemon juice, and rind. Chill until partially thick, then beat until light. Whip cream and fold into mixture. Pour into pie shell. Chill until firm. Garnish with a sprig of mint and orange slices.

Yield: 8 servings

RUM PIE
(VICKI FOSTER HARRIS)

PIE SHELL (9 or 10 inch):

1½ dozen graham crackers,
  crumbled
1 stick butter, melted

⅓ cup sugar
¼ teaspoon cinnamon

FILLING:

2 8-ounce packages cream
  cheese
2 eggs, well beaten

½ cup sugar
2 tablespoons dark rum

TOPPING:

1 cup sour cream
3 tablespoons sugar

1½ tablespoons dark rum

For the pie shell: place graham crackers on wax paper and crumble, using a rolling pin. Place in a bowl, add butter, sugar, and

238

cinnamon. Mix lightly with a fork until well blended. Place in a 10-inch pie plate and mash with a spoon to form a solid crust. For the filling: blend softened cream cheese with eggs and sugar until smooth. Stir in rum. Pour into graham cracker shell. Bake in a preheated 375° oven for 20–25 minutes. For the topping: remove pie from oven and top evenly with a mixture of sour cream, sugar, and rum. Return to the oven for 5 minutes. Serve chilled.

Yield: 8–10 servings.

NEW YEAR'S EGGNOG

1 dozen egg yolks	6 egg whites
1 heaping cup sugar	3 cups heavy cream
1 quart milk	Nutmeg
A fifth dark rum	

In a large bowl beat yolks with egg beater until light. Add sugar and beat until thick. Stir in milk, then rum. Beat egg whites until peaked. Fold into mixture. Pour into a punch bowl and chill (outdoors if cold enough) for at least 2 hours. Beat cream until it softly peaks, then gently fold into chilled mixture. Chill again for at least 2 more hours. When serving, garnish with nutmeg.

Funerals

Russell's grieving sweetheart

As granddaughters, nieces, and cousins of morticians, we have attended our share of funerals and surprisingly have found that some of the best Southern cooking is to be had during these times of sorrow. The custom of caring for the bereaved in this manner stems back to ancient Africa, where the family of the deceased was given not only food but items of value, including wardrobes, by the entire community in an effort to offset the loss in a practical manner. This was particularly important if the deceased was the head of a household and the continuation of family stability was a concern. In the antebellum South, churches, fraternal orders, and burial societies took over a similar function, and to a significant extent this continues today. Friends and neighbors also play an important role, each preparing and donating food to those who are grieving so that they need not have the burden of cooking for themselves or the many guests who will be visiting the home. Those closest to the bereaved family take up vigil in the home from morning till night to clean and prepare for visitors and to receive their gifts of food. Tables are arranged and the food tastefully displayed for the dinner following the funeral, when family and friends will come together to mourn, to comfort, and to share their feelings with one another.

It is a simple act of thoughtfulness to the living, but it takes the form of a feast. Turkeys, hams, roasts, and casseroles are given, but as children, we had a natural interest in the sweets and hot breads that were offered, and to this day we find it particularly appropriate to take a cake, a pie, or bread to the family of the departed.

CHOCOLATE CHIP CAKE

3 cups cake flour
3 teaspoons baking powder
½ pound lightly salted
    butter
2 cups sugar
4 eggs

1 cup milk
2 teaspoons vanilla extract
2 1-ounce squares
    unsweetened chocolate,
    grated

Sift, then measure flour. Add baking powder. Sift 3 times more. Cream butter and sugar until fluffy. Add 1 egg at a time; beat well after adding each egg. This mixture must be kept at a very light, fluffy consistency. Fold in dry ingredients, alternating with the milk. Add vanilla. Then fold in grated chocolate. Pour into a greased and lightly floured 10-inch funnel or 8″ × 10″ × 2½″ pan. Bake in a preheated 350° oven for 1 hour (funnel) or 40 minutes (flatpan). Serve plain or with chocolate frosting.

Courtesy: Sister Reta Rapp.

Papa Darden's widow visiting his grave

CHOCOLATE LAYER CAKE

2 cups sugar
3 sticks butter
1 3-ounce package cream
  cheese
6 eggs
4 cups all-purpose flour

1 heaping tablespoon baking
  powder
¼ teaspoon baking soda
¾ cup milk
1 teaspoon vanilla extract

Cream sugar, butter and cream cheese together. Beat eggs in a small bowl at high speed for about 5 minutes. Add to butter mixture and mix well. Sift flour, baking powder, and baking soda. Add half of flour mixture to the previous batter and mix for 10 minutes at low speed. Gradually add the milk. Then add the remaining flour, mixing thoroughly. Finally, add the vanilla extract. Mix thoroughly and pour into 3 buttered 9-inch cake pans. Bake in a preheated 350° oven for about 30 minutes. When cake is cool, frost with Chocolate Frosting (recipe follows).

CHOCOLATE FROSTING

7 1-ounce squares
   unsweetened chocolate
½ stick butter or margarine
2½ cups powdered sugar

½ cup milk
A few drops of vanilla
   extract

Melt the chocolate squares in a saucepan. Add butter or margarine, let simmer for about 1 minute over low heat. Add the powdered sugar. Then add the milk, stirring continuously. Let simmer for about 5 minutes and remove from heat. Stir in drops of vanilla. Let cool before frosting cake.

Courtesy: Cousin Lilly Tennessee.

§

CHOCOLATE CHERRY UPSIDE-DOWN CAKE

2 pounds black cherries or 2
   20-ounce cans pitted black
   cherries
6 tablespoons butter
¼ cup brown sugar
3 tablespoons butter
½ cup brown sugar
½ cup granulated sugar
1 egg yolk
2 squares bitter chocolate,
   melted in the top of a

   double boiler over
   simmering water
1 cup flour
1½ teaspoon baking powder
¼ teaspoon salt
½ teaspoon powdered
   cinnamon
¾ cup milk
1 teaspoon vanilla extract
1 egg white, beaten stiff
½ pint heavy cream

Carefully pit the black cherries, leaving them as close to whole as possible. This is painstaking. In a saucepan put the uncooked cherries, add a few tablespoons of water, and simmer for a few minutes until the cherries are a little soft but retain their shape. Remove from heat. Place the 6 tablespoons of butter in a heavy 9-inch skillet (preferably of black iron), add the ¼ cup of brown sugar, and turn on low heat until the butter and brown sugar are melted. Blend and spread evenly over the skillet, remove from heat. Carefully place the pitted cherries (fresh or canned) close together in the butter-sugar, with the uncut side down, because that is the side that will show when the cake is served. Reserve the cherry juice. Cream together the 3 tablespoons of butter, ½ cup of brown sugar, ½ cup of granulated sugar until very light. Add the egg yolk, melted chocolate, and mix thoroughly. Sift the flour, baking powder, salt, and cinnamon, and add to the butter-sugar mixture alternating with the milk. Add the vanilla, mix thoroughly. Fold in the stiffly beaten egg white. Carefully spoon the cake batter into the skillet so as not to disturb the cherries. Bake in a preheated 350° oven for 45 minutes. When the cake is springy to the touch, remove it from the oven, loosen the sides from the edge of the skillet if necessary, let the cake stand for 10 minutes. Place the cake serving plate upside down over the skillet, hold the skillet handle with one hand, the cake plate with the other, and flip the whole thing upside down. Leave the inverted skillet on the cake plate for 10 minutes, then slowly lift it off. Let the cake cool. Whip the cream till thick, adding every few seconds a teaspoon of cherry juice to give a rich flavor and a bright pink color. Spoon the whipped cream thickly around the edge of the top of the cake, leaving most of the cherries exposed. Cut with a sharp knife.

Courtesy: Deacon Cyrus Rogers.

CARROT CAKE

1½ cups sugar
3 egg yolks
1 cup vegetable oil
2½ tablespoons hot water
1½ cup all-purpose flour
1 teaspoon baking powder
1 teaspoon baking soda

½ teaspoon salt
½ teaspoon nutmeg
1 teaspoon cinnamon
1 cup grated carrots
1 cup chopped black walnuts
3 egg whites

Beat together the sugar, egg yolks, and oil along with the hot water. Sift together flour, baking powder, baking soda, salt, nutmeg, and cinnamon. Add to egg yolk mixture. Then add carrots and walnuts. Beat egg whites until stiff and gently fold into mixture. Bake in a preheated 350° oven in a well-greased tube pan for about 55 minutes. Let cool for 10 minutes before removing from pan.

Courtesy: Sister Effie Artis.

ANGEL BOX POUNDCAKE

1 pound butter
1 pound powdered sugar
8 eggs

1 box flour, loosely packed
 (use 1-pound powdered
 sugar box to measure)
1 tablespoon vanilla extract
1 tablespoon lemon extract

Cream butter and sugar together. Add eggs, one at a time, beating after each addition. Sift flour and add slowly, stirring at intervals. Add vanilla and lemon extract. Pour into a greased and lightly floured 10-inch funnel pan. Bake in a preheated 325° oven for 1 hour.

Courtesy: Sister Corrine Steele.

HEAVEN CAKE

4 eggs
½ pint heavy cream
1½ cups sugar

1½ cups self-rising flour
1 teaspoon vanilla extract

Break eggs in a mixing bowl and beat until light and foamy (at least 5 minutes). Add heavy cream and beat another 5 minutes. Pour in sugar, continuing to beat well. Last, blend in flour and vanilla. Bake in a greased tubular pan in a preheated 350° oven for 50 minutes, or in 2 8-inch cake pans for 30 minutes. Dust with confectioner's sugar or frost as desired.

Courtesy: Sister Hilda Lockett.

COLD OVEN CAKE

2 cups all-purpose flour
1 cup self-rising cake flour
2 sticks butter
½ cup shortening

3 cups sugar
1 cup milk
6 eggs
3 teaspoons lemon extract

Sift flours together 5 times. Cream butter and shortening well and add sugar gradually. Add flour, a small portion at a time, alternating with the milk. Add eggs one at a time, beating after each addition. Add lemon extract. Turn into a greased, floured 10-inch tube pan. Put in a cold oven. Light oven and set at 325°. Bake for 1 hour and 15 minutes.

Courtesy: Sister E. Mae McCarroll, M.D.

JIFFY NUTMEG CAKE—A ONE-BOWL CAKE

2 cups sifted all-purpose flour
1½ cups sugar
1 teaspoon salt
2 teaspoons baking powder
1½ cups heavy cream

3 eggs
2 teaspoons nutmeg
2 tablespoons dark rum or
  brandy

Sift flour, sugar, salt, and baking powder into a mixing bowl. Add cream, eggs, and nutmeg, and beat for 3 minutes. Add rum or brandy and beat for 1 minute longer. Then pour into a greased and floured 9″ × 5″ × 3″ loaf pan and bake in a preheated 350° oven for 1 hour or until an inserted toothpick comes out clean. Cool and frost or enjoy unfrosted.

Courtesy: Sister Virginia Savoy.

SHEET CAKE WITH YELLOW FROSTING

1 cup butter
2 cups sugar
4 eggs
4 cups all-purpose flour,
  sifted

½ teaspoon salt
6 teaspoons baking powder
1 cup milk
1 teaspoon vanilla extract

Cream butter and sugar until light. Beat in eggs, one at a time. Sift flour, salt, and baking powder together. Add these dry ingredients, alternating with milk. Stir in vanilla and blend well. Bake in a well-greased 18″× 10″ × 2½″ flat pan or 2 18″ × 10″ × 1″ sheet pans in a preheated 350° oven for 45 minutes. Let cake cool in its pan and frost the top with Yellow Frosting (recipe following).

YELLOW FROSTING

½ cup butter or margarine
Pinch of salt
1 egg white
3 cups confectioner's sugar
1 teaspoon vanilla or lemon
 extract

1–2 tablespoons milk,
 depending upon desired
 consistency
A few drops of yellow food
 coloring

With an electric beater, whip butter, salt, egg white, and 1½ cups confectioner's sugar until fluffy. Add vanilla or lemon extract, then remaining sugar, milk (if needed), and drops of yellow food coloring until desired shade is reached. Spread over the top of the Sheet Cake (preceding recipe).

Yield: 24 or 48 squares.
Courtesy: Sister Georgia Dupree.

PEACH-BLUEBERRY PIE

1 9-inch pastry shell,
 unbaked (see Index)
3 cups sliced fresh peaches
1 cup blueberries
¾–1 cup sugar, depending
 on sweetness of peaches

3 rounded tablespoons flour
¼ teaspoon salt
½ teaspoon cinnamon
⅛ teaspoon nutmeg
¾ cup heavy cream
2 tablespoons butter

Mix peaches and blueberries with dry ingredients and place in the unbaked pie shell. Pour heavy cream over fruit. Dot with butter. Bake in a preheated 450° oven until center of pie bubbles (about 15 minutes). Then reduce heat to 350° and continue baking until nicely browned (about 45 minutes). Serve warm or cold.

Yield: 6–8 servings.
Courtesy: Cousin Helen James.

DEEP DISH PLUM PIE

CRUST:

2½ cups flour	¾ cup shortening
1 teaspoon salt	4 tablespoons ice water

FILLING:

3 cups canned plums, drained, halved, and pitted	⅛ teaspoon salt
	1 tablespoon lemon juice
¾ cup reserved plum juice	¼ teaspoon almond extract
2½ tablespoons tapioca	1 tablespoon butter

For the crust: sift flour, then measure. Then add salt and sift into a mixing bowl. Cut in shortening with a pastry blender or 2 knives until mixture is the texture of small peas. Sprinkle ice water over mixture, stirring with a fork. Using your hands, pat dough into a ball, wrap in wax paper, and refrigerate until ready for use.
For the filling: prepare plums and set aside. Pour ¾ cup reserved plum juice into a small bowl. Add tapioca, salt, lemon juice, and almond extract. Blend well, then let stand for 10 minutes. Divide dough in half, roll out to ⅛-inch thickness. Line a deep pie dish with half of the pastry dough. Fill with plums. Pour over plum juice mixture and dot with butter. Top with upper crust and flute edges to seal. Cut a crisscross design in center of pie so that steam can escape. Bake in a preheated 425° oven for 50 minutes.

Courtesy: Sister Judy Haynes.

THE VERY BEST PUMPKIN PIE EVER

1 9-inch pie shell (see Index)	1 cup sugar
	Pinch of salt
2½ cups cooked, mashed fresh or canned pumpkin	1 stick butter
3 large eggs	1 teaspoon each powdered cinnamon, nutmeg, and allspice

If using fresh pumpkin, peel pumpkin, cut in thin slices, and put in a heavy saucepan with water to cover over low heat. Cook slowly until all water is absorbed. It is necessary to stir often when the water is almost absorbed to prevent sticking. Mash and set aside. Prepare pie shell. Beat eggs well. Add ¾ cup sugar, a pinch of salt, and ½ stick butter, melted, to eggs; add spices and blend. Then add mashed pumpkin and mix thoroughly. Turn into pie shell and pat pumpkin mixture even with edges of pastry. Sprinkle remaining ¼ cup sugar over top of pie and dribble remaining ½ stick of melted butter over sugar. Bake in a preheated 350° oven for about 45 minutes. (Note: The top of this pie is lightly browned and crunchy. Even if people don't like pumpkin pie, we suspect they'll decide this one is delicious.)

Courtesy: Brother Elroy Barnes.

DEEP DISH RHUBARB CRUNCH

⅓ cup sifted flour
¾ cup oatmeal
1 cup brown sugar
½ cup melted butter
1 teaspoon cinnamon
4 cups diced fresh rhubarb

¾ cup sugar
2 tablespoons cornstarch
1 cup water
1 tablespoon strawberry
  Jell-O

Mix flour, oatmeal, brown sugar, butter, and cinnamon. Then press half into the bottom of a buttered 9-inch deep pie dish or casserole. Cover with the rhubarb. Combine sugar, cornstarch, and 1 cup water and cook over low heat, stirring often until smooth, clear, and thick. Add Jell-O and pour over rhubarb. Cover with reserved crumbs and bake for 40 minutes in a preheated 350° oven.

Courtesy: Sister Ossie Mae Royal.

PEAR-CRANBERRY PIE

8 medium-size pears
(Anjou)
½ cup fresh cranberries
1 cup sugar
1 heaping tablespoon tapioca
1 teaspoon cinnamon
¼ teaspoon ginger

⅛ teaspoon salt
Juice of 1 orange
2 teaspoons grated orange
rind
Double crust for 10-inch pie
2 tablespoons butter

Peel and slice pears in a large bowl. Add cranberries, sugar, tapioca, cinnamon, ginger, salt, orange juice and rind. Mix well and pour into a pastry-lined 10-inch pie plate. Dot with butter, then cover with top crust and make air vents in an attractive design in the center. Bake in a preheated 425° oven for 45 minutes or until pie is nicely browned.

Yield: 8 large wedges.

Courtesy: Cousin Mary Sampson.

REFRIGERATOR ROLLS

1 cup mashed white potatoes
⅔ cup shortening
1½ teaspoons salt
⅔ cup sugar
2 eggs, beaten
1 yeast cake (or two ¼-
ounce packages active
dry yeast)

½ cup lukewarm water
1 cup milk, scalded and
cooled to lukewarm
6-8 cups sifted all-purpose
flour
Butter, melted

Peel, boil, and mash potatoes. While still warm, add shortening, salt, and sugar. Cream well, then beat in eggs. Dissolve yeast in lukewarm water. Stir lukewarm milk into potato mixture then add yeast. Add enough sifted flour to make a stiff dough. Place on a floured board and knead well. Then place in a large greased bowl and let rise until double in bulk. Knead slightly on floured board. Place back in the bowl and rub top with melted butter. Cover tightly and place in the refrigerator until ready to use (will keep for 5-6 days, supplying you with fresh rolls for the week). About 1½ hours before baking time pinch off desired amount of dough and either shape into cloverleaf or pocketbook rolls. To make cloverleaf rolls, form 1-inch balls and place 3 in each cup of a well-oiled muffin tin. To make pocketbooks, roll out a portion of the dough to ¼-inch thickness. Cut with a biscuit cutter and brush with melted butter. With a knife make an indentation across each roll just left or right of center. Fold the smaller half almost to the edge of the lower and pinch together. Place in a greased pan. Cover your rolls and let them rise in a warm place for about 1½ hours or until they double in size. Brush with melted butter. Bake in a preheated 400° oven for 15-20 minutes or until nicely browned.

Yield: 3 dozen rolls.
Courtesy: Sister Corrine Steele.

TINY BUTTER ROLLS

2 ¼-ounce packages dry
  active yeast
2 cups lukewarm water
2 eggs, well beaten
1 cup sugar
1 tablespoon salt

2 cups milk, scalded
1 cup butter, melted
8-10 cups sifted all-purpose
  flour
½ cup melted butter

Dissolve yeast in 2 cups lukewarm water. Add beaten eggs and blend. Now add sugar, salt, warm milk, and 1 cup melted butter. Gradually blend in flour. Mix well. Then knead on a heavily floured board. Place in a greased bowl and set in a warm place to rise for about 2 hours. When doubled in bulk, knead slightly and form into miniature cloverleaf or pocketbook rolls (see preceding recipe for instructions). Arrange in buttered pans and let rise until light, about 1 hour. Brush tops with the melted butter. Bake in preheated 425° oven for 15-20 minutes.

Yield: 50-60 rolls.
Courtesy: Sister Georgia Dupree.

On the Road

Norma Jean hitting the road

Summers in our childhood found us on the train going south, often by ourselves. It was not uncommon for children to be sent alone to stay with relatives—entrusted to the care of Pullman porters, gentlemen of color, whose concern and kindness for black travelers were legend. We boarded the night train in New York City with our mother, who introduced us to the porters, told them our destination, and settled us down. She then rode with us as far as Newark, our home, where our father was waiting, and there they waved us goodbye, knowing that we would be well taken care of—as indeed we were. Traveling at night in sleeping berths was one way black travelers could avoid the humiliation of sitting in the rear of the cars—a mandatory railroad practice that occurred after one reached Washington, D.C.

After our mother learned to drive and could share the responsibility with our father, car trips became more frequent and were incredible fun. We could hardly sleep the night before and would help pack our bags and lunches, which our mother put in shoe boxes with the name of the passenger Scotch-taped on so that special requests were not confused. We usually left very early in the morning, but when fully awake would make up songs, jokes, and games to amuse ourselves on the road. Big fun was waving at passers-by, then ducking out of sight in our seats. Our feelings of high excitement were unavoidably tinged with feelings of dread, however. These trips took place during the fifties, and one never knew what dangers or insults would be encountered along the way. Racist policies loomed like unidentified monsters in our childish imaginations and in reality. After the New Jersey Turnpike ended, we would have to be on the alert for the unexpected. So as we approached that last Howard Johnson's before Delaware, our father would make his inevitable announcement that we had to get out, stretch our legs, and go to the bathroom, whether we wanted to or not. This was a ritualized part of every trip, for, although there would be many restaurants along the route, this was the last one that didn't offer segregated facilities. From this point on, we pulled out our trusty shoe-box lunches.

Any discomfort during these yearly travels was balanced by a sense of adventure, for after we finished our shoe-box lunches we would have to keep our eyes peeled for black-owned establishments, which usually took us off the main route. If we needed a place to sleep before reaching our destination, we would have to ask random fellow blacks where accommodations could be found. Often total strangers would come to our rescue, offering lodging and feeding us as well. We made many new friends this way, as hospitality and solidarity were the byproducts of tight segregation.

How different traveling in the South is today! But, in spite of all the really remarkable changes, we have continued the habit of stopping with our old friends as we travel. They have shared many a fine meal with us, and for this reason we asked our friends on the road to contribute their favorite recipes. This chapter belongs to them.

Carole arriving at Aunt Norma's

SHOE-BOX LUNCH

Fried Chicken (see Index)
Peanut Butter and Jelly Sandwiches
Deviled Eggs (see Index)
Carrot and Celery Sticks
Salt and Pepper Packets
Chocolate Layer Cake (see Index)
Thermos of Lemonade

Everything was neatly wrapped in wax paper, with extra treats like
fresh fruit and small packs of nuts, raisins, and cheese. When it was
gone, we got by with a little help from our friends.

HOT CRAB-MEAT SALAD

It is always a pleasure to visit with our mother's friend Florence Byrd. They taught together in Petersburg, Virginia, where Florence still lives.

1 cup crab meat, flaked
1 cup soft bread crumbs
¼ cup light cream or top milk
1½ cups mayonnaise
5 hard-cooked eggs, diced
1 tablespoon minced parsley

½ teaspoon salt
⅛ teaspoon pepper
Red pepper to taste
½ cup buttered bread crumbs

Combine everything except buttered bread crumbs, and place in greased ramekin or a casserole; sprinkle with buttered crumbs. Bake in a preheated 350° oven for about 20 minutes or until crumbs are golden brown.

Yield: 8 servings.

AUNT RUBY'S SEAFOOD CASSEROLE

Our Aunt Ruby used to live in a little white wooden house at the tip of a small island, called Sullivans Island, off the coast of Charleston, South Carolina. The waters surrounding her home were filled with a variety of sea creatures. We would fish and crab in the mornings and she would transform our catch into the evening meal. This is one of Aunt Ruby's favorites.

1 pound fresh shrimp
1 pound fresh crab meat
8-ounces lobster meat
½ cup milk
1 can cream of mushroom soup

2 tablespoons flour
½ pound sharp cheese, grated
Worcestershire sauce or cooking sherry to taste
Salt and pepper to taste
Dash of turmeric

Peel and devein shrimp, set aside. Flake crab and lobster meats together with a fork, and place in a lightly greased casserole dish. Empty cream of mushroom soup into a saucepan and heat slowly. Use milk and flour to make a paste and add to mushroom soup, stirring constantly. Season with Worcestershire sauce or cooking sherry, salt, pepper, and turmeric. Add uncooked shrimp. Simmer for about 3 minutes, stirring constantly. Pour this mixture into the casserole and stir lightly, lifting gently from the bottom of the dish. Sprinkle grated cheese on top of casserole and bake in a preheated 375° oven until cheese melts and browns lightly.

Yield: 8–10 servings.

EDNA NEAL'S PAN-FRIED BLOWFISH

Easy and yet so hard . . . Few people can beat our friend Mrs. Edna Neal, from Warrenton, North Carolina in frying fish.

The blowfish is a delicious small, meaty fish that has only one neatly lined set of bones through its center. It is sometimes dubbed "chicken of the sea" because of its resemblance to the white meat of poultry. Blowfish used to be plentiful and inexpensive but have now grown somewhat scarce on the market. Nevertheless, if you should be so fortunate as to find some, this is a delicious way to prepare them:

Blowfish, allow at least 2
or 3 fish per person
Flour
Salt and pepper
Paprika

1 medium-size whole clove
of garlic
Fat for frying
Lemon wedges

Wash fish and pat dry. Coat lightly with flour, seasoned with salt and a spare amount of pepper and paprika. In a heavy skillet, heat a ½-inch level of fat until quite hot. Add the whole clove of garlic. Then add fish and fry until golden brown on both sides. Serve hot with lemon wedges

256

MRS. SHERIDAN'S NORTH CAROLINA DEVILED CRABS

Mrs. Sheridan was the short-order cook at the Wilson Drugstore. She loved to cook but didn't like her job. For months she prayed for a new one and her prayers were answered in the form of a suggestion from the Baptist minister, Reverend Watkins, who asked her if she would care for a member of his congregation who was too elderly to look after herself. Soon she had a full-scale home for the elderly, and the senior citizens are truly rejuvenated by her skills in the kitchen.

1 medium-size onion, minced
1 green pepper, diced
1 stick butter
4 cups cracker crumbs
1½ cups milk
4 eggs, well beaten
1 can cream of mushroom soup
2 pounds crab meat (save crab shells if possible)
1 tablespoon Worcestershire sauce
1½ tablespoons prepared mustard
Salt and cayenne pepper to taste
Additional cracker crumbs
Paprika
Lemon wedges

Sauté onion and green pepper in butter until almost limp. Remove from heat. In a large bowl, soak the cracker crumbs in milk until soft. Stir this into the skillet mixture. Add beaten eggs and cream of mushroom soup, blending well. Add crab meat by fluffing it into the mixture with a fork. Season with Worcestershire sauce, mustard, salt, and pepper. Stuff empty crab shells or ramekins with mixture. Sprinkle with additional cracker crumbs and paprika. Bake in a preheated 350° oven for 20 minutes. Serve with lemon wedges.

Yield: 10–12 servings.

CRAB MEAT LOAF

Follow the above recipe but increase the quantity of milk to 3 cups and add 5 eggs instead of 4. Pour into 2 greased loaf pans or a large casserole dish. Bake in a preheated 350° oven for 25–30 minutes or until set. Remove from loaf pans and slice.

257

SALMON CROQUETTES MCPHALE

Late in life, Papa Darden decided to remarry. His adult children were very upset, especially C.L. But when his new wife-to-be appeared with her two lovely daughters, they were all won over. Mrs. McPhale, of Wilson, North Carolina, was one of those daughters.

1 large and 1 small can
   salmon (15½ ounces and
   7¾ ounces)
2 small white potatoes,
   peeled, boiled, and mashed
2 eggs, well beaten

1 stalk celery, chopped fine
1 small onion, chopped fine
¼ cup evaporated milk
Salt and pepper to taste
Fat for deep frying

Mix first 7 ingredients well. Form into small croquettes and deep fry in hot fat, or form into patties and pan fry until golden brown. Excellent served for breakfast with hominy grits, eggs, and bacon, or for dinner as a main course.

Yield: Approximately 6 servings.

CONCH CHOWDER

We stayed in the guesthouse of Mrs. Harvey, of West Palm Beach, Florida, and she prepared this special dish.

2 cups conch
2 tablespoons cooking oil
¼ cup diced salt pork
1 large onion, diced
2 stalks celery with leaves,
   diced
⅓ cup diced green pepper
½ cup diced cooked ham
8 ripe tomatoes, peeled, cut
   in eighths

1 tablespoon tomato paste
½ teaspoon thyme
2 pinches basil
2 quarts water
2 carrots, cut in rounds
3 medium-size potatoes,
   cubed
Salt and pepper to taste
2 tablespoons Worcestershire
   sauce
Hot sauce to taste (optional)

Cook conch in water for 15 minutes or until tender; Mince and set aside. In a large pot, place cooking oil and salt pork. Cook until salt pork is crisp and brown. Remove and set aside. To the pot, add onion, celery, and green pepper. Sauté for about 5 minutes. Then add ham, tomatoes, tomato paste, thyme, and basil. Simmer, stirring frequently, for about 10 minutes. Then add 2 quarts water. Bring to a boil, then lower heat and allow mixture to simmer. Add carrots, potatoes, and minced conch. Cook for 45 minutes. Season with salt, pepper, Worcestershire sauce, and hot sauce. Simmer for another 30 minutes. Then remove from heat, cover, and let stand before serving.

Yield: 10–12 servings.

SHRIMP GUMBO

Mrs. Bessie Marsh, of Montclair, New Jersey, by way of Jackson, Tennessee, first introduced us to gumbo, and we've been fans ever since.

2 sliced salt pork, diced
1 pound fresh okra, sliced
Salt and pepper to taste
1 large onion, sliced
1 green pepper, sliced thin
1 cup ham or chicken diced
5 or 6 ripe tomatoes
1–2 tablespoons gumbo filé, according to taste (gumbo filé is a seasoning most easily obtained in Louisiana or in shops elsewhere that specialize in seasonings)
1 pound fresh shrimp, shelled and deveined with tails left on
5 slices bacon, fried crisp, then crumbled (optional)

In a large, heavy, skillet, cook the salt pork until crisp. Add okra, which has been salted and peppered, then onion and pepper. When okra is tender, add ham or chicken, tomatoes, and gumbo filé. Simmer slowly for approximately 1½ hours. Add shrimp. Cook until tender. Adjust seasoning.

Serve over steaming hot rice in wide soup bowls.

If using bacon, sprinkle over each serving.

Yield: 6–8 servings.

NORTH CAROLINA TURKEY BUTT SOUSE

Souse, sometimes called headcheese, is typically made from the head of a hog. The following variation is quite similar and just as tasty.

3 pounds turkey butts (knob at tail of turkey)
1 cup cider vinegar
1 small dried red pepper pod, crumbled
¼ teaspoon sage
Salt and pepper to taste

Simmer butts in water to cover until the meat falls off the bone (about 1½ hours). Remove meat, reserving broth. Pick out and discard any bones. Chop butts fine or put through a meat grinder. Return meat to broth and stir in the rest of the ingredients. Set aside and let cool to room temperature. Pour into a large, preferably lidded loaf pan. Let set in the refrigerator until completely firm. Souse is used as a luncheon meat. To serve, it should be sliced and eaten with crackers or corn bread. It will keep in the refrigerator for 2 months.

Yield: 12 generous servings.

OLD SOUTHERN WET HASH

Mrs. Alvin Martin, of Jersey City, New Jersey, by way of Alabama, shared a trip around the world with our mother. She is a Southern cook in the best tradition.

2 cups cubed lamb, beef, veal, or fowl
1 cup chopped onion
¼ cup chopped celery
3 medium-size white potatoes, diced fine
2 tablespoons margarine

2 tablespoons flour
2 cups stock (or 2 bouillon cubes dissolved in 1 cup water)
Salt and pepper to taste
Dash of soy sauce (optional)

Prepare meat. Sauté onion, celery, and potatoes in margarine until tender but not brown. Add flour to thicken. When flour browns, add stock and meat. Cook until sauce is thick and potatoes are tender. Season to taste. Aside from being an excellent way to use leftover foods this hash is good for any meal—over grits for breakfast, over toast for lunch.

Yield: 4 servings.

CORNFLAKE OMELET

We used to bill Cousin Charles, of Wilson, North Carolina, as "the ladies' pet and the man's threat" because he loved to wear white suits, shoes, ties, etc., and go calling on the womenfolk. He still likes to wear all white, but is now married. Charlie made this one up for a man on the go.

A beach party from Mother's scrapbook

4 eggs	½ teaspoon celery salt
⅓ cup crumbled cornflakes	Salt and pepper to taste
2 tablespoons milk	Bacon fat or butter
1½ teaspoons ketchup	

If you're in a hurry, you can have your eggs and cereal at the same time with this one. Just beat the first 6 ingredients together and scramble in bacon fat or butter.

Yield: 2 servings.

GINGERBREAD WAFFLES

Cousin Charles' wife, Edith, now makes him his Sunday favorite.

2 eggs	¼ teaspoon ground
¼ cup sugar	cinnamon
½ cup molasses	¼ teaspoon salt
1 cup sour milk (see page 279)	1 teaspoon baking soda
1½ cups all-purpose flour	1 teaspoon baking powder
1 teaspoon powdered ginger	⅓ cup melted butter
¼ teaspoon ground cloves	

261

Beat eggs until light. Add sugar, molasses, and sour milk. Sift dry ingredients. Add to egg mixture and beat together until smooth. Add butter. Cook as you would regular waffles.

Yield: 6–8 servings.

ᘀᘀᘀ

FILLED COFFEECAKE

This recipe comes from Gwen Kenney, a warm and vibrant mother of four dear friends whose house in Tuskegee was always a second home to us.

¼ cup butter
½ cup sugar
2 eggs, separated
1½ cups all-purpose flour
2 teaspoons baking powder

1 teaspoon salt
½ cup milk
1 teaspoon vanilla extract
Powdered sugar

FILLING:

½ cup brown sugar
1 tablespoon flour
1 teaspoon cinnamon

1 tablespoon melted butter
½ cup chopped nut meats

Cream butter and add sugar, and beat in egg yolks. Add sifted dry ingredients, alternating with milk. Add vanilla. Fold in egg whites, which have been beaten until stiff. Combine filling ingredients. Pour ⅔ of batter into a buttered 8-inch-square pan. Spread on the filling, and pour the rest of the batter over this. Bake in a preheated 350° oven for about 40 minutes. Cool and sprinkle with powdered sugar. Cut into squares and serve warm with butter.

❖❖❖❖❖❖❖❖❖❖❖❖❖❖❖❖❖❖❖❖❖❖❖❖❖❖❖❖❖❖❖❖❖❖❖

BRANDIED FRUIT

(A Love Potion)

When visiting Opelika, Alabama, we wouldn't miss a visit to Aunt Maude's neighbor, Mrs. Corrine Steele, for a dose of her wry humor and her latest recipes. This one is a magic potion and must be treated with respect. In a large apothecary jar, add the following ingredients in their listed order:

1 cup pineapple tidbits or chunks	1 cup maraschino cherries, halved
1 cup peaches, cut into small pieces	1 cup sugar
1 cup apricots, cut into small pieces	

Every 2 weeks you may add 1 cup of each fruit and 1 cup of sugar in the same order. If you are using canned fruit, drain before adding. *Never* add the juice. You *must not add more often than once every 2 weeks*, but you may delay adding ingredients for another day or two without disastrous results. If you do delay, you must, of course, change your calendar for later additions. Keep a calendar marked so as not to forget. You must never allow the contents to go below 3 cups, or fermentation will stop. Whenever you have over 6 cups of fruit, you may wish to divide it into 2 portions with at least 3 cups in each, one of which can be given to a friend as a starter. Bear in mind one condition about sharing this potion with others. The one you give it to must be worthy because it's a love potion. Always divide *before* adding more fruit and sugar, and *never, never* refrigerate. Keep in a warm place close to the oven. Never put a lid on tightly, as it may explode. Apothecary jars are best because there is room for expansion. Stir mixture occasionally to keep the contents down and the sugar dissolved.

This is delicious served over cake or ice cream or simply eaten by itself. It is ready to be eaten one month after starting and anytime thereafter, regardless of the adding schedule.

~~~~~~

CANDIED ORANGE PEEL

Sister Sally Gore of Aberdeen, North Carolina, is a minister in the rural part of that state. When we visited her and asked how to make sausage, she said, "Well, you let your hog get to be about 500 pounds before you kill him..." and we immediately became discouraged. It reminded us of Mrs. Elizabeth Sheridan, who told us that she remembered how to make molasses but that we'd need a mule. We had to abandon those recipes, but Reverend Gore was kind enough to give us this old-time favorite that was also a specialty of our Grandma Sampson.

263

| 1 cup orange peel (from about 4 oranges) | ½ cup water |
| 1 cup sugar, granulated | Sugar for coating, granulated or confectioner's |

Wash oranges. Remove peel and cut in narrow strips. Put in a pot, cover with water, and boil for 15 minutes or until tender. Drain off water. Then cover with water and again bring to a boil. Pour off water and set peels aside. Place sugar and ½ cup water in the pot and bring to a boil. Add orange peel and cook until syrup is almost gone, shaking the pan often to avoid scorching. Remove peels with a slotted spoon and place on waxed paper to cool. Roll in granulated or confectioner sugar. Dry and store in a covered jar or canister.

Yield: About 1 cup candied peel.

GINGER BEER

This thirst-quenching drink is from our Canadian-Trinidadian friends Albertha Jones and her mother, Alice Anderson.

¼ pound fresh gingerroot	¾ pound sugar
4 tablespoons lime juice	2 pints boiling water
Peel of 1 lime	

Peel the gingerroot and grate it into a large bowl. Place lime juice, peel, and sugar in the bowl and then pour in the boiling water. Cover the bowl and let stand in a warm draft-free place for 2 days. Then strain through a fine sieve into a bottle. Keep at room temperature for 3 days or longer. Serve chilled mixed with ginger ale, club soda, or over crushed ice.

Yield: 2½ pints.

CHITLINS

Mrs. Elizabeth Simmons, originally from North Carolina, now lives in Boston, but she hasn't forgotten how to turn out a chitlin.

10 pounds chitterlings (chitlins)	1 large onion, sliced or quartered
1 tablespoon salt	Vinegar to taste
	Hot sauce to taste

Wash chitterlings in warm water, rubbing as you would clothes, to remove all grease and residue. When washing water runs clear they are clean. Place the chitterlings in a large pot. Do not add water. The chitterlings will produce their own water, aided by the dampness produced from the washing. Add salt and onion (it is the onion that reduces the odor). Simmer slowly for 2 hours, removing water as it builds up, so that mixture remains watery but does not run over. Stir every half hour or so to prevent sticking. After 2 hours cut chitterlings into smaller pieces with a two-pronged fork and a knife. Continue cooking for 1–2 more hours or until completely tender. Remove excess liquid. Adjust seasoning, using salt, vinegar, and hot sauce to taste. Serve with greens, potato salad, and corn bread.

Yield: 6 servings.

CHITLIN SALAD

Thelma Byers, of Charlotte, North Carolina, and daughter of Annie Darden Barnes, inherited her mother's ability to take one food and present it in many new and exciting ways. Here are some of her chitlin and acorn squash recipes and her best corn pone.

2 cups cooked chitterlings (chitlins), cut into small pieces
Juice of ½ lemon
½ cup diced celery

½–¾ cup mayonnaise
Salt and pepper to taste
Lettuce
Paprika

Sprinkle the chitterlings with lemon juice and let stand for at least 1 hour. Add celery, mayonnaise, salt and pepper. Serve on beds of lettuce. Dust with paprika.

Yield: 2–3 servings.

FRENCH FRIED CHITLINS

10 pounds chitterlings (chitlins)
4 tablespoons vinegar

1 medium-size onion
2 tablespoons salt

Uncle C.L. (center front) arranged for Booker T. Washington (second row center) and Dr. John Kenney (fifth from left) of Tuskegee, Alabama, to address North Carolina businessmen in Wilson.

Clean and cook chitterlings in the manner described in the recipe for Chitlins (see Index). However, do not cut chitterlings into small pieces, but leave whole. Cook for 3–4 hours or until tender. Drain, cool, and cut into finger-length pieces.

BATTER:

¾ cup milk	½ teaspoon baking powder
1 egg, beaten	¼ teaspoon salt
¾ cup flour	Fat for deep frying

Mix milk and egg together and add dry ingredients. Stir until a smooth consistency is reached. Dip chitterlings in batter. Fry in very hot, deep fat until brown.

Yield: 6 servings.

FRENCH FRIED ACORN SQUASH

4 young tender acorn squash, peeled or unpeeled	¾ cup cracker crumbs
2 eggs, beaten	Fat for deep frying

Slice squash in pieces ¼–½ inch thick. Remove seeds and fiber. Soak in salt water for about 20 minutes. Drain and pat dry with paper towels. Dip in beaten eggs, then in cracker crumbs. Fry in deep fat until golden brown and drain on paper towels.

Yield: 6–8 servings.

STUFFED ACORN SQUASH

2 small or 1 medium-size
  acorn squash (about 1½
  pounds)
½ teaspoon salt
2 eggs
1 tablespoon grated onion

1 cup grated Cheddar cheese
2 tablespoons fine bread
  crumbs
Salt and pepper to taste
Butter

Boil whole squash in salted water until almost tender. Remove tops
to make cavities for stuffing. Scoop out stringy insides and discard.
Drain water that collects. Beat eggs until frothy. Add grated onion,
cheese, bread crumbs, and salt and pepper. Put bits of butter in each
cavity of squash. Fill with stuffing. Place butter and bread crumbs
on top of each. Place in a foil-lined pan and bake in a preheated
350° oven for 30 minutes.

Yield: 4 servings.

THELMA'S TOP-OF-THE-STOVE
EASTERN NORTH CAROLINA CORN PONE

1½ cups unbolted cornmeal
Warm water
½ teaspoon salt

Sift unbolted cornmeal and measure out 1½ cups into a bowl.
Discard husk. Add salt and enough warm water to make a slightly
stiff batter. Grease a medium size iron skillet and heat on the stove.
When it begins to smoke, pour on batter. Cover with a lid and cook
over medium heat until mixture is set and underside is brown. Slide
pone onto a plate and return to hot skillet with the uncooked side
down. Cover and finish cooking in like manner. Cut in wedges. This
bread is very good with fish, barbecue, collard greens, turnips, and
chitterlings.

Yield: 6–8 wedges.

MARCUS GARVEY BEAN SALAD AND DRESSING

Hattie Gossett, of Harlem, U.S.A., is an untraditional traditional cook
who is not afraid to experiment with black culinary classics. Her Marcus
Garvey Bean Salad uses the black, red, and green colors of the Afro-
American flag that the nationalist leader designed.

Motoring 1920s style

1 medium-size can (1 pound) snap string beans, washed and drained

1 medium-size can (15 ounces) red kidney beans, washed and drained

1 small can (7½ ounces) black beans, washed and drained

½ medium-size green pepper, diced

2 scallions, diced

1 stalk celery, diced

Chopped fresh parsley and pimentos as garnish

Combine all the above ingredients except garnish. Add Peanut Oil and Lime Juice Dressing (recipe follows) and mix it in well. Add garnish.

Yield: 6–8 servings.

PEANUT OIL AND LIME JUICE DRESSING

In keeping with the spirit of the salad, Hattie uses peanut oil because it was promoted by an Afro-American, George Washington Carver, and because it's a frequently used ingredient in West African cooking.

¼ teaspoon each of salt, pepper, and garlic powder
3 tablespoons lime juice
4 tablespoons peanut oil

1 teaspoon prepared mustard
Pinch of basil
Pinch of dried parsley

Put salt, pepper, and garlic powder into a mixing jar; add lime juice and shake until seasonings have blended with juice; add peanut oil, mustard, basil, and parsley. Shake again.

Yield: About ½ cup of dressing.

HATTIE'S MARINATED FRIED FISH

Use any kind of boned whole fish, allowing 1 or 2 per person
Salt and pepper

Lemon or lime juice
Soy sauce
Paprika

About 2 hours before frying, wash fish and pat dry. Sprinkle with salt and pepper and place a single layer of fish in a shallow pan. Use 2 parts lemon or lime juice to 1 part soy sauce as a marinade, pouring in enough liquid to half cover fish. Be sure to turn fish 2–3 times while marinating so that it is evenly coated. After 2 hours, remove fish from marinade, sprinkle liberally with paprika, and fry in shallow hot fat until brown on each side. Serve immediately.

SISTER HATTIE GOSSETT'S COLESLAW

1 medium-size head of cabbage
4 carrots
1 cup mayonnaise
6 tablespoons lemon juice

1 teaspoon celery seed
4 tablespoons sweet pickle relish
Salt and pepper to taste

Remove the outer leaves of the cabbage and quarter the head. Shred, using the largest sized holes on the grater. To shred the carrots, use the next smallest size. Place these vegetables in a salad bowl and toss them lightly together. In a small bowl, mix the remaining ingredients together until smooth and creamy. Blend this into the cabbage mixture, using only a small amount at a time. You may not have to use all of it. Simply keep in mind that the mixture should be wet enough to hold everything together without being soupy.

Yield: 8 servings.

CAULIFLOWER AU GRATIN

Charlotte Kyle of North Carolina, Newark, and now New York City, keeps moving, but we never loose touch with her or her wonderful cuisine.

1 large cauliflower	¼ teaspoon pepper
2 tablespoons butter	Pinch of nutmeg
⅓ cup flour	1 cup grated Cheddar cheese
2 cups milk, scalded	¼ cup bread crumbs
½ teaspoon salt	

Trim and wash cauliflower. Separate flowerets. Cook in boiling salted water for 15 minutes, or until tender but not soft. Drain. In a small, heavy saucepan melt 1 tablespoon butter. Add flour. Stir in scalded milk. Add salt, pepper, nutmeg, and cheese. Cook over low flame, stirring constantly until smooth. Place cauliflower in a shallow ovenproof dish. Cover with cheese sauce. Sprinkle with bread crumbs. Dot with remaining butter. Broil under broiler flame until browned.

Yield: 6 servings.

NORTH CAROLINA CHOPPED BARBECUED PORK

From Alvis Hines, Wilson's own Barbecue King.

1 pork shoulder roast	½ teaspoon chili powder
1 teaspoon salt	½ teaspoon nutmeg
1 teaspoon celery seed	½ teaspoon sugar
⅛ teaspoon cinnamon	1 cup water
⅓ cup cider vinegar	Additional vinegar to taste
½ cup ketchup	Hot sauce to taste

Brown roast in a small amount of fat and place in a Dutch oven. Mix the next 9 ingredients in a saucepan and bring to a boil. Pour over roast and cover. Bake in a preheated 325° oven, 40 minutes to the pound, until done, basting occasionally with drippings. Transfer roast to a chopping board. Remove meat from the bone and chop into fairly fine pieces. Season to taste with additional vinegar and hot sauce. Serve hot with coleslaw and corn bread. This is the most popular barbecue dish in North Carolina, and, as far as we know, it is indigenous to that state.

❧❧❧❧❧❧❧❧❧❧❧❧❧❧❧❧❧❧❧❧❧❧❧❧❧❧❧❧❧❧❧❧❧❧❧❧❧❧

PIG'S EARS AND LENTIL STEW

Cousin Josiane is an import to our family from Paris. After fifteen years on these shores, her French food has a decided touch of "soul."

6 pigs' ears (or tails)
½ pound lentils
2 carrots, sliced
2 onions, quartered
6 cups water

¼ pound salt pork
1 bay leaf
¼ teaspoon thyme
Salt to taste

Wash pigs' ears under running water, cleaning well. Place in a Dutch oven or heavy kettle with lentils, carrots slices, onions, 2½ cups water, salt pork, and seasoning. Bring to a boil. Then lower heat and cook, covered, very slowly for 3 hours. Adjust seasoning, remove salt pork, and serve in soup bowls.

Yield: 4–6 servings.

COUSIN JOSIE'S CARROT SALAD

6 young carrots, finely grated
  or minced (use blender if
  available)
1 small onion, grated

1 stalk celery, grated
1 teaspoon finely chopped
  parsley

Mix all gredients well with vinaigrette sauce (recipe follows).

VINAIGRETTE SAUCE

Mix 1 teaspoon prepared mustard with 2 tablespoons vinegar. Add salt and a pinch of pepper. Mix well. Add 6 tablespoons oil. Mix well. Pour over carrot mixture.

Yield: 4–6 servings.

COUSIN JOSIE'S BABA AU RHUM

4 eggs
½ cup sugar
1¼ cups sifted all-purpose
   flour
3 teaspoons baking powder

6 tablespoons butter, melted
½ cup lukewarm milk
Rum Syrup (recipe follows)
1 cup heavy cream, whipped

In an electric mixer, beat eggs with sugar until fluffy. Add flour and baking powder that have been sifted together. Mix at medium speed. Add melted butter and lukewarm milk. Mix at high speed. Pour into a buttered and floured ring mold. Bake in a preheated 325° oven for 35–40 minutes. Remove from oven, unmold, and pour rum syrup slowly on baba while still hot. Serve cold topped with whipped cream.

RUM SYRUP

½ cup sugar
½ cup water
1 cup dark rum

Cook sugar and water until a thin syrup is formed. Remove from heat and add rum and pour over cake.

☆

Our cousin Emma Reno Connor, who is a poet and lives with her husband in St. Albans, New York, recently wrote us that "things certainly don't taste the same as when I lived in Elizabethtown, Kentucky, where the food was grown on lush, blue-green land. I sometimes long for a pot of succotash, just as my Mom, Rutelia, used to make. It was usually served with a salad of lettuce, tomatoes and cucumbers fresh from the garden, cornbread, and was topped off with a dessert of a fresh fruit cobbler. This was my favorite meal."

OKRA SUCCOTASH

4 ham hocks	Salt to taste
2 pounds string beans	8 small new potatoes
1 medium-size onion,	4 cobs of corn
sliced, and slices halved	1 pound okra

Simmer ham hocks in water to cover for about 1 hour. Prepare beans by washing them and breaking or cutting into desired lengths, add to ham hocks with onion and a little salt. Peel new potatoes and add to one side of the pot. Simmer for 15 minutes. In the meantime, cut corn from the cobs and set aside. Carefully trim pods of okra and leave whole. Then add okra and corn to the pot. Let all cook together until desired tenderness is achieved. Adjust seasonings and serve hot with corn bread and salad.

Yield: 4 servings.

BLACKBERRY COBBLER

Garnett Henderson, of Montclair, New Jersey, our neighbor and friend, remembers her mother making her favorite cobbler dessert. "My mother had no cookbooks or menus as guides, but her food was delicious. I try every so often to make her cobbler and have decided that the following turns out tasty and delicious."

3 cups fresh blackberries	4 tablespoons butter, melted
1 cup sugar	4 tablespoons sugar
1 teaspoon lemon juice	1 cup sifted flour
2 tablespoons flour	2 teaspoons baking powder
Butter for dotting	½ teaspoon salt
1 or 2 eggs, beaten	

Mix berries, sugar, lemon juice, and 2 tablespoons flour. Spread over the bottom of a well-greased deep pie dish and dot with butter. Combine beaten eggs, melted butter and sugar. Sift flour and then measure 1 cup. Add baking powder and salt and sift twice again. Stir a little at a time into egg mixture until well blended. Spread over berries. Bake in a preheated 375° oven for 30 minutes. Serve warm with light cream.

Yield: 6 servings.

MISS MARY'S BANANA PUDDING

Mrs. Mary Alexander owned a hotel in Birmingham, Alabama. Many weary travelers, particularly gospel and rhythm-and-blues singers, and those touring on the black baseball circuit, pressed on a few extra miles just to reach her well-known kitchen. Everyone called her Miss Mary.

2 cups milk
2 eggs, plus 2 egg yolks
½ cup sugar
2 tablespoons flour
1 tablespoon butter
1 teaspoon vanilla extract

1 box vanilla wafers
6 bananas, cut in round slices
2 egg whites, beaten stiff
2 tablespoons sugar

Pour milk into the top of a double boiler. Beat eggs well, then add sugar and flour and blend. Pour the egg mixture into milk and let simmer for 20 minutes stirring constantly. Add butter and vanilla, stir, and remove from heat. In a deep ovenproof dish place a layer of vanilla wafers. Cover them with a layer of sliced bananas, and pour over them a portion of the custard. Continue layers 3 times. Cover with meringue composed of beaten egg whites and sugar. Then bake in a preheated 375° oven for 15 minutes or until top is golden brown.

~~~~

FLOSSIE BARNES'S SOUTH CAROLINA CORN PIE

On Saturdays we used to go to the Ritz, Wilson's "colored" movie house on Nash Street, with Flossie's children, John Howard, Helen, and Boisie, Jr. We paid twenty-five cents to see Captain Video and Lash LaRue serials and the fabulous so-called "race movies" with Lena Horne and Ethel Waters. After the movies, we would go to Flossie's for supper.

4 cups corn, cut from the cob
⅓ cup butter, melted
3 eggs, beaten
1½ cups whole milk

½ cup evaporated milk
1–3 teaspoons sugar to taste
Salt to taste

Place corn in a medium-size casserole dish. Stir in melted butter. In a separate bowl, beat eggs until light. Add whole milk, sugar, and salt. When well blended, pour over corn. Then pour ½ cup evaporated milk over the entire mixture. Bake in a preheated 325° oven for 30–40 minutes until set. Serve hot.

Yield: 6 servings.

TAMALE PIE

Mrs. Marie Kellar, now of San Francisco, was one of the most renowned cooks in Newark, before she decided to move West. All appreciators of great food were truly sad to see her leave.

FILLING:

1 pound ground lean beef
2 large onions, chopped
1 green pepper, chopped
4 cloves garlic, minced
¼ cup vegetable oil
1 16-ounce can tomato sauce
1 3-ounce bottle chili powder

1 tablespoon ground cumin
1 tablespoon sugar
1 tablespoon salt
½ teaspoon black pepper
2 cups water
1 cup grated Cheddar cheese
1 cup pitted black olives

CORNMEAL CRUST:

5 cups cold water
2 teaspoons salt

1 teaspoon chili powder
2½ cups yellow cornmeal

For the filling: in a skillet brown meat, onions, pepper, and garlic in the oil. When well browned blend in tomato sauce, spices, sugar, salt, and pepper. Add the 2 cups water and simmer for about 30 minutes. For the cornmeal crust: combine the 5 cups water, salt, chili powder, and cornmeal in a saucepan and place over medium heat. Stir frequently and cook until thick enough to form a crust. Line the bottom and sides of a buttered 2-quart casserole with ⅔ of the cornmeal mixture. Place the filling in the lined casserole and top with remaining cornmeal. Sprinkle with grated cheese and black olives. Bake in a preheated 350° oven for 45 minutes.

Yield: 6 servings.

✿◇✿◇✿◇✿◇✿◇✿◇✿◇✿◇✿◇✿◇✿◇✿◇✿◇✿◇✿◇✿◇✿◇✿◇✿

FIESTA RICE

2 tablespoons butter
½ cup chopped celery
1 large green pepper, chopped
1 medium-size onion, chopped

1 clove garlic, minced
4 cups cooked rice (firm, not overcooked)
1½ cups grated sharp cheese
Pimento for garnish

Melt butter in a large skillet. Add celery, green pepper, onion, and garlic. Sauté over low heat until tender. Fold in rice and cheese. Blend well. Spoon into a lightly buttered medium-size casserole dish. Garnish with pimento. Cover and bake in a preheated 325° oven for 30 minutes.

Yield: 6–8 servings.

DELUXE FRUIT SALAD
(In Honeydew Bowl)

1 honeydew melon	2 cups chopped walnuts
¼ cup milk	2 quarts mixed fresh fruit
12-ounces cream cheese	of the season
cheese	Sugar to taste

Pare skin from the entire melon. Cut off top and scoop out the seeds. Cut off just enough of the bottom so that melon will stand up. Blend milk and cream cheese to a smooth consistency and spread over outside of the melon. Sprinkle with chopped nuts. Refrigerate until ready for use. In a large bowl slice and mix peaches, plums, apples, melon balls, blueberries, strawberries, pineapple, grapes, cherries, bananas, oranges, or any other fruit in season. Add sugar to taste and keep cold. When ready to serve, fill honeydew bowl with fruit and place remaining fruit around it on a large platter. Slice a wedge of melon and scoop the fruit around it on each plate.

Yield: 6–8 servings.

CREAM CHEESE SOUFFLÉ
(With Black Cherry Sauce)

1 8-ounce package cream	⅛ teaspoon salt
cheese, softened	3 egg yolks, beaten
1 cup sour cream	3 egg whites
1 tablespoon honey	2 tablespoons sugar

Whip cream cheese, sour cream, honey, salt, and egg yolks until smooth. Then beat the egg whites until soft peaks are formed. Gradually add sugar to egg whites, beating until stiff peaks form. Then fold into cheese mixture. Pour into a lightly buttered 1½-quart casserole and bake in a preheated 425° for 45 minutes. Serve immediately with Black Cherry Sauce (recipe follows).

BLACK CHERRY SAUCE

¾ cup orange juice
2 tablespoons sugar
1 tablespoon cornstarch
¼ cup water

1 8-ounce can black cherries
and their syrup
3 tablespoons brandy

In the top of a double boiler heat orange juice and sugar. Add cornstarch to the ¼ cup water, blend, and stir into orange juice mixture. Cook until thick, then add cherries and their syrup. Reheat, add brandy, and remove from stove. Serve hot or cold over cream cheese soufflé (recipe above).

Yield: 6 servings.

CHICKEN CURRY FOR 50

Marie Kellar's *pièce de résistance* was a dish she made with our mother for a bon voyage party. It took them two days to get it together. This is a mild curry. Add extra curry powder for a more pungent taste.

20 pounds chicken pieces
 (legs, thighs, and breasts)
7 quarts water
1 lemon, sliced
15 medium-size onions
2 bunches celery
12 green apples, cored and
 diced
2½ cups vegetable oil
½ cup curry powder
1½ teaspoons black pepper
1 tablespoon powdered
 ginger

2 teaspoons Tabasco
5 tablespoons Worcestershire
 sauce
1½ cups flour
2½ cups water
3 coconuts (grated meat and
 milk)
1 dozen egg yolks, beaten
4 cups evaporated milk
1 pound seedless raisins
1 pound unsalted peanuts
2 pints chutney

SPOONBREAD AND STRAWBERRY WINE

The Sampsons picnicking at roadside

Cook chicken in 7 quarts of water with lemon slices, 1 onion, and 2 celery stalks until chicken is falling from the bones. Then reserve stock and prepare the chicken by removing skin, bones, and gristle. Dice the meat. In a large skillet (or 2) sauté the minced onions and minced remaining celery with the apples in the oil until translucent. Add curry powder and simmer for 5 minutes more. Add pepper, ginger, Tabasco, Worcestershire sauce and stir in. Pour in reserved chicken stock and cook for 20 minutes. Blend flour with 2½ cups water, add to vegetables and cook until thick. Now add diced chicken and 2 of the grated coconuts and their milk. Heat through, then remove from heat and refrigerate overnight or let stand for at least 3 hours. Just before serving, add egg yolks and evaporated milk. Heat thoroughly, add salt to taste, and serve in chafing dishes. Use remaining grated coconut, chutney, peanuts, and raisins for condiments. Serve with steaming hot rice.

Yield: 50 servings.

GLOSSARY OF COOKING TERMS

Baste: To moisten meat by pouring pan juices or additional liquid over it while roasting or baking.

Blanche: To remove skins of fruits or nuts by dipping in hot water, then cold water.

Cream: To make shortening fluffy and smooth with an electric mixer or by beating with a spoon against the side of the bowl.

Cut: To combine shortening and dry ingredients by slicing through mixture with two knives or pastry blender.

Dice: To cut into small cubes.

Dredge: To coat with flour.

Fold in: To gently add whipped cream or beaten egg white to other ingredients with an under-and-over motion so that airiness will not be lost.

Fricassee: To stew in liquid over low heat.

Knead: To prepare dough by pressing it away with the palms and heels of hands and doubling it over with the fingertips while rotating it in a circle. (Note: A good place to pick up this skill is by observation in your local pizza parlor.)

Marinate: To soak in a liquid, usually juice, wine, or vinegar, for flavoring purposes.

Parboil: To boil until only partially done.

Pare: To cut off skin.

Purée: To liquefy cooked foods in a blender or through a sieve.

Sauté: To fry to a golden brown in a little fat.

Scald: To heat liquid until bubbly around the edges of the pot but not boiling.

Sour milk: Old milk that has a sour taste. Regular milk can be soured by adding 1 tablespoon of vinegar or lemon juice to a cup of milk.

Sweet milk: Old term for regular milk that set it apart from buttermilk or sour milk.

EQUIVALENTS

Brown sugar—1 pound = about 2¼ cups packed
Butter, shortening—1 pound = 2 cups
   1 stick = ¼ pound = 8 tablespoons = 4 ounces = ½ cup
Cheese, hard—1 pound = 4 cups grated
Confectioner's Sugar—1 pound = 3¾ cups
Chocolate—1 square = 1 ounce = 1 tablespoon melted = 4
   tablespoons grated
Cornmeal—1 cup uncooked = 3½ cups cooked
Cream (heavy)—1 cup = 2 cups whipped
Flour, all-purpose—1 pound = 4 cups sifted
Flour, cake—1 pound = 4½ cups sifted
Granulated sugar—1 pound = 2 cups
Lemon or lime—1 medium = 3–4 tablespoons juice
Lemon rind—1 medium = 2–3 teaspoons grated
Meat—1 pound = 2 cups diced
Onions—1 medium = ½ cup chopped
Orange—1 medium = ⅓ cup juice
Potatoes—1 pound = 4 medium = 2½ cups diced = 2 cups mashed
Raisins—1 pound = 3 cups
Rice, raw—1¾ cups = ½ pound = 4 cups cooked
  precooked—1 cup = 2 cups cooked
Tomatoes—1 pound = 5 medium = 1⅔ cups chopped

WEIGHTS AND MEASURES

In the event that some of you wish to prepare portions of recipes and run into odd amounts, we have included this list.

A pinch = less than ⅛ teaspoon
3 teaspoons = 1 tablespoon
2 tablespoons plus 2 teaspoons = ⅙ cup
4 tablespoons = ¼ cup
5 tablespoons plus 1 teaspoon = ⅓ cup
8 tablespoons = ½ cup
12 tablespoons = ¾ cup
⅜ cup = ¼ cup plus 2 tablespoons
⅝ cup = ½ cup plus 2 tablespoons
⅞ cup = ¾ cup plus 2 tablespoons
16 tablespoons = 1 cup = 8 ounces
2 cups = 1 pint = 16 ounces
2 pints = 1 quart
4 quarts = 1 gallon
1 ounce = 2 tablespoons (liquid)

Happiness is remembering
A garden tilled and harvested for food·
Brought in by Papa's toil-worn hands
Cooked lovingly by Mama for her brood.
—Cousin Emma Connor

Recipe Index

SPOONBREAD AND STRAWBERRY WINE

AN AVON TRUE ROMANCE

Gwyneth and the Thief

MARGARET MOORE

AVON BOOKS

An Imprint of HarperCollins*Publishers*

FIND TRUE LOVE!
www.avontrueromance.com

An Avon True Romance is a trademark of HarperCollins Publishers Inc.

Gwyneth and the Thief

Copyright © 2002 by Margaret Wilkins

Printed in the United States of America.
For information address HarperCollins Children's Books,
a division of HarperCollins Publishers, 1350 Avenue of the Americas,
New York, NY 10019.

Library of Congress Catalog Card Number: 2001118667
ISBN 0-06-447337-6

First Avon edition, 2002

❖

Visit us on the World Wide Web!
www.harperteen.com